Expert JavaScript

Mark E. Daggett

Apress*

Expert JavaScript

ISBN-13 (pbk): 978-1-4302-6097-4

ISBN-13 (electronic): 978-1-4302-6098-1

President and Publisher: Paul Manning
Lead Editor: Louise Corrigan
Technical Reviewer: Jonathan Fielding
Editorial Board: Steve Anglin, Mark Beckner, Ewan Buckingham, Gary Cornell, Louise Corrigan, Morgan Ertel,
   Jonathan Gennick, Jonathan Hassell, Robert Hutchinson, Michelle Lowman, James Markham,
   Matthew Moodie, Jeff Olson, Jeffrey Pepper, Douglas Pundick, Ben Renow-Clarke, Dominic Shakeshaft,
   Gwenan Spearing, Matt Wade, Tom Welsh
Coordinating Editor: Katie Sullivan
Copy Editor: Nancy Sixsmith
Compositor: SPi Global
Indexer: SPi Global
Artist: SPi Global
Cover Designer: Anna Ishchenko

Distributed to the book trade worldwide by Springer Science+Business Media New York, 233 Spring Street, 6th Floor, New York, NY 10013. Phone 1-800-SPRINGER, fax (201) 348-4505, e-mail orders-ny@springer-sbm.com, or visit www.springeronline.com. Apress Media, LLC is a California LLC and the sole member (owner) is Springer Science + Business Media Finance Inc (SSBM Finance Inc). SSBM Finance Inc is a Delaware corporation.

For information on translations, please e-mail rights@apress.com, or visit www.apress.com.

Apress and friends of ED books may be purchased in bulk for academic, corporate, or promotional use. eBook versions and licenses are also available for most titles. For more information, reference our Special Bulk Sales–eBook Licensing web page at www.apress.com/bulk-sales.

Any source code or other supplementary materials referenced by the author in this text is available to readers at www.apress.com. For detailed information about how to locate your book's source code, go to www.apress.com/source-code/.

For Erika, who knew me before I could program and probably liked me better that way.

Contents at a Glance

Contents

CONTENTS

About the Author

Mark Daggett is a pioneering New Media artist, professional developer, and CEO of Humansized Inc., a social innovations lab in Kansas City. He is a co-creator of Pledgie.com, the popular crowdfunding platform, and an adjunct professor of art. He has worked for nearly two decades within the fields of experience and user interaction design, concept development and strategy, through a variety of startup ventures, consulting, and advisory roles. He is a Rockefeller New Media Grant nominee, and has been profiled in The *New York Times, Le Monde, WIRED Magazine*, and *Surface Magazine*, among others. You can find Mark on his web site, http://www.markdaggett.com, and on Twitter as @heavysixer."

About the Technical Reviewer

Jonathan Fielding is a web developer based in the UK, working in the marketing industry as a Senior Developer. He is the lead developer on the responsive SimpleStateManager open-source project along with regularly contributing to a variety of other open-source projects.

Acknowledgments

Much of this book was informed and influenced by a group of JavaScript experts, without whom I would have made several colossal missteps during the writing of this text. Specifically, I would like to thank Rick Waldron, Chris Williams, and Raquel Vélez for help on the Nodebots chapter. Rick, in particular, graciously pored over several revisions of this chapter and greatly improved the example code. I would also like to thank Kris Kowal for his detailed review of my chapter on Asynchronous JavaScript and Tim Caswell for his insights on how to explain coroutines and generators clearly. Jarrod Overson offered very helpful insight on the code quality chapter, and Jason Huggins very graciously provided me plenty of resources on his Tapster bot. Additional thanks goes to Bliksem Tobey, who provided the initial encouragement to start writing this book.

Special thanks goes to my mother, Patricia Daggett, who started proofreading my work when I was writing marginally intelligible essays in elementary school, and continues to this day. She is a deeply curious person and a female trailblazer in the computer industry. I tapped her fount of nearly 40 years of professional experience in product quality assurance and testing repeatedly during the writing of this book. I love you, Mom!

Introduction

In my mind, good technical books are part mixtape, treasure map, and field journal. *Expert JavaScript* is the result of my efforts to successfully weave these forms together into a compelling and information-rich book about JavaScript.

A mixtape, for those old enough to remember, is a curated collection of songs. These tapes were often made as gifts for friends, lovers, and those in between. The mixer would craft the tape by selecting personal favorites or organizing tracks along a conceptual thread. Often these tapes were a surrogate for the mixer, a way to be remembered by the listener when the tape was playing. This book is a mixtape for JavaScript that I made for you. These chapters cover some of my favorite aspects of the language, but also includes less-understood topics because they are not easily explained in a tweet or blog post. The long form format of a book affords these subjects the necessary room to breathe.

As a child, I found the idea of finding a treasure map a thrilling prospect. I was captivated by the idea that anyone could become rich as long as they followed the map. This book will not lead you to buried treasure, but it is a map of sorts. I laid out these chapters to chart the inner workings of the language, which you can follow to the end. Dig through these concepts with me and you will unearth a deeper understanding of JavaScript than when you started.

A field journal is kept by scientists. They are taught to keep a log of their thoughts, observations, and hunches about their subject. They may even tape leaves, petals, or other artifacts of nature between its pages. It's a highly contextual diary about a subject of study filtered through a specific point of view. The purpose of the field journal is to be a wealth of information that the scientist can continually mine when they are no longer in the field.

Expert JavaScript is my field journal of JavaScript, which I wrote to return to often. I will use it to help me remember and understand the particulars of the language. I encourage you to do the same. Scribble in the margins, highlight sections, and bookmark pages. It is not a precious object; it is meant to be a living document that is improved through your use.

CHAPTER 1

■ ■ ■

Objects and Prototyping

Practice does not make perfect. Only perfect practice makes perfect.

—Vince Lombardi

It may seem odd to include three chapters on core concepts of JavaScript in a book for experts. After all, these topics are some of the most rudimentary components of the language. My assertion is this: just as a person can speak a language without the ability to read or write it, so too can developers use the fundamental features of JavaScript and yet be blissfully unaware of their complexities.

The goal of these chapters is to shine a light on some of the more shadowy portions of the language. These are the concepts that you may have always intended to learn or even assumed you already understood. Think of it as if you are descending into your brain's basement, in which JavaScript is stored. Use this text like a flashlight to check for cracks in the foundation of your knowledge. This chapter and the next are meant to fill any fissures that might be revealed. Do not think of it as a needless review, but rather a structural assessment of your understanding of JavaScript.

I will start with a high-level overview of the goals of the language. But before you know it, you will be flat on your belly, commando-crawling your way through the lesser-known concepts of JavaScript. I will describe in detail the important ideas related to objects and prototypes. Then, in the next chapters you'll look at functions and closures, which are the building blocks of JavaScript.

JavaScript from a Bird's-Eye View

What we call JavaScript is actually an implementation of the ECMAScript language specification. For JavaScript to be considered a valid version of ECMAScript, it must provide mechanisms to support the syntax and semantics defined in the spec. JavaScript as an implementation must provide the programmer affordances to use the various types, properties, values, functions, and reserved words that make up ECMAScript.

Once a version of JavaScript conforms to ECMAScript, language designers are free to embellish their version with extra features and methods as they see fit. The ECMAScript specification explicitly allows this kind of flourish, as you can read here:

> *A conforming implementation of ECMAScript is permitted to provide additional types, values, objects, properties, and functions beyond those described in this specification. In particular, a conforming implementation of ECMAScript is permitted to provide properties not described in this specification, and values for those properties, for objects that are described in this specification. A conforming implementation of ECMAScript is permitted to support program and regular expression syntax not described in this specification.*

1

The fact that these extra features can exist in parallel with the core elements and still be considered a valid implementation is a sign of how progressive the ECMAScript standards body is. The looseness of what qualifies as ECMAScript is simultaneously a benefit and a drawback. Although the flexibility to add new features encourages language designers to innovate, it can leave developers in a bad spot trying to write clever polyfills[1] to support the differences between the various implementations and runtime environments.

The ECMAScript specifications change over time, and occur for a variety of reasons (too many to enumerate here). Primarily, though, these changes are an attempt to codify new approaches to old problems or to support advancements in the larger computing ecosystem. The changing specification represents an attempt to formalize the evolutionary processes within the language. Therefore, although I'm talking about "core concepts" as if they are immutable, in reality they are not. The concepts explored in this chapter are foundational and important, but my advice to the reader is to stay on your toes.

Scripting by Design

As its name implies, ECMAScript is a scripting language used to interact with a host environment programmatically. A host system, be it a browser, a server, or piece of hardware, exposes control points for JavaScript to manipulate. Most host environments allow JavaScript to trigger only aspects of the system that are already under the user's control (albeit manually). For example, where a user of a browser might click a link on a web page using a mouse or finger, JavaScript could trigger the same event programmatically:

```
document.getElementById('search').click();
```

Traditionally, ECMAScript was almost exclusively intended as a tool for web scripting within browsers. Developers employed it to enhance the user's experience when browsing a web page. Today, ECMAScript is equally at home on the server as it is in the browser, thanks to stand-alone engines such as V8 or TraceMonkey.

The ECMAScript standards body foresaw this growing divergence between how developers have traditionally used JavaScript, and where much of the recent growth has been. Wisely when defining what "web scripting" is in the most recent specification, it provided two examples that present the various contexts in which ECMAScript is popular today:

> *A web browser provides an ECMAScript host environment for client-side computation including, for instance, objects that represent windows, menus, pop-ups, dialog boxes, text areas, anchors, frames, history, cookies, and input/output. Further, the host environment provides a means to attach scripting code to events such as change of focus, page and image loading, unloading, error and abort, selection, form submission, and mouse actions. Scripting code appears within the HTML and the displayed page is a combination of user interface elements and fixed and computed text and images. The scripting code is reactive to user interaction and there is no need for a main program.*

> *A web server provides a different host environment for server-side computation including objects representing requests, clients, and files; and mechanisms to lock and share data. By using browser-side and server-side scripting together, it is possible to distribute computation between the client and server while providing a customized user interface for a Web-based application.*

> *Each Web browser and server that supports ECMAScript supplies its own host environment, completing the ECMAScript execution environment.*

---

[1]`http://remysharp.com/2010/10/08/what-is-a-polyfill/`

■ **Note** At the time of this writing, the arrival of the newest version of ECMAScript 6 (named "Harmony") was imminent, and although not officially released, many of the proposed changes are already being supported by runtime engines and browsers. This chapter is an exhaustive look at the core of the language, which also includes some of the new features introduced in Harmony. I will take special care to alert the reader when I am explaining a proposed feature that may have limited support.

Objects Overview

JavaScript is an object-oriented programming (OOP) language created by Brendan Eich, which he released after a few weeks of development while working for Netscape. Although JavaScript has "Java" in the name, it has little to do with the Java language. In an interview with *InfoWorld*, Eich explained the turn of events that lead to the language being renamed "JavaScript:"

> *InfoWorld: As I understand it, JavaScript started out as Mocha, then became LiveScript and then became JavaScript when Netscape and Sun got together. But it actually has nothing to do with Java or not much to do with it, correct?*
>
> *Eich: That's right. It was all within six months from May till December (1995) that it was Mocha and then LiveScript. And then in early December, Netscape and Sun did a license agreement and it became JavaScript. And the idea was to make it a complementary scripting language to go with Java, with the compiled language.*[2]

Even a casual comparison of the two languages reveals glaring differences. Unlike Java, JavaScript is not complied, does not enforce strict typing, or have a formal class–based inheritance mechanism. Instead, JavaScript is executed in the context of a host environment (e.g., a web browser), supports dynamic typing of variables, and implements inheritance through a prototype chain instead of classes. Therefore, we should probably chalk up the similarities between the names as the desire for a marketing synergy instead of an attempt to create a meaningful linkage between the two languages.

Yet for all their differences, both Java and JavaScript are members of the OOP family. Being object oriented means objects control a program's operation by communicating with each other. OOP languages are some of several popular programming paradigms that include, among others, Functional, Imperative, and Declarative.

■ **Note** Just because JavaScript is conceived as an object-oriented language does not mean that it is restricted to that paradigm. For example, the popular library Underscore.js[3] is written in the Functional programming style.

Objectified

What does it mean to be an OOP language? This may seem like an unnecessary question to ask experienced programmers, but the act of answering this question gives you the space needed to evaluate JavaScript's approach to OOP. You will spend the bulk of this book designing and thinking in terms of objects and their interrelationships, but it is important to remember that objects are just one of many possible metaphors used to model programs.

---

[2]http://www.infoworld.com/d/developer-world/javascript-creator-ponders-past-future-704
[3]http://underscorejs.org/

Metaphors are seductive and often obscure as much as they reveal; their affordances may allow you to cleanly conceive a solution for one problem while needlessly complicating another. As you answer what it means to be OOP, reflect on your own understandings and presuppositions. You may find that you've biased your own outlook on the concept.

Objects in JavaScript are little more than containers for properties. I've heard programmers describe them as "property bags," which evokes a pleasing visual. Every object can have zero or more properties, which can either hold a primitive value or pointer that references a complex object. JavaScript can create objects in three ways: using literal notation, the new() operator, or the create() function. In their simplest form, these three approaches can be expressed like this:

```
var foo = {},
    bar = new Object(),
    baz = Object.create(null);
```

The difference between these approaches is how the object is initialized, which we'll sift through later. For now, I will describe the ways to embellish objects by assigning them custom properties.

Property Manager

Many developers assume that an object's property is only a container that can be assigned a name and a value. In actuality though, JavaScript gives the developer a series of powerful property descriptors that further shape how the property behaves. Let's iterate over them now:

configurable

When this attribute is set to true, the affected property can be deleted from the parent object, and the property's descriptor can be modified later. When set to false, the property's descriptor is sealed from further modifications. Here is a simple example:

```
var car = {};

// A car can have any number of doors
Object.defineProperty(car, 'doors', {
    configurable: true,
    value: 4
});

// A car must have only four wheels
Object.defineProperty(car, 'wheels', {
    configurable: false,
    value: 4
});

delete car.doors;

// => "undefined"
console.log(car.doors);

delete car.wheels;
// => "4"
console.log(car.wheels);
```

```
Object.defineProperty(car, 'doors', {
    configurable: true,
    value: 5
});

// => "5"
console.log(car.doors);

// => Uncaught TypeError: Cannot redefine property: wheels
Object.defineProperty(car, 'wheels', {
    configurable: true,
    value: 4
});
```

As you can see in the previous example, wheels becomes fixed while doors remains malleable. A programmer might want to revoke the configurable attribute of a property as a form of defensive programming to prevent an object from being modified much like built-in objects of the language do.

enumerable

Enumerable properties appear if an object's properties are iterated over using code. When set to false, those properties cannot be iterated over. Here is an example:

```
var car = {};

Object.defineProperty(car, 'doors', {
  writable: true,
  configurable: true,
  enumerable: true,
  value: 4
});

Object.defineProperty(car, 'wheels', {
  writable: true,
  configurable: true,
  enumerable: true,
  value: 4
});

Object.defineProperty(car, 'secretTrackingDeviceEnabled', {
  enumerable: false,
  value: true
});

// => doors
// => wheels
for (var x in car) {
  console.log(x);
}
```

```
// => ["doors", "wheels"]
console.log(Object.keys(car));

// => ["doors", "wheels", "secretTrackingDeviceEnabled"]
console.log(Object.getOwnPropertyNames(car));

// => false
console.log(car.propertyIsEnumerable('secretTrackingDeviceEnabled'));

// => true
console.log(car.secretTrackingDeviceEnabled);
```

As you can see from the previous example, even though a property is not enumerable it does not mean the property is hidden altogether. The enumerable attribute can be used to dissuade a programmer from using the property, but should not be used as a method to secure an object's properties from inspection.

writable

When true, the value associated with the property can be changed; otherwise, the value remains constant.

```
var car = {};

Object.defineProperty(car, 'wheels', {
  value: 4,
  writable: false
});

// => 4
console.log(car.wheels);

car.wheels = 5;

// => 4
console.log(car.wheels);
```

Inspecting Objects

In the last section, you learned how to define your own properties on objects you create. Just as in life, it's helpful to know how to read *and* write, so in this section you'll learn how to dig through the underbrush of objects in JavaScript. What follows is a list of functions and properties worth knowing when it comes to inspecting objects.

Object.getOwnPropertyDescriptor

In the last section, you saw the various ways to set the attributes of a property. Object.getOwnPropertyDescriptor gives you a detailed description of those settings for any property of an object:

```
var o = {foo : 'bar'};

// Object {value: "bar", writable: true, enumerable: true, configurable: true}
Object.getOwnPropertyDescriptor(o,'foo');
```

Object.getOwnPropertyNames

This method returns all the property names of an object, even the ones that cannot be enumerated:

```
var box = Object.create({}, {
    openLid: {
        value: function () {
            return "nothing";
        },
        enumerable: true
    },
    openSecretCompartment: {
        value: function () {
            return 'treasure';
        },
        enumerable: false
    }
});

// => ["openLid", "openSecretCompartment"]
console.log(Object.getOwnPropertyNames(box).sort());
```

Object.getPrototypeOf

This method is used to return the prototype of a particular object. In lieu of this method, it may be possible to use the __proto__ method, which many interpreters implemented as a means of getting access to the object's prototype. However, __proto__ was always considered somewhat of a hack, and the JavaScript community used it mainly as a stopgap. It is worth noting, however, that even if Object.getPrototypeOf gives you access to the prototype of an object, the only way to set the prototype of an object instance is by using the __proto__ property.

```
var a = {};

// => true
console.log(Object.getPrototypeOf(a) === Object.prototype && Object.prototype === a.__proto__);
```

Object.hasOwnProperty

JavaScript's prototype chain allows you to iterate over an instance of an object and return all properties that are enumerable. It includes properties that are not present on the object but somewhere in the prototype chain. The hasOwnProperty method allows you to identify whether the property in question is present on the object instance:

```
var foo = {
    foo: 'foo'
};
var bar = Object.create(foo, {
    bar: {
        enumerable: true,
        value: 'bar'
    }
});
```

CHAPTER 1 ■ OBJECTS AND PROTOTYPING

```
// => bar
// => foo
for (var x in bar) {
    console.log(x);
}

var myProps = Object.getOwnPropertyNames(bar).map(function (i) {
    return bar.hasOwnProperty(i) ? i : undefined;
});

// => ['bar']
console.log(myProps);
```

Object.keys

This method returns a list of only the enumerable properties of an object:

```
var box = Object.create({}, {
    openLid: {
        value: function () {
            return "nothing";
        },
        enumerable: true
    },
    openSecretCompartment: {
        value: function () {
            return 'treasure';
        },
        enumerable: false
    }
});

// => ["openLid"]
console.log(Object.keys(box));
```

Object.isFrozen

This method returns true or false if the object being checked cannot be extended and its properties cannot be modified:

```
var bombPop = {
    wrapping: 'plastic',
    flavors: ['Cherry', 'Lime', 'Blue Raspberry']
};

// => false
console.log(Object.isFrozen(bombPop));

delete bombPop.wrapping;
```

```
// undefined;
console.log(bombPop.wrapping);

// prevent further modifications
Object.freeze(bombPop);

delete bombPop.flavors;

// => ["Cherry", "Lime", "Blue Raspberry"]
console.log(bombPop.flavors);

// => true
console.log(Object.isFrozen(bombPop));
```

Object.isPrototypeOf

This method checks every link in a given object's prototype chain for the existence of another object:

```
// => true
Object.prototype.isPrototypeOf([]);

// => true
Function.prototype.isPrototypeOf(()=>{});

// => true
Function.prototype.isPrototypeOf(function(){});

// => true
Object.prototype.isPrototypeOf(()=>{});
```

▪ **Note**   At the time of this writing, the so-called fat arrow syntax was supported only in browsers like Firefox 22 (SpiderMonkey 22). Running arrow functions in unsupported browsers produce a syntax error.

Object.isExtensible

By default, new objects in JavaScript are extensible, meaning that new properties can be added. However, an object can be marked to prevent it from being extended in the future. In some environments, setting a property on an inextensible object throws an error. You can use Object.isExtensible to check an object before trying to modify it:

```
var car = {
    doors: 4
};

// => true
console.log(Object.isExtensible(car) === true);

Object.preventExtensions(car);

// => false
console.log(Object.isExtensible(car) === true);
```

Object.isSealed

This function returns true or false depending on whether an object cannot be extended and all its properties are nonconfigurable:

```
var ziplockBag = {};

// => false
console.log(Object.isSealed(ziplockBag) === true);

// => true
console.log(Object.isExtensible(ziplockBag));

Object.seal(ziplockBag);

// => true
console.log(Object.isSealed(ziplockBag) === true);

// => false
console.log(Object.isExtensible(ziplockBag));
```

Object.valueOf

If you have ever tried to inspect an object only to see it spit out "[object Object]", you have seen the handiwork of this function. Object.valueOf is used to describe an object with a primitive value. All objects receive this function, but it is essentially a stub, meant to be overridden by a custom function later. Creating your own valueOf function provides a way to give an extra layer of descriptive detail to your custom objects:

```
var Car = function (name) {
    this.name = name;
}

var tesla = Object.create(Car.prototype, {
    name: {
        value: 'tesla'
    }
});

// => [Object object]
console.log(tesla.valueOf());

Car.prototype.valueOf = function () {
    return this.name;
}

// => tesla
console.log(tesla.valueOf());
```

Object.is (ECMAScript 6)

Testing equality of two values has long been a sore spot for some developers in JavaScript because JavaScript actually supports two forms of equality comparison. For checking abstract equality, JavaScript uses the double equal syntax ==. When checking strict equality, JavaScript uses the triple equal syntax ===. The major difference between the two is that by default the abstract equality operator coerces some values in order to make the comparison. The Object.is method determines whether the two supplied arguments have the same value without the need of coercing. Here are some examples of how to use the Object.is method:

```
// True because both strings use the same characters and length.
Object.is('true', 'true')

// False because type case counts as a difference.
Object.is('True', 'true')

// True because function is coerced to true using the logical not operator.
Object.is(!function(){}(), true)

// True because the built-in Math object has no prototype.
Object.is(undefined, Math.prototype);
```

Do not confuse this behavior with the strict equality comparison operator, which returns true only if the two share the same type, not the same value. It can be represented easily with the following example:

```
// => false
console.log(NaN === 0/0);

// => true
Object.is(NaN,0/0);
```

Modifying Objects

In addition to being able to explore the structures of existing objects, it is also essential to be able to modify (or prevent modification). This section explains the various mechanisms available to bend objects to your will.

Object.freeze

Freezing an object prevents it from being changed again. Frozen objects cannot accept new properties, have existing properties deleted, or have their values changed:

```
var bombPop = {
    wrapping: 'plastic',
    flavors: ['Cherry', 'Lime', 'Blue Raspberry']
};

// => false
console.log(Object.isFrozen(bombPop));

delete bombPop.wrapping;

// undefined;
console.log(bombPop.wrapping);
```

```
// prevent further modifications
Object.freeze(bombPop);

delete bombPop.flavors;

// => ["Cherry", "Lime", "Blue Raspberry"]
console.log(bombPop.flavors);

// => true
console.log(Object.isFrozen(bombPop));
```

Object.defineProperties

This function allows new properties to be defined or existing properties to be modified:

```
var car = {};

Object.defineProperties(car, {
    'wheels': {
        writable: true,
        configurable: true,
        enumerable: true,
        value: 4
    },
        'doors': {
        writable: true,
        configurable: true,
        enumerable: true,
        value: 4
    }
});

// => 4
console.log(car.doors);

// => 4
console.log(car.wheels);
```

Object.defineProperty

This function allows a single property to be added to an object or an existing property to be modified:

```
var car = {};

Object.defineProperty(car, 'doors', {
  writable: true,
  configurable: true,
  enumerable: true,
  value: 4
});
```

Object.preventExtensions

This function prevents new properties from being added to an existing object. Do not confuse this method with freezing an object, though. Although an object cannot be extended, it can be reduced, meaning that properties are removable.

```
var car = {
    doors: 4
};

// => true
console.log(Object.isExtensible(car) === true);

Object.preventExtensions(car);

// => false
console.log(Object.isExtensible(car) === true);

// => 4
console.log(car.doors);
delete car.doors;

// => undefined
console.log(car.doors);

car.tires = 4;

// => undefined
console.log(car.tires);
```

Object.prototype

Setting the prototype of an object decouples the object from its existing prototype chain and appends it to the end of the new object specified. This is useful for imbuing objects with the properties and methods of another object and those in its chain.

```
var Dog = function () {};
Dog.prototype.speak = function () {
    return "woof";
};

var Cat = function () {};
Cat.prototype.speak = function () {
    return "meow";
};

var Tabby = function () {};
Tabby.prototype = new Cat();
var tabbyCat = new Tabby();
```

13

```
// => 'meow'
console.log(tabbyCat.speak());

// => undefined
console.log(tabbyCat.prototype);

// Setting the prototype of an object instance will not affect the instantiated properties
tabbyCat.prototype = new Dog();

// => Dog { speak: function }
console.log(tabbyCat.prototype);

// => 'meow'
console.log(tabbyCat.speak());
```

Object.seal *(properties can still be modified)*

Sealing an object makes it immutable, meaning that new properties cannot be added, and existing properties are marked as nonconfigurable. This is not the same as freezing an object that prevents the object from being modified further, as you can see in the following example:

```
var envelope = {
    letter: 'To whom it may concern'
};

// => false
Object.isSealed(envelope);

Object.seal(envelope);

envelope.letter = "Oh Hai";
envelope.stamped = true;

// => Oh Hai
console.log(envelope.letter);

// => undefined
console.log(envelope.stamped);
```

Calling Objects

It is useful at times for one object to borrow the function of another object, meaning that the borrowing object simply executes the lent function as if it were its own. Think of this the same way as you might borrow a sweater from a friend. You use the sweater temporarily to warm yourself, but give it back when you are done. Sweater borrowing in JavaScript is accomplished through the call() and apply() functions, respectively. They act very similar except that the call() function accepts an argument list, and the apply() function expects a single array of arguments. These methods are very useful for imbuing objects with temporary functionality, such as using built-in functions from core objects or chaining calls to constructors.

Function.call and Function.apply

```
var friend = {
    warmth: 0,
    useSweater: function (level) {
        this.warmth = level;
    }
};
var me = {
    warmth: 0,
    isWarm: function () {
        return this.warmth === 100;
    }

};

// => false
console.log(me.isWarm());

try {
    me.useSweater(100);
} catch (e) {
    // => Object #<Object> has no method 'useSweater'
    console.log(e.message);
}

friend.useSweater.call(me, 100);

// => true
console.log(me.isWarm());

me.warmth = 0;

// => false
console.log(me.isWarm());

friend.useSweater.apply(me, [100]);

// => true
console.log(me.isWarm());
```

Creating Objects

JavaScript treats nearly everything as an object, so almost every element of the language can be created, assigned properties, and linked to a prototype chain. The only exceptions are the hungry ghosts of the language null and undefined. When objects are created in JavaScript, they are not made from whole cloth. In this section, I'll explain the three methods for object creation and why more than one method is even needed.

■ **Note**   I once incorrectly thought that numbers were not objects because I could not call methods on them using the dot syntax—for example, 1.toString(). As it turns out, most interpreters assume that the period is the point of delineation between whole and fractional numbers. If you call your method using grouped parentheses (1).toString() or double periods 1..toString(), it works!

Object Literals

The literal syntax describes objects in-line with the rest of the code as a series of comma-delineated properties, which are wrapped inside curly brackets. Unlike the new Object() and Object.create() syntax, the literal syntax is not explicitly invoked because the literal notation is actually a syntactic shortcut for using the Object.create method in a specific context. Here is an example:

```
var foo = {
    bar: 'baz'
};

var foo2 = Object.create(Object.prototype, {
    bar: {
        writable: true,
        configurable: true,
        value: 'baz'
    }
});

// => baz
console.log(foo.bar);

// => baz
console.log(foo2.bar);
```

The literal syntax is clear, expressive, and compact. You can describe and create your object in-line, and do so in one shot. This quality makes the literal notation syntax a great choice for simple one-off objects used to handle events, marshal state changes between objects, or to compartmentalize functionality while keeping the code visually grouped together. Another subtle difference between the literal syntax and new Object() form is that the literal syntax's constructor cannot be redefined. However, the native Object constructor function belongs to the global namespace, and if modified can result in unexpected behavior that can be hard to trace. The fact that the literal syntax is invoked implicitly affords the code a bit of defensive programming.

```
var foo = new Object();
var bar = {};

// => object
console.log(typeof(foo))

// => object
console.log(typeof(bar))
```

```
window.Object = function(){ arguments.callee.call() };

// => Uncaught RangeError: Maximum call stack size exceeded
var foo = new Object();
```

The literal syntax is not good for every use case; for example, there is no way to create an object whose prototype is anything other than the built-in object. Moreover, because the literal syntax is invoked implicitly, there is no explicit constructor function meaning that object literals make poor object factories.

■ **Note** Object literals are not JSON. Many people confuse the Object literal syntax with JSON, and even if they look similar, they are not the same. JSON is only a data description language, so it cannot contain functions. Additionally, many JSON parsers expect properties to be defined using double quotes that the literal syntax does not require.

---

new Object()

When I talk about new Object(), what I am really discussing is the new operator. This operator creates an instance of an object on demand. It accepts a constructor function and a series of optional arguments to be used during initialization. Upon creation the newly created object inherits from the constructor function's prototype.

```
var Animal, cat, dog;

Animal = function (inLove) {
    this.lovesHumans = inLove || false;
};
cat = new Animal();
dog = new Animal(true);

// => false
console.log(cat.lovesHumans);

// => true
console.log(dog.lovesHumans);
```

The new operator is a vestigial structure of JavaScript's attempt to be like Java. Many people are confused by the new operator because it imposes a pseudo-classical vocabulary onto JavaScript, which does not have a formalized class-based inheritance methodology. To better understand what new does behind the scenes, let's take the previous example and dissect what new is doing for us. Hopefully, this clears up any potential ambiguities introduced by its semantics.

1. JavaScript Creates a New Object

This is equivalent to creating an object literal { }.

2. JavaScript Links the Constructor of the Newly Created Object to the Animal Function

```
/*
 * function (inLove) {
 *    this.lovesHumans = inLove || false;
 * }
 */
console.log(cat.constructor);
```

3. JavaScript Links the Object's Prototype to Animal.prototype

During the construction process, the newly created object gets a reference to the previous constructor's properties. They are a shallow copy, and if modified later, what actually happens is the reference to the constructor's properties are now obscured by a local reference.

```javascript
var Animal, cat, dog;

Animal = function (inLove) {
    this.lovesHumans = inLove || false;
};
cat = new Animal();
dog = new Animal(true);

// capture the errors so our script will continue to execute.
try {
    // => Uncaught TypeError: Object [object Object] has no method 'jump'
    console.log(cat.jump());
} catch (e) {}

/*
 * We can change the base object and have the changes reflected downward even
 * to objects who have already been instantiated.
 */
Animal.prototype.jump = function () {
    return "how high?!";
};

// => how high?!
console.log(cat.jump());

// => how high?!
console.log(dog.jump());

/*
 * Changes to the local property do not propagate up the prototype chain.
 * Instead, the reference to the prototype's property is blocked by the new local
 * property of the same name.
 */
cat.jump = function () {
    return "no";
}

// => no
console.log(cat.jump());

// => how high?!
console.log(dog.jump());
```

4. JavaScript Assigns Any Supplied Arguments to the Newly Created Object

The new operator marshals the initialization of an arbitrary number of properties on the newly created object. They are supplied as arguments passed into the constructor function.

```
var Animal, dog;

Animal = function (inLove) {
    this.lovesHumans = inLove || false;
};

// `new` is essentially doing this:
// dog = {}
// dog.lovesHumans = true;
dog = new Animal(true);
```

If you think of new as a helpful worker elf that creates objects for you by following a recipe, you'll be fine. However, if you assume that new behaves as it does in other languages such as Java, you will have a bad time.

Object.create

Until the introduction of Object.create in ECMAScript 5, the only way to create prototypical inheritance was through the use of the new operator. For all intents and purposes, though, Object.create() and the literal notation should be used in place of new Object(). Object.create() affords the developer the same benefits of new, but with a method signature more consistent with the rest of the language. The advantages of Object.create go beyond just semantic improvements, Object.create is actually much more powerful, mostly in terms of how it supports inheritance. Object.create takes two parameters: an object to serve as a prototype and an optional property object that contains values to configure the newly created object with.

```
var Car = {
    drive: function (miles) {
        return this.odometer += miles;
    }
};

var tesla = Object.create(Car, {
    'odometer': {
        value: 0,
        enumerable: true
    }
});

// => 10
console.log(tesla.drive(10));
```

This section investigated various ways objects are created, accessed, and modified using JavaScript. Along the way, I hinted at how the prototype concept works. The next section explains how JavaScript implements common strategies in OOP, such as inheritance, and some of the common ways developers get tripped up trying to use it.

Programming Prototypically

The purpose of an OOP language is to create virtual objects with the ability to communicate together to accomplish a task. Typically, this means modeling a representation of an entity in code and then having the software *use* it to accomplish the developer's goals. Although the previous definition sounds straightforward, the reality is that there is often an unavoidable messiness in orchestrating the interchange of data and state between objects. This is especially true when translating a complex real-world problem domain into a series of objects that depend on each other. Generally, OOP languages mitigate some of the organizational complexity inherent in translating the entities into code through the application of higher-order concepts including abstraction, encapsulation, inheritance, and polymorphism. In most OOP languages, these techniques are applied using classes.

Classes in languages such as C++, JAVA, and Ruby are descriptions of objects, but not objects in and of themselves. In the same way you would not get brain freeze by eating a recipe for ice cream, neither can you use a class to perform work. Classes are purposely abstract because they must define all characteristics, capabilities, and affordances of the potential object they create. Proponents of class-based languages say they offer a clear delineation between the structure and state. The counter argument is that classes force an unnecessarily rigid ontology to categorizing objects.

In JavaScript, there is no such thing as a class definition. Objects inherit their functionality from other objects through a prototypical link (if desired). These prototype links can in turn form chains of dependencies between each other, which enables sophisticated behavior though composition. This section explains in detail the intricacies of the prototype concept and how to maximize its effectiveness in JavaScript.

To fully explain the benefits of programming using prototypes, you first need to understand the goals of *abstraction, encapsulation, inheritance,* and *polymorphism* as it applies to JavaScript. As part of the explanation of each of the four concepts, I will use programming examples to help clearly delineate the difference between JavaScript's prototype and what for many other programmers may be the more familiar class-based approach.

Abstraction

Abstractions in programming are invented constructs that mentally transform a real-world object or process into a computational analog. Abstractions afford the programmer a mechanism to begin to break up complexities of their subject into smaller discrete parts. This process is referred to as *decoupling* in most OOP languages. Thinking about a problem in terms of classes or prototypes are abstractions because they give a convenient metaphor to organize our programs while hiding the actual low-level code that talks to the machine. A common misconception about abstractions is that they are only for hiding information, decoupling contents into modules, or defining a clear interface between objects. Although these are strategic goals of abstractions, the tactics to achieve them can vary depending on the language. In JavaScript, all abstractions have at their root the use of the prototype, which is the actual mechanism that handles encapsulation, inheritance, and polymorphism.

Encapsulation

Encapsulation in software design has three goals: hide implementation, promote modularity, and protect the internal state of an object. Well-designed objects hide unneeded or privileged information from public consumption. Encapsulation does this by defining a public interface that gives the programmer just enough information on how to use the object, while hiding the specifics of how it works. Information hiding through encapsulation also allows the implementation of business logic to change over time without affecting the public interface that is exposed to the user. This is like users learning to drive a car: once they understand how to use the steering wheel and the pedals, it doesn't matter how many valves the engine has.

If we extend the previous example, I will wager that you could swap out the engines between cars without the driver needing to relearn anything about how to steer the car. They may notice a difference in how the car performs, but the interface stays the same. This observation hints at the next benefit of encapsulation, which is that it promotes modularity in code design.

True encapsulation also provides a third benefit, which is that it prevents private logic from being accessed or modified by other objects. In this way, encapsulation works like a protective barrier around the class, ensuring that the inner workings of the object remain unmolested.

A popular way to hide the implementation in class-based languages is through the use of private and public functions. The private qualities of functions are restrictions enforced by the language, which makes certain code available to the class instance but inaccessible to outside objects. Here is an example in Java:

```java
public class Car{

    private String name;
    private int wheelCount;

    public String getName(){
        return name;
    }

    public void setName(String newName){
        name = newName;
    }

    public String getWheelCount(){
        return wheelCount;
    }

    public void setWheelCount( String wheels){
        wheelCount = wheels;
    }
}
```

As you can see in the previous example, it is impossible to directly access the name or wheelCount variables because Java allows them to be declared private. To access them, you must instead use the public methods of the class. Typically, these proxy methods are known as getters and setters. In this way, the variables can still be used, albeit through a controlled interface.

One consequence of JavaScript's prototype-based approach is that it prevents objects from designating properties as private, which makes encapsulation harder (but not impossible!).

```javascript
var Car = function(){
    var name = 'Tesla';
    var wheelCount = '4';
    this.getName = function(){
        return name;
    }
    this.getWheelCount = function() {
        return wheelCount;
    }
    this.setName = function(newName) {
        name = newName;
    }
    this.setWheelCount = function(newCount) {
        wheelCount = newCount;
    }
}
var myCar = new Car();
```

```
// #=> undefined
console.log(myCar.name);

myCar.name = "Corvette";

// #=> 'Corvette'
console.log(myCar.name);

// #=> 'Tesla'
console.log(myCar.getName());

// #=> 'Corvette'
myCar.setName('Corvette');
console.log(myCar.getName());
```

In this script, you can see that there are two local variables defined inside the function body. These two variables are implicitly private because of the way that JavaScript's function level scoping works. To expose their values to the outside, you can create your own getter and setter methods. The key takeaway is that by using local variables instead of object properties, their value stays inaccessible to the outside.

This approach gives good encapsulation because it promotes modularity through information hiding and protects the inner state of the object from unwanted global access.

Polymorphism

Polymorphism describes the capability of one object to act like another in certain contexts. There are many types of polymorphisms in OOP languages, but "ad hoc polymorphism"[4] is particularly prevalent and useful in JavaScript. This section explores how ad hoc polymorphism works.

Ad Hoc Polymorphism

Ad hoc polymorphism affords an object the ability to use the context of the call to shape the outcome. The context may include the calling object or the type of arguments supplied to the method. Ad hoc polymorphism is sometimes referred to as function overloading or operator overloading because these techniques are a common way to implement this form of polymorphism.

Function Overloading

In statically typed languages such as C++, function overloading allows the developer to define multiple functions of the same name as long as their method signatures differs from each other. The distinction between the functions is achieved by requiring a different number of arguments or arguments of a different type. Once implemented, it is up to the compiler to choose the correct function based on the number and type of arguments provided.

JavaScript functions do not enforce type checking and can receive an arbitrary number of arguments. This flexibility means that function overloading works out of the box without needing to declare multiple flavors of the same function.

Operator Overloading

Many languages support operator overloading, whereby a developer can redefine how an operator functions. JavaScript does not support this level of overloading but does allow the operators to shift their behavior based on the context of how they are used. Consider how the "+" operator behaves, depending on the situation in which it is used.

---

[4]http://en.wikipedia.org/wiki/Ad_hoc_polymorphism

```
// summation
// => 2
console.log(1+1);

// concatenation
// => "foo bar"
console.log("foo " + "bar");

// accumulation
// => 2
var num = 1;
console.log(num++);
```

Inheritance

> *Inheritance defines semantic hierarchies between objects, by allowing children to create specializations, generalizations or variations of the parent class.*[5]

The definition of *inheritance* literally means to pass down rights, properties, and obligations to another party (typically after death)[6]. In class-based languages inheritance is described as forming an "*is-a*"[7] relationship between objects (class Dog *is a* subclass of Mammal, while Animal *is a* superclass of Mammal).

The fact that children can inherit specifications from their parents leads many developers to believe that inheritance also affords the programmer a conduit for code reuse within their system. Intuitively this makes sense; imagine a collection of objects all sharing attributes among one another. By extracting those common features into a base class, each child would benefit from those features automatically, while not having to redefine those features internally.

However, code reuse through inheritance is severely crippled because in most languages, a child can inherit from only one parent. This limitation can cause classes to inherit code it doesn't need or needing to override a feature of the parent class. Angus Croll describes the problems with using inheritance for code reuse succinctly when he writes this:

> *Using inheritance as a vehicle for code reuse is a bit like ordering a happy meal because you wanted the plastic toy. Sure a circle is a shape and a dog is a mammal—but once we get past those textbook examples most of our hierarchies get arbitrary and tenuous–built for manipulating behaviour even as we pretend we are representing reality. Successive descendants are saddled with an ever increasing number of unexpected or irrelevant behaviours for the sake of re-using a few.*[8]

The need to alter the inherited qualities of a class muddies the is-a relationship between a parent and child. Additionally, by omitting or overriding aspects of the parent, the child also breaks encapsulation and promotes brittle code through tight coupling[9].

Inheritance is by no means perfect in JavaScript, either. JavaScript uses differential inheritance[10], in which all objects are derived from a generic base object instead of some parent class. Each object that is created keeps a reference to the object that created it, which is that object's prototype. Where class-based inheritance defines the relationship between objects based on similarities, differential inheritance uses the small differences between the prototype and the offspring as a dividing line.

---

[5]http://isase.us/wisr3/7.pdf
[6]http://en.wikipedia.org/wiki/Inheritance
[7]http://en.wikipedia.org/wiki/Is-a
[8]http://javascriptweblog.wordpress.com/2010/12/22/delegation-vs-inheritance-in-javascript/
[9]http://en.wikipedia.org/wiki/Coupling_(computer_programming)
[10]https://developer.mozilla.org/en/docs/Differential_inheritance_in_JavaScript

Power of Prototype

Prototype-based languages including JavaScript build up complexity in objects by allowing one object to reference another through a prototype link. JavaScript uses the prototype chain as a mechanism for dynamic delegation between objects, where an attempt to reference a property travels up the prototype chain until it reaches the last link. Practically speaking, prototypes offer the developer a flexible tool to organize and reuse code. This section explores how to access and augment an object's prototype chain.

Understanding Prototypes

In JavaScript, a prototype can be accessed in three ways:

- `Foo.prototype` defines the prototype for objects instantiated using the new operator; for example, `new Foo()`.

- `Object.getPrototypeOf(foo)` returns the prototype reference for a given object.

- `Foo.__proto__` is a property that points to the object constructor's own prototype object. This property reference is nonstandard, but older engines may depend on it. As such, `__proto__` has now been codified in the most recent version of ECMAScript (ES6). I am mentioning this property for the sake of completeness only. If you have need to reference an object's prototype, you should prefer the standardized `Object.getPrototypeOf()` over this `__proto__`.

The following code demonstrates the various ways the prototype object can be read:

```
var Car = function (wheelCount) {
    this.odometer = 0;
    this.wheels = wheelCount || 4;
};
Car.prototype.drive = function (miles) {
    this.odometer += miles;
    return this.odometer;
};
var tesla = new Car();

// => true
console.log(Object.getPrototypeOf(tesla) === Car.prototype);

// => true
console.log(tesla.__proto__ === Car.prototype);
```

It may seem that having a prototype object is somewhat dangerous because what happens if an object unintentionally modifies one of the properties of the prototype? As it turns out, JavaScript protects against this sort of thing; any attempt to set a property of the prototype in effect makes a new property on the object instance that obscures access to the property somewhere in the prototype chain. Continuing with the car example, you can see this play out:

```
var tesla = new Car();

// => 4
console.log(tesla.wheels);
var isetta = new Car(3);
```

```
// =>3
console.log(isetta.wheels);
isetta.drive = function (miles) {
    this.odometer -= miles;
    return this.odometer;
};

// => -10
console.log(isetta.drive(10));

// => 10
console.log(tesla.drive(10));

// Changes made to the prototype are propagated throughout the chain.
Car.prototype.drive = function (miles) {
    this.odometer += miles * 2;
    return this.odometer;
};

// However it cannot propagate changes to properties defined inside the constructor.
Car.prototype.odometer = 0;

// => -20 no change because the local function obscures the prototype's new version
console.log(isetta.drive(10));

// => 30
console.log(tesla.drive(10));
```

There are several advantages to this approach:

- Properties of the prototype accessed through the linked object are merely a shallow reference, which adds a layer of defense against unintended changes.

- Shallow property references conserve memory because there is only one instance of a given property or function.

- Properties added to the prototype object immediately propagate downward to objects lower on the property chain.

The last example of the car constructor tried to reset the value of the odometer at runtime in the hopes that it would reset the values for all instances. It failed because the odometer property was defined inside the constructor. However, if you had defined odometer on the prototype the same way as the drive method, the change would have taken effect as long as the object instance has not defined its own local copy of odometer, which occurs during the drive() function.

```
var Car = function (wheelCount) {
    this.wheels = wheelCount || 4;
};
Car.prototype.odometer = 0;
Car.prototype.drive = function (miles) {
    this.odometer += miles;
    return this.odometer;
};
var tesla = new Car();
```

```
// assign the odometer a new default value.
Car.prototype.odometer = 200;

// => 210
console.log(tesla.drive(10));

// assign it yet again.
Car.prototype.odometer = 2000;

// This change fails because the drive function set a local variable for odometer as it runs.

// => 220
console.log(tesla.drive(10));
```

Class by Convention

JavaScript has no formal class-based structure. Even though the last section proved this fact, I don't blame some readers for having a twinge of doubt in the back of their minds. Maybe this disbelief is because the JavaScript landscape is littered with references to classes or class-based terminology. To make things even more confusing, the language has a reserved class keyword, which does nothing! Douglas Crockford refers to JavaScript as being pseudoclassical because of what he sees as "an unnecessary level of indirection" (Crockford, 2008) due to the fact that objects are produced by constructor functions. Whenever people talk about classes in JavaScript, they are talking about class as a convention of style, not a feature of the language.

It is important to make this distinction because those familiar with classes from other languages bring with them certain mental artifacts and expectations of how they work. These preconceptions may derail a developer who expects the same behavior from JavaScript. What follows is a discussion for JavaScript developers who think in terms of classes, about how they can implement class-like behavior using a design pattern. This pattern is a mixture of built-in language features and coding conventions.

> In a class-based object-oriented language, in general, state is carried by instances, methods are carried by classes, and inheritance is only of structure and behaviour. In ECMAScript, the state and methods are carried by objects, while structure, behaviour, and state are all inherited.[11]

Constructors

Intuitively, it would seem that the goal of a constructor is to construct an object. In JavaScript constructors are nothing more than functions, that when invoked with a new operator return an instance object. *In JavaScript, any function invoked using the* new() *operator is a constructor*. The purpose of the constructor is to initialize the newly created object with sensible defaults. As a rule of thumb, define only the properties and functions needed by all instances that are derived from the constructor.

```
var Car = function(){

    // Instance Property
    this.running = false;
```

---

[11]ECMA 262 edition working draft

```
    // Instance Method
    this.start = function(){
        return this.running = true;
    }
}

var tesla = new Car();

// => false
console.log(tesla.running);

// => true
console.log(tesla.start());
```

Not all built-in functions can be invoked without the new operator. Often this is because there is no sensible default to return by the built-in object. Invoking the Date() function returns a string representing the current date and time, while calling the Math() function will return an error.

```
// => "Wed May 15 2013 15:42:24 GMT-0400 (EDT)"
Date()

// => TypeError: object is not a function
Math();
```

Where possible, it is best to return a similar result from a constructor regardless of whether it is called within the context of the new operator or not. David Herman goes into detail on this topic in his section "Make Your Constructors new-Agnostic" (Herman, 2013). However, many of the built-in objects of JavaScript don't adhere to this convention.

```
// Zero is returned as specified by the built-in Number object's constructor.
// => 0
var num = Number();

// A new instance of the number object is returned.
// => Number {}
var num = new Number();
```

▓ **Note**   JavaScript doesn't have formal classes, but it does follow the naming convention used in other languages in which they use uppercase names to (e.g., "Foo" designate a class-like object).

Instance Properties

Instance properties are any publicly accessible variable that describes a quality of the object instance. Instance properties are those values that may vary from object to object. In the previous example, `this.running` is an instance property. Instance properties can be defined inside the constructor function or separately as part of the prototype object.

```
var Car = function(wheelCount){
    this.wheels = wheelCount || 4
}
Car.prototype.odometer = 0;

var tesla = new Car();

// => 4
console.log(tesla.wheels);

// => 0
console.log(tesla.odometer);
```

Instance Methods

Instance methods provide functionality useful to the object instance. The instance method also has access to instance properties. Instance methods can be defined in two ways: it can extend the instance by referencing the `this` keyword or set the property directly to the prototype chain.

```
var Car = function(){

    // Instance Property
    this.running = false;

    // Instance Method
    this.start = function(){
        return this.running = true;
    }
}

Car.prototype.stop = function() {
    return this.running = false;
}

var tesla = new Car();

// => false
console.log(tesla.running);

// => true
console.log(tesla.start());

// => false
console.log(tesla.stop());
```

Class Properties

Class properties are variables that belong to the class object itself. They are useful for properties that will never change, such as constants. The core Math object has a class property PI, which has a default value of 3.141592653589793. In JavaScript, class properties can be set directly on the constructor function.

```
var Cake = function () {};
Cake.isLie = true;
```

Class Methods

Class methods, which are sometimes called *static methods*, are functions available only to the class itself. Class methods can access class properties, but not properties of an object instance. Class methods are typically utility functions that perform calculations upon supplied arguments and return a result. For example, consider the various class methods of the core Math object. Class methods are defined in the same manner as class properties. If you want to add a reverse class method to the built-in String object, you could simply write this:

```
String.reverse = function (s) {
    return s.split("").reverse().join("");
};

// => secret message
console.log(String.reverse("egassem terces"));
```

■ **Note**   You would not actually want to extend a core JavaScript object like this even though it is allowed. It is considered at a minimum to be bad etiquette, but can potentially introduce errors into your code or others'. An exception to this rule is when an object is extended through the use of a polyfill in an effort to fill in missing functionality that other code expects.

Summary

Objects are the building blocks of JavaScript and to ensure that your construction is as sturdy as possible, consider these key concepts:

- Objects are bags that hold zero or more properties.

- Object properties are either a primitive or complex type. Objects can hold their own copy of a primitive type, but can only point to complex types. For this reason, JavaScript properties are considered either pass by reference or pass by value.

- Object properties can have flags that alter the behavior and capabilities of an object when modified.

- Objects can be created in one of three ways:
    - Using the literal syntax '{}'
    - Using the new operator in conjunction with an constructor function 'new Foo()'
    - Using the built in `Object.create()` function.
- JavaScript is a prototype-based language, in which objects are related to one another through the links of a prototype chain.
- When an object is inspected for a property, it queries each step of the prototype chain until it is returned or determined to be undefined.
- When a property is set on an object that exists somewhere in the prototype chain, the prototype property is not changed; instead, a new property is defined on the local object that blocks access to the remote prototype property.
- JavaScript has no formal Class mechanisms; all uses of class-like code are conventions, not properties of the language.
- JavaScript's use of differential inheritance means that the memory footprint is often much smaller than if it were using abstract classes.
- JavaScript is an object-oriented language, but that doesn't prevent you from writing JavaScript in many other programming paradigms.

CHAPTER 2

■ ■ ■

Functions

As you learned in the previous chapter, almost everything in JavaScript is an object, including functions. However, functions are much more than just bags for containing properties; they are how work gets done in the language. Typically, developers become aware of the specifics of functions only when something they wrote explodes in their face. My goal in this chapter is to expose the intricacies of JavaScript functions to you, which will hopefully save you from having to pull syntactic shrapnel from your codebase.

A word of caution before I begin: JavaScript is only as good as its interpreter. Although the concepts discussed here are well-covered in the language spec, it does not mean that all host environments will work the same way. In other words, your mileage may vary. This section will discuss common misconceptions of JavaScript functions and the silent bugs they introduce. However, debugging functions in detail is not covered. Fortunately, correcting errors in functions has been documented by others in the JavaScript community especially in Juriy Zaytsev's excellent article, "Named Function Expressions Demystified".[1]

Blocks in JavaScript

Before you can understand functions in JavaScript, you have to appreciate blocks. JavaScript blocks are nothing more than statements grouped together. Blocks start with a left curly bracket "{" and end with a right one "}". Simply put, blocks allow statements inside the brackets to be executed together. Blocks form the most basic control structure in JavaScript. The following are a few examples of how blocks work in JavaScript:

```
// Immediately invoked function expression
;!function () {
    var triumph = false,
        cake = false,
        satisfaction = 0,
        isLie,
        note;

    // Block used as part of a function expression
    var isLie = function (val) {
        return val === false;
    }

    // Block used as part of a conditional statement
    if (isLie(cake)) {
        triumph = true;
```

---

[1]http://kangax.github.com/nfe/

```
        makeNote('huge success');
        satisfaction += 10;
    }

    // Block used as part of a function declaration
    function makeNote(message) {
        note = message;
    }
}();
```

As you saw previously, functions are essentially named blocks that the developer can invoke on demand. This is easy to demonstrate:

```
// The inline conditional block statement is executed only once per cycle.
if (isLie(cake)) {
    ...
}

function makeNote(message) {
    ...
}

// The function declaration is executed as many times as it is called.
makeNote("Moderate Success");
makeNote("Huge Success");
```

Function Arguments

Functions such as control flow statements (if, for, while, etc.) can be initialized by passing arguments into the function body. In JavaScript, variables are either a complex type (e.g., Object, Array) or a primitive type (e.g., String, Integer). When a complex object is supplied as an argument, it is passed by reference to the function body. Instead of sending a copy of the variable, JavaScript sends a pointer to its location in the memory heap. Conversely, when passing a primitive type to a function, JavaScript passes by value. This difference can lead to subtle bugs because conceptually functions are often treated as a black box and assume that they can affect only the enclosing scope by returning a variable. With pass by reference, the argument object is modified, even if it may not be returned by the function. Pass by reference and pass by value are demonstrated here:

```
var object = {
    'foo': 'bar'
},
num = 1;

// Passed by reference
;!function(obj) {
    obj.foo = 'baz';
}(object);

// => Object {foo: "baz"}
console.log(object);
```

```
// Passed by value;
;!function(num) {
    num = 2;
}(num);

// => 1
console.log(num);
```

Winning Arguments

The arguments object is a useful tool for designing functions that do not require a predetermined number of arguments as part of their method signature. The idea behind the arguments object is that it acts like a wildcard that allows you to access any number of supplied arguments by iterating over this special object just like an array. Here's an example:

```
var sum = function () {
    var len = arguments.length,
        total = 0;
    for (var x = 0; x < len; x++) {
        total += arguments[x];
    }
    return total;
};

// => 6
console.log(sum(1, 2, 3));
```

However, one of the most frustrating aspects of the arguments object is that it has just enough array-like behavior to trip up developers. If you rewrite the function to use more array methods, the script will fail:

```
var sum = function () {
    var total = 0;
    while (arguments.length > 0) {
        total += arguments.pop();
    }
    return total;
};

// Uncaught TypeError: Object #<Object> has no method 'pop'
sum(1, 2, 3);
```

Fortunately, ESCMAScript 6 improves the way functions take arguments to the point where there is very little use for the original arguments object anymore. Let's look at a couple of the new features added to support arguments.

defaultParameters (ECMAScript 6)

Many languages allow you to choose default values for arguments in the method signature. Finally, in ECMAScript 6 (ES 6), JavaScript will be one of those languages.

```
var join = function (foo = 'foo', baz = (foo === 'foo') ? join(foo + "!") : 'baz') {
    return foo + ":" + baz;
}

// => hi:there
console.log(join("hi", "there"));

// Use the default parameter when not supplied
// => hi:baz
console.log(join("hi"));

// Use the default parameter when undefined is supplied
// => foo:there
console.log(join(undefined, "there"));

// Use an expression which has access to the current set of arguments
// => foo:foo!:baz
console.log(join('foo'));
```

rest (ECMAScript 6)

Sometimes it's useful, even necessary, to design functions that take an arbitrary number of arguments. This can be tricky because of the wonkiness of the argument object, however.

```
var dispatcher = {
    join: function (before, after) {
        return before + ':' + after
    },
    sum: function () {
        var args = Array.prototype.slice.call(arguments);
        return args.reduce(function (previousValue, currentValue, index, array) {
            return previousValue + currentValue;
        });
    }
};
var proxy = {
    relay: function (method) {
        var args;
        args = Array.prototype.splice.call(arguments, 1);
        return dispatcher[method].apply(dispatcher, args);
    }
};

// => bar:baz
console.log(proxy.relay('join', 'bar', 'baz'));

// => 28
console.log(proxy.relay('sum', 1, 2, 3, 4, 5, 6, 7));
```

In the previous example, our proxy object expects a single argument that is the method to call on dispatcher. It has no clue how many other arguments are needed by the function it is calling. As you know, the argument object is not an array and therefore doesn't have useful methods such as splice, map, or reduce. In order to send the remaining arbitrary number of arguments to the dispatcher, you must process them with an array.

The rest parameters get rid of the nerdy secret handshake between functions. Here is the previous method rewritten using the rest parameters:

```
var dispatcher = {
    join: function (before, after) {
        return before + ':' + after
    },
    sum: function (...rest) {
        return rest.reduce(function (previousValue, currentValue, index, array) {
            return previousValue + currentValue;
        });
    }
};
var proxy = {
    relay: function (method, ...goodies) {
        return dispatcher[method].apply(dispatcher, goodies);
    }
};

// => bar:baz
console.log(proxy.relay('join', 'bar', 'baz'));

// => 28
console.log(proxy.relay('sum', 1, 2, 3, 4, 5, 6, 7));
```

Function Types

Now that you have a better understanding of blocks and arguments, let's dive deeper into function declarations and function expressions, the two types of functions used in JavaScript. To the casual reader, the two appear very similar:

```
// Function Declaration
function isLie(cake){
    return cake === true;
}

// Function Expression
var isLie = function(cake){
    return cake === true;
}
```

The only real difference between the two is when they are evaluated. A function declaration can be accessed by the interpreter as it is being parsed. The function expression, on the other hand, is part of an assignment expression, which prevents JavaScript from evaluating it until the program has completed the assignment. This difference may seem minor, but implications are huge; consider the following example:

```
// => Hi, I'm a function declaration!
declaration();
```

```
function declaration() {
    console.log("Hi, I'm a function declaration!");
}

// => Uncaught TypeError: undefined is not a function
expression();

var expression = function () {
    console.log("Hi, I'm a function expression!");
}
```

As you can see in the previous example, the function expression threw an exception when it was invoked, but the function declaration executed just fine. This exception gets to the heart of the difference between declaration and expression functions. JavaScript knows about the declaration function and can parse it before the program executes. Therefore, it doesn't matter if the program invokes the function before it is defined because JavaScript has *hoisted* the function to the top of the current scope behind the scenes. The function expression is not evaluated until it is assigned to a variable; therefore, it is still undefined when invoked. This is why good code style is to define all variables at the top of the current scope. Had you done this then, your script would visually match what JavaScript is doing during parse time.

The concept to take away is that during parse time, JavaScript moves all function declarations to the top of the current scope. This is why it doesn't matter where declarative functions appear in the script body. To further explore the distinctions between declarations and expressions, consider the following:

```
function sayHi() {
    console.log("hi");
}

var hi = function sayHi() {
    console.log("hello");
}

// => "hello"
hi();

// => 'hi'
sayHi();
```

If you are casually reading this code, you might assume that the declaration function would get clobbered because its function expression has an identical name. However, because the second function is part of an assignment expression, it is given its own scope, and JavaScript treats them as separate entities. To make things even more confusing, look at this example:

```
var sayHo

// => function
console.log(typeof (sayHey))

// => undefined
console.log(typeof (sayHo))
```

```
if (true) {
    function sayHey() {
        console.log("hey");
    }

    sayHo = function sayHo() {
        console.log("ho");
    }

} else {
    function sayHey() {
        console.log("no");
    }

    sayHo = function sayHo() {
        console.log("no");
    }

}

// => no
sayHey();

// => ho
sayHo();
```

In the previous example, you saw that functions of the same name were considered differently if one was an expression and the other was a declaration. In this example, I am attempting to conditionally define the function based on how the program executes. Reading the script's control flow, you'd expect sayHey to return "hey" because the conditional statement evaluates true. Instead, it returns "no", meaning the second version of the sayHey function clobbered the first. Even more confusing is that the sayHo function behaves the opposite way! Again, the difference comes down to parse time versus runtime.

You already learned that when JavaScript parses the script, it collects all the function declarations and hoists them to the top of the current scope. When this happens it clobbers the first version of sayHey with the second because they exist in the same scope. This explains why it returns "no." You also know that function expressions are ignored by the parser until the assignment process completes. Assignment happens during runtime, which is also when the conditional statement is evaluated. That explains why the sayHo function could be conditionally defined. The key to remember here is that function declarations cannot be conditionally defined. If you need conditional definition use a function expression. Furthermore, function declarations should *never* be made inside a control flow statement, due to the different ways interpreters handle it.

Function Scopes

Unlike many other languages that are scoped to the block, JavaScript is scoped to the function. In Ruby (version 1.9.X), you can write this:

```
x = 20
10.times do |x|

  # => 0..9
  puts x
end
```

```
# => 20
puts x
```

What this demonstrates is that each block gets its own scope. Conversely, you can write a similar code in JavaScript:

```
var x = 20;

// Functions have their own scope
;!function() {
    var x = "foo";

    // => "foo"
    console.log(x);
}();

// => 20
console.log(x);

for (x = 0; x < 10; x++) {

    // => 0..9
    console.log(x);
}

// => 10
console.log(x);
```

In JavaScript, x is available inside the for loop because as a control statement it belongs to the enclosing scope. This is not intuitive to many developers who are used to block level scope. JavaScript handles the need of block level scope at least partially through the use of closures, which I'll discuss later.

Arrow Prone (ECMAScript 6)

As of ES 5, JavaScript only supports function level scope. This means that this always references the scope inside the function body. This quality of function level scope has always been an awkward fact of life for developers who are used to block level scope. Many developers resort to routing around this behavior by using free variables or using bound functions.

```
// Option 1: Use a local free variable to bypass the need to reference this.
var VendingMachine = function () {
    this.stock = ["Sgt. Pepper", "Choke", "Spite"];
    var that = this;
    return {
        dispense: function () {
            if (that.stock.length > 0) {
                return that.stock.pop();
            }
        }
    };
};
```

```
var popMachine = new VendingMachine();

// => 'Spite'
console.log(popMachine.dispense());

// Option 2: Use a bound function to reference this.
var VendingMachine = function () {
    this.stock = ["Sgt. Pepper", "Choke", "Spite"];
    var dispense = function () {
        if (this.stock.length > 0) {
            return this.stock.pop();
        }
    };
    return {
        dispense: dispense.bind(this)
    };
};

var popMachine = new VendingMachine();

// => 'Spite'
console.log(popMachine.dispense());
```

Fortunately, one of the major new features of ES 6 is meant to clear up the ambiguities of lexical this—through the use of the so-called *fat arrow*. The fat arrow is a new shorter way to write functions using `=>` instead of `function()` `{}`, and will look familiar to anyone who has used CoffeeScript. As with any change, some developers bemoan what they see as unnecessary complexity in how functions work. However, when used for the correct problem, the fat arrow does have its advantages. Here is how you might rewrite the VendingMachine function using the fat arrow:

```
// Option 3: Use a fat arrow to supply the lexical this.
var VendingMachine = function () {
    this.stock = ["Sgt. Pepper", "Choke", "Spite"];
    return {
        dispense: () => {
            if (this.stock.length > 0) {
                return this.stock.pop();
            }
        }
    };
};

var popMachine = new VendingMachine();

// => 'Spite'
console.log(popMachine.dispense());
```

In addition to the shorter syntax, the fat arrow also makes reading code clearer because the this argument is visually linked to the rest of the code. The fat arrow also enables the developer to write shorter more terse (yet readable) code (for example, map and reduce require iterator functions, which look needlessly complex when written using the older function paradigm). Now using the fat arrow you can write simple functions all on one line, which allows for the of omission implied requirements such as the return statement. This is another convention that CoffeeScripters are familiar with because the last statement in a CoffeeScript function is always the return value.

```
// function classic
var sum = [1, 2, 3, 4, 5].reduce(function (last, curr) {
    return last + curr;
});

// => 15
console.log(sum);

// now with 100% more fat arrow.
var sum = [1, 2, 3, 4, 5].reduce((last, curr) => last + curr);

// => 15
console.log(sum);
```

Function Fu

Functions in JavaScript are the glue that binds the whole language together, and mastering functions go a long way toward conquering the language as a whole. With that in mind, you can now investigate several advanced uses of functions in JavaScript that can really improve not only the quality of the code but also the clarity in reading it.

Expression Closures

Expression closures are a shortcut for writing simple functions. If expression closures look familiar to you, it is because they are very similar to how lambda expressions work in other languages such as Lisp.

```
// => 10
[1, 2, 3, 4].reduceRight(function(curr, val) curr + val);
```

Using the new fat arrow syntax in ES 6, you can save even more characters.

```
// => 10
[1,2,3,4].reduceRight((curr, val) => curr + val);
```

■ **Note** Presently, expression closures have limited support in most browsers. Mozilla based browsers are the only ones with full implementation of this syntax.

Immediately Invoked Function Expressions

The immediately invoked function expression (IIFE) is one pattern you will see various libraries and frameworks use repeatedly. In its most basic form, it can be written in a couple of ways:

```
;(function(){
    ...
})();
```

```
;!function(){
    ...
}();
```

```
;-function(){
    ...
}();

;+function(){
    ...
}();

;~function(){
    ...
}();

// Not Recommended
;void function(){
    ...
}();

// Not Recommended
;delete function(){
    ...
}();
```

The beauty of the IIFE is that it uses a unary expression to coerce a function declaration, which would normally need to be explicitly called into a function expression that can self-execute. Internally, JavaScript is running a unary operation on the function declaration. The result of that operation is the function expression, which is immediately invoked with the trailing parentheses (). Besides being elegant code, the IIFE also affords the following:

- It provides a closure that prevents naming conflicts.
- It provides elegant block scoping.
- It prevents pollution of the global namespace.
- It promotes the developer to think in terms of modular code.

▒ **Note**   One other point worth mentioning is the use of the semicolon prepending the statement. Adding it provides a bit of defensive programming against other malformed modules that might not have a trailing semicolon. If this were just a function declaration, it would be absorbed into the preceding module, which can often occur when multiple scripts are concatenated together as part of a deploy process. It is highly recommended that you follow this convention to protect yourself against mystery bugs in production.

Recursive Functions

Recursive functions are simply functions that have the capability to call themselves. You can think of them as controlled loops. This capability to self-execute proves to be an excellent tool for making code more succinct while reducing complexity. However, recursive functions are not without their potential peril; when used incorrectly, recursive functions can become memory black holes that engulf resources until your script fails. Let's explore the correct ways to use recursive functions while avoiding infinite recursion.

Consider the following example:

```
var tree = {
    name: 'Users',
    children: [{
        name: 'heavysixer',
        children: [{
            name: 'Applications',
            children: []
        }, {
            name: 'Downloads',
            children: []
        }, {
            name: 'Library',
            children: [{
                name: 'Accounts',
                children: []
            }, {
                name: 'Arduino',
                children: []
            }]
        }]
    }, {
        name: 'root',
        children: []
    }]
};

var walker = function walk(branch, newDepth) {
    var depth = newDepth || 0;
    var len = branch.children.length;
    console.log(depth + ':' + branch.name);
    while (len > 0) {
        len--;
        walker(branch.children[len], depth + 1);
    }
};

/*
  => 0:Users
  => 1:root
  => 1:heavysixer
  => 2:Library
  => 3:Arduino
  => 3:Accounts
  => 2:Downloads
  => 2:Applications
*/
walker(tree);
```

In this example, the walker function takes a JSON object that represents a directory tree; iterates over each node; and outputs a list of all the directory names and their depth, respectively. You could have written a series of nested for loops and arrived at the same output. However, to do that you would have had to first calculate the absolute depth of the tree to know the number of loops required. This process is, of course, completely the wrong approach because it makes the code comically brittle. Using the recursive function, you can achieve the same effect in a flexible fashion because you can test for the existence of children and only then recursively call the function over again, this time supplying the current branch as the root node.

You may wonder whether you can simplify the recursive function even further by using the callee reference inside the arguments object:

```
// reference the callee object from the arguments object
arguments.callee(branch.children[len], depth + 1);
```

Unfortunately, using arguments.callee doesn't work in strict mode; it throws an error: "Uncaught TypeError: 'caller', 'callee', and 'arguments' properties may not be accessed on strict mode functions or the arguments objects for calls to them."

▓ **Note**   For more info on recursion, see the Function Fu section of the Functions chapter.

Higher-Order Functions

When people describe JavaScript as having "first-class functions," all that means is that JavaScript allows functions to be supplied as arguments to other functions. First-class functions are a hallmark of the functional programming paradigm, which JavaScript also supports indirectly. Functional programming promotes the use and execution of functions as a unit of abstraction. This is in contrast to object-oriented programming (OOP), which uses objects to both manipulate and store the changing state of data as the means of abstraction.

One great feature of first-class functions is that they allow JavaScript to be used to create higher-order functions, which are functions that accept functions as arguments or return functions as return values. There are many advantages of higher-order functions, but one of the primary uses is to abstract common functionality into one place. Therefore, it is not surprising that many of the uses of higher-order functions in JavaScript are for so-called utility functions. For example, Jeremy Ashkenas' project underscore.js refers to itself as "a utility-belt library for JavaScript that provides a lot of the functional programming support that you would expect in Prototype.js (or Ruby), but without extending any of the built-in JavaScript objects.[2]"

Not surprisingly, underscore.js makes good use of higher-order functions. I have included two such functions here:

```
// The cornerstone, an `each` implementation, aka `forEach`.
  // Handles objects with the built-in `forEach`, arrays, and raw objects.
  // Delegates to **ECMAScript 5**'s native `forEach` if available.
  var each = _.each = _.forEach = function(obj, iterator, context) {
    if (obj == null) return;
    if (nativeForEach && obj.forEach === nativeForEach) {
      obj.forEach(iterator, context);
    } else if (obj.length === +obj.length) {
      for (var i = 0, l = obj.length; i < l; i++) {
        if (iterator.call(context, obj[i], i, obj) === breaker) return;
      }
```

---

[2]http://underscorejs.org/

```
    } else {
      for (var key in obj) {
        if (_.has(obj, key)) {
          if (iterator.call(context, obj[key], key, obj) === breaker) return;
        }
      }
    }
  };

  // Return the results of applying the iterator to each element.
  // Delegates to **ECMAScript 5**'s native `map` if available.
  _.map = _.collect = function(obj, iterator, context) {
    var results = [];
    if (obj == null) return results;
    if (nativeMap && obj.map === nativeMap) return obj.map(iterator, context);
    each(obj, function(value, index, list) {
      results.push(iterator.call(context, value, index, list));
    });
    return results;
  };
```

You can use the _.map() like this:

```
// => [2,3,6]
var doubled = _.map([1, 2, 3], function(num){ return num * this.multiplier; }, {multiplier : 2});
```

As you unpack the _.map() higher-order function, you'll see a couple of features that make it so powerful:

- Because the data, iterator, and context are passed in as parameters to the map command, using the function becomes very expressive. This is because the transparency of intent is provided by the parameters.

- The function becomes implementation-agnostic, allowing it to act as a polyfill when a native implementation of the method is not available and otherwise deferring to the built-in version.

- The fact that you can pass in the iterator and the executing context as parameters means that the map function stays pleasingly generic. This allows the method to be used in a wide variety of circumstances, which reduces the chances of code duplication occurring.

Debugging Functions

Before I wrap this topic up, let's briefly touch on debugging functions. In JavaScript naming, a function expression is completely optional. So why do it? The answer is to aid the debugging process. Named function expressions have access to their name within the newly defined scope, but not in the enclosing scope. Without a name, their anonymous nature can make them feel a bit like ghosts in the machine when it comes to debugging.

```
var namedFunction = function named() {

    // => function
    console.log(typeof(named));
}
namedFunction();
```

```
// => undefined
console.log(typeof(named));
```

Nameless function expressions display in the stack trace as "(anonymous function)" or something similar. Naming your function expression gives you clarity when trying to unwind an exception whose call stack may feel miles long:

```
/*
 * It is much harder to debug anonymous function expressions
 * Uncaught boom
 *     - (anonymous function)
 *     - window.onload
 */
;!function(){
    throw("boom");
}();

/*
 * Naming your function expressions give you a place to start looking when debugging.
 * Uncaught boom
 *     - goBoom
 *     - window.onload
 */
;!function goBoom() {
    throw("boom")
}();
```

Summary

There are several key concepts to remember when using functions in JavaScript:

- With few exceptions (such as the let operator), JavaScript has function level scope, which is unlike many other languages that are primarily scoped at the block level.

- Functions come in two flavors: function declarations and function expressions. Function declarations are hoisted during runtime, which allows you to call them from anywhere within the local block; function expressions throw an error if you invoke them before they are defined.

- The argument object is just enough like an array to get you into trouble.

- ES 6 adds a way to specify default arguments as part of your function signature.

- ES 6 introduces the rest operator, which gives you an easy way handle an arbitrary number of arguments in a function.

- Fat arrow functions can be used as a succinct way to specify the value of this within the function body.

- There are many wonderful conceptual paradigms such as IIFEs that you can use to make your functions more powerful and easier to manage.

- Use named functions wherever possible because they make a stack trace more readable.

CHAPTER 3

■ ■ ■

Getting Closure

"No matter where you go, there you are."

— Buckaroo Banzai

The purpose of this chapter is to explain how closures work in plain English and to give a few compelling examples in which the use of closures really improves the quality of your code. Along the way, you'll also explore whether any of the improvements in ECMAScript 6 mean that closures will not need to be the Swiss army knife of JavaScript.

Like many others, I am a self-taught programmer. A little more than a decade ago, I was also a freshly minted Creative Director working in Los Angeles. I was employed by a large company and inherited a team of very bright and technically gifted programmers. I felt that I needed to learn enough code to speak intelligently to them. I didn't want to propose a feature that wasn't possible, but more importantly I wanted to understand the promise and the problems inherent in the medium in which we were building. More generally, though, I am just a very curious person who likes to learn, and once I started to pull the thread of JavaScript, the world of programming began to unwind for me. Now years later, here I sit writing about the internals of the language, hoping to pass that thread along to you.

Being that my computer science education has been *ad hoc*, there are many core concepts in JavaScript (and programming in general) that I wanted to understand better. My hypothesis is that there are others like me who have been using and abusing JavaScript for years. For this reason, I decided to write on closures, an often-used and yet misunderstood concept in JavaScript. Closures are important for a variety of reasons:

- They are both a feature and a philosophy that, once understood, make many other concepts (e.g., data binding, asynchronous programming, and promise objects) in JavaScript easier.

- They are one of the most powerful components of the language, which many other so-called real languages don't support.

- When used correctly, they afford developers a mechanism to make their code more expressive, compact, and reusable.

For all the potential benefits that closures offer, there is a black magic quality to them that can make them hard to understand. Let's start with a definition:

> *A closure is the act of binding all free variables and functions into a closed expression that persist beyond the lexical scope from which they were created.*

Although this is a succinct definition, it is pretty impenetrable for the uninitiated; let's dig deeper.

The Straight Dope on Scope

Before you can truly understand closures, you must take a step back and look at how scope works in JavaScript. Writers about JavaScript will sometimes make reference to *lexical scope*, or the *current and/or executing scope*.

Lexical scope simply means that the placement of a statement within the body of the code is important. The location of the statement affects how it can be accessed and what, in turn, it has access to. Before the release of ES 6, JavaScript could create a new scope only through a function invocation.[1] This fact often tripped up developers used to block-level scope, which is the standard in many other languages. The following example demonstrates lexical scope:

```
// Free Variable
var iAmFree = 'Free to be me!';

function canHazAccess(notFree){

  var notSoFree = "i am bound to this scope";

  // => "Free to be me!"
  console.log(iAmFree);
}

// => ReferenceError: notSoFree is not defined
console.log(notSoFree)

canHazAccess();
```

As you can see, the function declaration canHazAccess() can reference the iAmFree variable because the variable belongs to the enclosing scope. The iAmFree variable is an example of what in JavaScript is called a free variable.[2] Free variables are any nonlocal variables that the function body has access to. To qualify as a free variable, it must be defined outside the function body and not be passed as a function argument.

Conversely, referencing notSoFree from outside the enclosing scope produces an error because at the point at which this variable was defined, it was inside a new lexical scope. (Remember that prior to ES 6, function invocation created a new scope.)

Function level scopes act like one-way mirrors; they let elements inside the function body spy on variables in the outer scope, while they remain hidden. As you'll see, closures short-circuit this relationship and provide a mechanism whereby the inner scopes internals can be accessed by the outer scope.

Thisunderstandings

One feature of scope that routinely throws developers off (even seasoned ones) is the use of the this keyword as it pertains to the lexical scope. In JavaScript, the this keyword always refers to the owner of scope from which the script is executing. Misunderstanding how this works can cause all sorts of weird errors in which developers assume that they are accessing a particular scope but are actually using another. Here is how this might happen:

```
var Car, tesla;
Car = function() {
  this.start = function() {
    console.log("car started");
  };
```

---

[1] http://howtonode.org/what-is-this
[2] http://en.wikipedia.org/wiki/Free_variable

```
  this.turnKey = function() {
    var carKey = document.getElementById('car_key');
    carKey.onclick = function(event) {
      this.start();
    };
  };
  return this;
};
tesla = new Car();

// Once a user clicks the #carKey element they will see "Uncaught TypeError: Object has no method
'start'"
tesla.turnKey();
```

The developers who wrote this were headed in the right direction, but ultimately a *thisunderstanding* forced them off the rails. They correctly bound the click event to the car_key DOM element. However, they assumed that nesting the click binding inside the car class would give the DOM element a reference to the car's this context. The approach is intuitive and looks legit, especially based on what we know about free variables and lexical scope. Unfortunately, it is hopelessly borked; because as we learned earlier a new scope is created each time a function is invoked. Once the onclick event fired this now referred to the DOM element not the Car class.

Developers sometimes get around this scoping confusion by assigning this to a local free variable (e.g., that, _this, self, me). Here is the previous method rewritten to use a local free variable instead of the this variable:

```
var Car, tesla;
Car = function() {
  this.start = function() {
    console.log("car started");
  };
  this.turnKey = function() {
    var that = this;
    var carKey = document.getElementById('carKey');
    carKey.onclick = function(event) {
      that.start();
    };
  };
  return this;
};
tesla = new Car();

// Once a user click's the #carKey element they will see "car started"
tesla.turnKey();
```

Because that is a free variable, it won't be redefined when the onclick event is triggered. Instead, it remains as a pointer to the previous this context. Technically, casting this to a local variable solves the problem, and I am going to resist the urge of calling this an antipattern (for now). I have used this technique thousands of times over the years. However, it always felt like a hack, and fortunately, closures can help us marshal scopes in a much more elegant way.

Let There Be Block Scope

ES 6 introduces two new variable types, "let" and "const", both of which allow developers to use block-level scope. This is a huge improvement because it clears up some of the ambiguity of how variable hoisting is applied and will allow JavaScript to be much easier to understand. Consider the following example, which shows how block scope works in Ruby:

```
10.times do |x|
   foo = 'bar'
end

# => undefined local variable or method `foo' for main:Object (NameError)
puts foo
```

In the following example, the Ruby interpreter explodes trying to reference the local variable foo outside the loop statement because Ruby uses block-level scope. In JavaScript, however, the variable is happily returned outside of the loop block:

```
for (var x = 0; x < 10; x++){
   var foo = "bar";
}

// => 'bar'
console.log(foo);
```

JavaScript's function level scoping of local variables means behind the scenes the interpreter actually hoists the variable outside of the block. What actually gets interpreted looks more like this:

```
var x, foo;
for (x = 0; x < 10; x++) {
   foo = "bar";
}

// => 'bar'
console.log(foo);
```

With the introduction of the let declaration, JavaScript can now use true block-level scoping. Here is an example:

```
for (var x = 0; x < 10; x++) {
   let foo = "bar";

   // => bar
   console.log(foo);
}
// => ReferenceError: foo is not defined
console.log(foo);
```

The introduction of these new declarations not only makes JavaScript clearer to programmers who understand block scoping, but also aids compilers in the pursuit of improved runtime performance.

Now that you understand how scoping works in JavaScript, you can continue exploring closures.

My First Closure

In its most basic form, a closure is simply an outer function that returns an inner function. Doing this creates a mechanism to return an enclosed scope on demand. Here is a simple closure:

```
function outer(name) {
  var hello = "hi",
  inner;

  return inner = function() {
    return hello + " " + name;
  };
}

// Create and use the closure
var name = outer("mark")();

// => 'hi mark'
console.log(name);
```

As you learned in the previous chapter, JavaScript introduced a new function style: the so-called fat arrow. Let's rewrite the previous example using the fat arrow:

```
var outer (name) => {
  var hello = "hi",
  inner;

  inner => hello + " " + name;
}
var name = outer("mark")();

// => 'hi mark'
console.log(name);
```

In these two examples, you can see that the local variable hello can be used in the return statement of the inner function. At the point of execution, hello is a free variable belonging to the enclosing scope. This example borders on meaninglessness, though, so let's look at a slightly more complex closure:

```
var car;
function carFactory(kind) {
  var wheelCount, start;
  wheelCount = 4;
  start = function() {
    console.log('started with ' + wheelCount + ' wheels.');
  };

  // Closure created here.
  return (function() {
    return {
      make: kind,
```

```
      wheels: wheelCount,
      startEngine: start
    };
  }());
}

car = carFactory('Tesla');

// => Tesla
console.log(car.make);

// => started with 4 wheels.
car.startEngine();
```

Why Use Closures?

Now that you have a basic definition of what closures are, let's look at some use cases on where they can elegantly solve common problems in JavaScript.

Object Factories

The previous closure implements what is commonly known as the Factory Pattern.[3] In keeping with a Factory Pattern, the internals of the factory can be quite complex, but are abstracted away, thanks in part to the closure. This highlights one of the best features of closures: their capability to hide state. JavaScript doesn't have the concept of private or protected contexts, but using closures give us a good way to emulate some level of privacy.

Create a Binding Proxy

As promised, let's revisit the preceding Car class. The scoping problem was solved by assigning the outer function's this reference to a that free variable. Instead of that approach we'll solve it through the use of closures. First, you create a reusable closure function called proxy, which takes a function and a context and returns a new function with the supplied context applied. Then you wrap the onclick function with your proxy and pass in the this, which references the current instance of the Car class. Coincidentally, this is a simplified version of what jQuery does in its own proxy function:[4]

```
var Car, proxy, tesla;
Car = function() {
  this.start = function() {
    return console.log("car started");
  };
  this.turnKey = function() {
    var carKey;
    carKey = document.getElementById("carKey");
    carKey.onclick = proxy(function(event) {
```

---

[3]http://en.wikipedia.org/wiki/Factory_method_pattern
[4]https://github.com/jquery/jquery/blob/master/src/core.js#L685

```
      this.start();
    }, this);
  };
  return this;
};

// Use a closure to bind the outer scope's reference to this into the newly created inner scope.
proxy = function(callback, self) {
  return function() {
    return callback.apply(self, arguments);
  };
};

tesla = new Car();

// Once a user click's the #carKey element they will see "car started"
tesla.turnKey();
```

▓ **Note** ES 5 introduced a `bind` function that acts as a binding proxy for you. The previous example was used merely to explore in detail how a binding proxy works. However, in production code, you should defer to the native *Function. prototype.bind* interface.

Contextually Aware DOM Manipulation

This example comes directly from Juriy Zaytsev's excellent article "Use Cases for JavaScript Closures."[5] His example code demonstrates how to use a closure to ensure a DOM element has a unique ID. The larger takeaway is that you can use closures as a way to maintain internal states about your program in an encapsulated manner.

```
var getUniqueId = (function() {
  var id = 0;
  return function(element) {
    if (!element.id) {
      element.id = 'generated-uid-' + id++;
    }
    return element.id;
  };
})();

var elementWithId = document.createElement('p');
elementWithId.id = 'foo-bar';
var elementWithoutId = document.createElement('p');
```

---

[5]http://msdn.microsoft.com/en-us/magazine/ff696765.aspx

```
// => 'foo-bar'
getUniqueId(elementWithId);

// => 'generated-id-0'
getUniqueId(elementWithoutId);
```

Singleton Module Pattern

Modules are used to encapsulate and organize related code together under one roof. Using modules keeps your codebase cleaner, and easier to test and reuse. Attribution for the Module Pattern is typically given to Richard Conford,[6] though a number of people, most notably Douglas Crockford, are responsible for popularizing it. The Singleton Module is a flavor that restricts more than one instance of the object from existing. It is very useful for times when you want several objects to share a resource. A much more in-depth example of the Singleton Module can be found here,[7] but for now, consider the following example:

```
// Create a closure
var SecretStore = (function() {
  var data, secret, newSecret;

  // Emulation of a private variables and functions
  data = 'secret';
  secret = function() {
    return data;
  }
  newSecret = function(newValue) {
    data = newValue;
    return secret();
  }

  // Return an object literal which is the only way to access the private data.
  return {
    getSecret: secret,
    setSecret: newSecret,
  };
})();

var secret = SecretStore;

// => "secret"
console.log(secret.getSecret());

// => "foo"
console.log(secret.setSecret("foo"));

// => "foo"
console.log(secret.getSecret());
```

---

[6]http://groups.google.com/group/comp.lang.javascript/msg/9f58bd11bd67d937
[7]http://www.addyosmani.com/resources/essentialjsdesignpatterns/book/#singletonpatternjavascript

```
var secret2 = SecretStore;

// => "foo"
console.log(secret2.getSecret());
```

Summary

In this chapter, you learned about the dark arts of JavaScript closures. Closures are one of the most misunderstood concepts in JavaScript because they involve many of the less-understood particulars of the language, including free variables, lexical scope, and function level scope.

Closures are powerful because they allow free variables to persist outside of their lexical scope. However, they are often easy to create by mistake and can lead to misunderstandings about how the this operator functions. This ambiguity is likely to increase at least in the short run with the introduction to block-level scope in ES 6.

■ ■ ■

## CHAPTER 4

Jargon and Slang

"One of the reasons there are so many terms for conditions of ice is that the mariners observing it were often trapped in it, and had nothing to do except look at it."

—Alec Wilkinson, The Ice Balloon: S. A. Andrée and the Heroic Age of Arctic Exploration

Several months ago, I came across a presentation by Gary Bernhardt, simply titled "Wat." *Wat* is a colloquialism used on the Internet to describe confusion or amused disbelief toward a subject, in this case JavaScript. Bernhardt's presentation used a question-and-answer format. First, he displayed a seemingly reasonable line of JavaScript and then asked the audience to give him the output. In one case, he asked the audience what {}+[] would produce. Most in the audience thought the result would be some sort of error because it didn't make sense that you could add a literal object and array together. Instead, the result was '0'. The audience groaned and laughed in bemusement. The presentation continued on this way, asking questions and then giving results that seemed to be too wrong to be correct.

To the chagrin of many defenders of JavaScript, this presentation went viral, mostly because it is funny and lighthearted, and gave the JavaScript community a vehicle to laugh at themselves. Eventually, even Brendan Eich—the creator of JavaScript—joined the fray, making a half-hearted effort in a recent presentation to explain some of the seemingly idiotic things that his language did in Bernhardt's presentation.

I originally, thought this chapter was going to be spent unpacking and then explaining examples of *Wat* within JavaScript. However, as I dug deeper into the various examples used in Bernhardt's presentation, I began to realize that many of these inconsistencies were not defects of the language, but instead a secret handshake inside the language, a kind of programmatic jargon. At that point, my direction for this chapter shifted, and now the goal is to define jargon as it relates to programming. I will give examples of jargon in JavaScript, how to embrace it or avoid it, depending on your own style.

Jargon.prototype = new Slang()

Before accurately defining jargon, you must first understand what constitutes slang. *Slang* is the use of words or expressions that are outside of the normal, and standard vocabulary of a culture. Slang's capability to transmit meaning depends on the receiver's ability to unpack the often highly contextual references in the words or expression. In an effort to codify the mechanics of slang, Bethany K. Dumas and Jonathan Lighter (Duman & Lighter, 1978) suggest that an example of slang must meet at least two of the following criteria:

- It lowers, if temporarily, "the dignity of formal or serious speech or writing." In other words, it is likely to be considered in those contexts a "glaring misuse of register."

- Its use implies that the user is familiar with whatever is referred to, or with a group of people who are familiar with it and use the term.

- "It's a taboo term in ordinary discourse with people of a higher social status or greater responsibility."

- It replaces "a well-known conventional synonym." This is done primarily to avoid discomfort caused by conventional phrases or by further elaboration.

As you can see from these rules, Jargon meets only the second criterion. However, even this is enough to begin to see the faint outlines of what might be called programmatic jargon.

What Is Programmatic Jargon?

Programmatic jargon is a compression of code through the use of highly specific often technical rules of the language. Like other forms of jargon, the programmatic form is used to efficiently reference complex ideas between members of a community. It can become a kind of shorthand used to reference complex concepts among its members. However, because jargon is so highly contextual, it often acts as a social divider or lingual border guard between communities. This can be what makes jargon feel so impenetrable by outsiders. Knowing this, you can begin to identify criteria for defining programmatic jargon:

- It short-circuits mechanics of the language.
- It is confusing or easily misunderstood by the casual member of the community.
- It subverts visual clarity in the service some other goal (e.g., smaller code or faster execution).
- It serves as a means for stratification within a community.

Jargon gets a bad reputation because it is often used by those who have only an inkling of what the terms mean. In these cases, jargon becomes noise in the conversation, verbal filler to make the speaker seem more intelligent. In the case of programmatic slang, it could be represented by the misapplication or misuse of a programming concept in the hopes of appearing clever. Of course, the misuse of jargon makes the speaker seem like a fraud and an idiot. Richard Mitchell sums up this sentiment when he writes the following:

> *His jargon conceals, from him, but not from us, the deep, empty hole in his mind. He uses technological language as a substitute for technique.*

> —Richard Mitchell, "Less Than Words Can Say"

In JavaScript, there are three components of the language that especially lend themselves to the creation of jargon: coercion, logical operators, and bitwise manipulations (pejoratively known as bit twiddling.) Now that you have a basis for recognizing programmatic jargon, you will spend the rest of the chapter exploring and understanding specific examples of how it occurs in JavaScript.

▦ **Note** Jargon is often used in a derogatory way to describe the use of technical terminology to make a speaker seem intelligent or expert. However, jargon used correctly can be a succinct pointer to a concept that an experienced listener need not have explained. In this chapter, jargon simply means highly contextual code that is often impenetrable to the uninitiated, but not necessarily inherently bad.

Coercion

In JavaScript as in most other languages, *coercion* is the act of forcing an object or entity of one type into another. This is not to be confused with *type conversion*, which is the explicit transformation between types. In JavaScript, explicit type conversion would look like this:

```
// => "1"
var a = (1).toString();
console.log(a);
```

However, the number can also be implicitly coerced into a string this way:

```
// => "1"
var a = 1 + "";
console.log(a);
```

Many of the most cryptic code examples that have puzzled me over the years have involved coercion at some level. Much of my confusion was due to how JavaScript handles ad hoc polymorphism. If you think back to the core concepts chapter, you will remember that this form of polymorphism uses the context of execution to help shape the outcome. Specifically, JavaScript uses overloading to shift the behavior of its operators, depending on how they are called.

For example, the binary operator can be used for summation or concatenation, but it also coerces values in the process. Much of the confusion over coercion is knowing how or when it occurs. ***In JavaScript, coercion is always about simplifying complex objects to a primitive form or converting between two primitive types.*** You cannot coerce a number into an array, but you can coerce an array into a number. The following examples help explain the various ways JavaScript coerces values.

To String

JavaScript uses the binary operator to concatenate two values together. However, to make this work, JavaScript first silently coerces the zero into a string. When JavaScript attempts to convert an object to a string, it calls the `toString()` method first. If `toString()` does not return a primitive representation, it defers to the `valueOf()` function. If the `valueOf()` function cannot produce a primitive value either, JavaScript throws a `TypeError` exception:

```
// => '0'
var s = ''+0;
console.log(s);
```

To number

The unary operator's job is to convert the operand that follows into a number. Like the concatenation process, it also involves coercing the object into a primitive form, this time a number. This is the equivalent of writing `1*'10'`. Just as in the string conversion process, JavaScript relies on the results of `toString()` or `valueOf()`. However, the order is reversed: JavaScript calls `valueOf()` first and then `toString()`. Here is a simple example:

```
// => 10
console.log(+'10');
```

Context-Aware Coercion

Many built-in core objects can be coerced and therefore support unary and binary operations. The coerced object tailors the return values of valueOf() and toString() to be contextually meaningful. Take the built-in Date object, for example. When converting the object to a primitive number, it returns the milliseconds since epoch, which is a useful result for performing calculations:

```
// => 1373558473636
console.log(+new Date());
```

However, a string representation of epoch is not as useful, so when a date is converted to a string, the object returns a textual representation of the current date and time:

```
// => Thu Jul 11 2013 11:01:13 GMT-0500 (CDT)
console.log(new Date() + '');
```

Coercion Gotchas

Knowing the order of operations for type conversion should enable you to create meaningful conversion values for your own objects. That way, when your object is coerced, just like the built-in Date object it can return a contextually aware result. However, as you'll see in the following code it turns out to be harder to do than it appears at first blush:

```
var Money = function (val, sym) {
    this.currencySymbol = sym;
    this.cents = val;
};

var dollar = new Money(100, '$');

// Not helpful
// => NaN
console.log(+dollar);

// Not helpful
// => Total: [object Object]
console.log("Total: " + dollar);

Money.prototype.toString = function () {
    return this.currencySymbol + (this.cents / 100).toFixed(2);
};

Money.prototype.valueOf = function () {
    return this.cents;
};

// Helpful!
// => 100
console.log(+dollar);

// Wait what?! I wanted $1.00
// => 100
console.log(dollar + '');
```

```
// Now I am totally confused!
// => $1.00
console.log([dollar] + '');
```

The order in which the conversion occurs seems to be at odds with what you learned in the Date examples. To get an answer, you need to look at the steps JavaScript takes when coercing this object into a String. Here, operator overloading again is the problem. You might assume that because you are concatenating a string, JavaScript would use toString() instead of valueOf(), like it does for the Date object. Here is what the spec says in regards to type conversion:

> *The abstract operation ToPrimitive takes an input argument and an optional argument PreferredType. The abstract operation ToPrimitive converts its input argument to a non-Object type. If an object is capable of converting to more than one primitive type, it may use the optional hint PreferredType to favour that type.*

In this case, conversion of the object follows the following sequence:

> *Return a default value for the Object. The default value of an object is retrieved by calling the [[DefaultValue]] internal method of the object, passing the optional hint PreferredType. The behaviour of the [[DefaultValue]] internal method is defined by this specification for all native ECMAScript objects in 8.12.8.*

So it seems that you need to understand how DefaultValue is derived in the object. Digging ever deeper in the spec, you find that JavaScript has two ways of determining a DefaultValue: one for string and the other for numbers. It makes this decision based on the hint argument supplied to the DefaultValue method. If hint is not supplied, JavaScript defaults to a Number. Following is what a hypothetical version of the ToPrimitive() method might look like:

```
var ToPrimitive;

ToPrimitive = function (obj) {
    var funct, functions, val, _i, _len;
    functions = ["valueOf", "toString"];
    if (typeof obj === "object") {
        if (obj instanceof Date) {
            functions = ["toString", "valueOf"];
        }
        for (_i = 0, _len = functions.length; _i < _len; _i++) {
            funct = functions[_i];
            if (typeof obj[funct] === "function") {
                val = obj[funct]();
                if (typeof val === "string" || typeof val === "number" || typeof val ===
"boolean") {
                    return val;
                }
            }
        }
        throw new Error("DefaultValue is ambigious.");
    }
    return obj;
};
```

```
// => 1 (as string)
console.log(ToPrimitive([1]));
```

```
// => Thu Jul 11 2013 15:55:11 GMT-0500 (CDT)
console.log(ToPrimitive(new Date()));
```

Now you understand why the concatenation of the object fails to use the custom `toString()` method: because without specifying a hint for the internal `DefaultValue` function, JavaScript assumes you want a number. This results in a call to `valueOf()` instead. All you need to do now is figure out how to set the hint to a string, the same way the built-in `Date` object does. Unfortunately, there is no way to specify a hint for custom objects! At the bottom of the `DefaultValue` method description, you find this warning:

> *When the [[DefaultValue]] internal method of O is called with no hint, then it behaves as if the hint were Number, unless O is a Date object (see 15.9.6), in which case it behaves as if the hint were String.*

> *The above specification of [[DefaultValue]] for native objects can return only primitive values. If a host object implements its own [[DefaultValue]] internal method, it must ensure that its [[DefaultValue]] internal method can return only primitive values.*

You have now found a limitation in JavaScript that you cannot get around (at least not in an elegant way). With no built-in way to specify a hint to the `DefaultValue` function, the object cannot prefer `toString()` the same way the `Date` object does. All is not lost, though; if you refer to the previous example, you see that you did ultimately find a way to get the `dollar` object to concatenate in the manner you wanted. Oddly, it works if you first wrap the object in an array. Only then would JavaScript correctly coerce the value using the `toString()` method, but why? Here is a hint:

```
// => object
console.log(typeof [1].valueOf());
```

```
// => string
console.log(typeof [1].toString())
```

Did you figure it out? Remember that the rules of `ToPrimitive` say that the function must return a primitive value. The Array's `valueOf()` method however returns an object, which causes the `ToPrimitive` function to move on and call `toString()`. The subsequent call to `toString()` does return the desired primitive value. Internally, the array's `toString()` function must be iterating over all the elements in its collection and calling `toString()` on each of them. This theory is easy to test; you can simply push an object into an array that cannot be coerced into a string:

```
var noConversions = [{
    toString: undefined
}];
```

```
// => Uncaught TypeError: Cannot convert object to primitive value
console.log(noConversions + '');
```

As expected, the attempted coercion throws an error.

Mixed Type Comparison Through Coercion

Up to this point, I have been talking about coercion as it applies to type conversion for summation or concatenation. However, the equals operator also coerces the operands into primitive values before performing the equality test. Consider the following examples:

```
// => true
console.log([1] == 1);

// => true
console.log([1] == "1");

// => true
console.log([{
    toString: function () {
        return 1;
    }
}] == "1");

// => false
console.log([1] === 1);

// => false
console.log([1] === "1");

// => false
console.log([{
    toString: function () {
        return 1;
    }
}] === "1");
```

It can be worrisome that an object can essentially be equal to a primitive value through coercion, but at least now you know when that occurs. Moreover, you can see why comparing values using the strictly equals operator is promoted so heavily in JavaScript best practices.

Complex Coercion

Now that you have the basics of coercion down let's try an advanced example (by *advanced*, I mean mind-numbingly obtuse). Consider this gem:

```
// => '10'
++[[]][+[]]+[+[]]
```

The best way to understand what is going on is to unpack the innards first and work outward. First, look at the inner arrays starting from left to right:

```
// => [Array[0]]
[[]]
```

```
// An array which contains a single value, a coerced zero thanks to the unary operation.
// => [0]
[+[]]

// A second array also containing a coerced zero.
// => [0]
[+[]]
```

Next, ponder the two operands on either side of the binary operator. Starting with the left:

```
// => 1
++[[]]['0']
```

This statement is a tiny bit tricky. Essentially what is happening is that the inner array is being accessed at index '0' and being returned. At the point of return, the left unary operator is incrementing it, which also changes it to a number. Then the two values are combined. Since the left operand is a number and the right is an array, the combination will be through concatenation, not summation. Therefore the final sequence looks like this:

```
// => '10'
1 + ['0']
```

Now that you have an understanding of why this is jargon—because it performs tasks through a deep understanding of the internal coercion mechanics. Let's move on to the topic of logical operators to understand the role they play in programmatic jargon.

Logical Operators

Logical operators are used to return Boolean values, but under certain conditions they can be used to short-circuit control flows within a statement. This short-circuiting often shortens code, but at the expense of being expressive. In this way, logical operators are perfect for creating programmatic jargon. The following section steps through the various logical operators to explain how they can be used to produce jargon.

Logical AND (&&)

The logical OR and logical AND are both used for chaining comparisons that return a Boolean. In the case of logical AND, all conditional evaluations must be true; otherwise, false is returned.

Assignments Through Comparisons or Implicit Fallback

Knowing the behavior of &&, it becomes possible to leverage both the chaining and the return value in a single statement:

```
var car = {
    hasWheels: function () {
        return true;
    },
    engineRunning: function () {
        return true;
    },
```

```
    wheelsTurning: function () {
        return true;
    }

};

if (car.inMotion = car.hasWheels() && car.engineRunning() && car.wheelsTurning()) {
    console.log('vrrrrooooommmm');
}
```

Though the code above is technically correct, it is not considered good practice to have an assignment statement inside a conditional expression because people often misread assignment statements as an equality comparison, which can lead to confusion.

Logical OR (||)

Much like the logical AND operator, the logical OR operator can be used as a control flow mechanism, one that compares operands from left to right looking for the first true value. Unlike the AND operator, the OR operator needs only one operand to be true for a success.

Default Values

A common way that the logical OR is used is to assign default values to variables that may be considered optional in the method signature. The OR operator tests the left operand, and finding an undefined will look for a value that can be coerced into a Boolean. Once found, the value is assigned the variable.

```
var Car = function(){
    var args = Array.prototype.slice.call(arguments);

    this.name = args[0] || 'tesla'
    this.mpg = args[1] || 100
    this.mph = args[2] || 80

    // => Volt
    console.log(this.name);

    // => 90
    console.log(this.mpg);

    // => 80
    console.log(this.mph);
}

new Car('Volt',90);
```

Logical NOT (!)

The logical NOT operator expects a single right operand, that is a Boolean value or can be coerced into one. It returns true only if the operand is false.

Shorthand Boolean

As you saw in the section on coercion, implicit type conversion can be hard to understand by just reading the code. One of the most widespread conventions I see in JavaScript is using the logical NOT as a shortcut to a Boolean. Consider the following ways the NOT operator can coerce and then express Boolean values:

```
// number is coerced to a Boolean false
// NOT inverts it to true
// => true
console.log(!0);

// number is coerced to a Boolean true
// NOT inverts it to false
// => false
console.log(!1);

// number is coerced to a Boolean true
// NOT inverts it to false
// => false
console.log(!-1);

// string is coerced to a Boolean truthy *something*
// NOT inverts it to false
// => false
console.log(!'0');

// string is coerced to a Boolean truthy *something*
// NOT inverts it to false
// => false
console.log(!'1');

// this is coerced to a Boolean falsey *nothing*
// NOT inverts it to true
// => true
console.log(!undefined);

// this is coerced to a Boolean truthy *something*
// NOT inverts it to true
// => false
console.log(!this);

// unary operator coerces empty array into zero
// zero is coerced into Boolean false
// NOT inverts it to true
// => true
console.log(!+[]);
```

```
// inner NOT coerces the empty array to false
// false is not a valid array index so undefined is returned
// undefined is coerced into Boolean false
// NOT inverts it to true
// => true
console.log(![][![]]);
```

Double NOTs

As you saw in the last example, the logical NOT operator can cast many kinds of entities to variables, including undefined variables. Knowing this allows you to treat the lack of a variable as a *de facto* false variable. In the following example, you can see how the use of double NOTs allow the code to treat both the undefined and explicit false Boolean the same way. However, this code is very opaque; what it saves in visual space, it loses in conceptual clarity.

```
var user = {
    isAdmin: function () {
        return !!this.admin;
    }
};

// undefined this.admin is coerced to false
// then inverted to true
// then inverted again to false
// => false
console.log(user.isAdmin());

user.admin = true;

// this.admin is true without coercion
// inverted to false
// inverted back to true
// => true
console.log(user.isAdmin());

user.admin = false;

// => false
console.log(user.isAdmin());
```

Immediately Invoked Function Expression

Using the logical NOT operator, you can write a more succinct version of an immediately invoked function expression. In this case, the logical NOT operator tells the parser to treat the function not as a function declaration, but an expression that affords a new execution context:

```
// Uncaught SyntaxError: Unexpected token (
function(){console.log('foo');}();

// => foo
!function(){console.log('foo');}();
```

Now that you have taken this section to its *logical* conclusion, you can transition to some of the real back roads of JavaScript, better known as bitwise operations.

Bit Twiddling

Just like it sounds, a *bitwise operation* is the process of working with data at the bit level. Generally, this is useful for algorithms that require fast execution and/or have limited resources in which to operate. Specifically, these operations must require only primitive transformations to data to benefit from this kind of manipulation. Bitwise operations are standard fare for many low-level tasks, including communicating over sockets, compressing or encrypting information, or manipulating bitmap graphics. It is also very common to see bitwise operations used to implement role based access control (RBAC) systems because their access permissions can be described using only a bit field and yet remain a single number in the database.

The bitwise operators come in four distinct flavors: NOT, AND, OR and XOR, respectively. In addition to the logical operators, JavaScript has left and right bit shifting operators, too. As you might expect, properly explaining the hows and whys of these operators is quite involved and must also include understanding how bit shifting works in general. As such, it is outside the scope of this chapter. Instead, you will maintain your focus on jargon expressions, but now with an emphasis on the use of bitwise operations. What follows are examples and explanations of bit twiddling jargon.

Bitwise AND (&)

The bitwise OR function returns a 1 in each bit position in which both operands have a 1 in the specified position.

Converting Hex to RGB

Occasionally, it's useful to convert a hex number to an RGB value; for example, in the service of a CSS class:

```
// my favorite hex color
var color = 0xCOFFEE;

// Red
// => 192
console.log((color>>16) & 0xFF);

// Green
// => 255
console.log((color>>8) & 0xFF);

// Blue
// => 238
console.log(color & 0xFF);
```

You can extend this function a bit further and create a gradient factory[1] that returns a gradient of colors: when given a beginning and end color and a number of stops.

---

[1] http://markdaggett.com/blog/2012/03/23/generate-beautiful-gradients-using-javascript/

```javascript
var GradientFactory = (function () {
    var _beginColor = {
        red: 0,
        green: 0,
        blue: 0
    };
    var _endColor = {
        red: 255,
        green: 255,
        blue: 255
    };
    var _colorStops = 24;
    var _colors = [];
    var _colorKeys = ['red', 'green', 'blue'];
    var _rgbToHex = function (r, g, b) {
        return '#' + _byteToHex(r) + _byteToHex(g) + _byteToHex(b);
    };
    var _byteToHex = function (n) {
        var hexVals = "0123456789ABCDEF";
        return String(hexVals.substr((n >> 4) & 0x0F, 1)) + hexVals.substr(n & 0x0F, 1);
    };
    var _parseColor = function (color) {
        if ((color).toString() === "[object Object]") {
            return color;
        } else {
            color = (color.charAt(0) == "#") ? color.substring(1, 7) : color;
            return {
                red: parseInt((color).substring(0, 2), 16),
                green: parseInt((color).substring(2, 4), 16),
                blue: parseInt((color).substring(4, 6), 16)
            };
        }
    };
    var _generate = function (opts) {
        var _colors = [];
        var options = opts || {};
        var diff = {
            red: 0,
            green: 0,
            blue: 0
        };
        var len = _colorKeys.length;
        var pOffset = 0;
        if (typeof (options.from) !== 'undefined') {
            _beginColor = _parseColor(options.from);
        }
        if (typeof (options.to) !== 'undefined') {
            _endColor = _parseColor(options.to);
        }
        if (typeof (options.stops) !== 'undefined') {
            _colorStops = options.stops;
        }
```

```
            _colorStops = Math.max(1, _colorStops - 1);
            for (var x = 0; x < _colorStops; x++) {
                pOffset = parseFloat(x, 10) / _colorStops;
                for (var y = 0; y < len; y++) {
                    diff[_colorKeys[y]] = _endColor[_colorKeys[y]] - _beginColor[_colorKeys[y]];
                    diff[_colorKeys[y]] = (diff[_colorKeys[y]] * pOffset) + _beginColor[_colorKeys[y]];

                }
                _colors.push(_rgbToHex(diff.red, diff.green, diff.blue));
            }
            _colors.push(_rgbToHex(_endColor.red, _endColor.green, _endColor.blue));
            return _colors;
        };
        return {
            generate: _generate
        };
}).call(this);


// From hex to hex
// => ["#000000", "#262626", "#4C4C4C", "#727272", "#999999"]
console.log(GradientFactory.generate({
    from: '#000000',
    to: '#999999',
    stops: 5
}));


// From color object to hex
// => ["#C0FFEE", "#CFFFF2", "#DFFFF6", "#EFFFFA", "#FFFFFF"]
console.log(GradientFactory.generate({
    from: {
        red: 192,
        green: 255,
        blue: 238
    },
    to: {
        red: 255,
        green: 255,
        blue: 255
    },
    stops: 5
}));
```

Bitwise OR (|)

The bitwise OR function returns a 1 in each bit position in which either of the two operands has a 1 in the specified position.

Truncating Numbers

As you learned in the previous section, this function performs a bitwise OR operation on a pair of bits. It can also be used to round numbers down.

```
// => 30
var x = (30.9 | 0);
console.log(x);
```

Bitwise XOR (^)

The following examples make use of the fact that the bitwise XOR operator returns a 1 in the place in which a specific bit of 2-bit patterns do not match.

Determining Sign Equality

This expression is an easy way to determine whether two operands have opposing signs. It works because JavaScript uses two's compliment to represent negative numbers, which makes the XOR possible.

```
var signsMatch = function (x, y) {
    return !((x ^ y) < 0);
};

// => false
console.log(signsMatch(10, -10));

// => true
console.log(signsMatch(0, 0));

// => true
console.log(signsMatch(0, -0));

// => true
console.log(signsMatch(-10, -10));

// => true
console.log(signsMatch(1, 1e0));

// => false
console.log(signsMatch(-1, 1e0));
```

Toggling Bits

Occasionally, you see the XOR operator used to toggle bits, which can be helpful for toggling the state of an object. Here's an example:

```
var light = {
    on: 1,
    toggle: function () {
        return this.on ^= 1;
    }
};

// => 0
console.log(light.toggle());
```

```
// => 1
console.log(light.toggle());

// => 0
console.log(light.toggle());
```

Bitwise NOT (~)

The bitwise NOT function essentially swaps the sign of a number and then subtracts 1 from it. Behind the scenes, JavaScript converts the operand into a binary representation and then computes a new number by swapping all the bits from 1 to zero and vice versa. This new number is called the one's complement of the original. Finally, the one's complement is converted back into a base 10 number. Knowing the behavior of NOT gives you some clever ways to exploit it.

Bitwise Arithmetic

Occasionally, you see developers using the bitwise NOT to perform arithmetic on a variable. Here's an example:

```
// => 9
~-10

// => 11
-~10

// => 18
2*~-10
```

Parsing Strings into Numbers

The bitwise NOT operator returns the inverted value of the operand, and strings are coerced as part of this process. Therefore, supplying a double NOT returns the number to its original sign.

```
var num = "100.7"

// => true
console.log(parseInt(num,10) === ~~num);
```

Bitwise Shifting (<<, >>, >>>)

Bit shifting is the use of bitwise operators to manipulate integers by *shifting* their binary representations an arbitrary number of bit positions left or right in the bit field. The process of shifting results in a new number being formed. Bit shifting is quite common when interacting with hardware devices because they often lack the support of floating point numbers. Bit shifting is also quite useful in image processing, for example, when bit shifting is used to handle translations between color profiles, or to handle bitmap manipulations of a field of pixels.

Bit shifting is less frequently used in JavaScript but can still be quite useful for performing simple arithmetic shifts on a number or as part of a larger function as you'll see in the signum function example next.

Signum Function

The purpose of the signum (also called sign) function is to determine whether a number is less, equal to or greater than zero; and therefore can return -1, 0, or 1 as a result.

```
var sign = function(x) {
    return (x >> 31) | ((-x) >>> 31);
};
```

```
// => -1
console.log(sign(-100));
```

```
// => 0
console.log(sign(0));
```

```
// => 1
console.log(sign(100));
```

Although you used bit shifting to calculate the number's sign, you can also use two plain old terinary expressions grouped together:

```
// => 1
console.log(100 ? 100 < 0 ? -1 : 1 : 0);
```

Now that you know that the function works, let's figure out why. First, consider the right shift operator. The job of this operator is to shift the operand the specified number of bits, in this case 31 places. Because you are using the end of the bit field, positive numbers always return 0, and negative numbers always return -1. Here are a couple of examples:

```
// => -1
console.log(-200 >> 31);
```

```
// => -1
console.log(-100 >> 31);
```

```
// => 0
console.log(0 >> 31);
```

```
// => 0
console.log(100 >> 31);
```

```
// => 0
console.log(200 >> 31);
```

Next, you use the zero-fill right shift operator >>> to shift 31 bits to the right and shift any zeros needed in from the left. Again, you can see this play out in the following code:

```
// => 1
console.log(-200 >>> 31);
```

```
// => 1
console.log(-100 >>> 31);
```

```
// => 0
console.log(0 >>> 31);

// => 0
console.log(100 >>> 31);

// => 0
console.log(200 >>> 31);
```

Finally, to get the return value, you use the bitwise OR operator. However, you do not get the expected results unless you reverse the sign of the number to the right of the OR operand. The simplified function looks like this:

```
// => -1
console.log(-200 >> 31 | 200 >>> 31);

// => -1
console.log(-100 >> 31 | 100 >>> 31);

// => 0
console.log(0 >> 31 | 0 >>> 31);

// => 1
console.log(100 >> 31 | -100 >>> 31);

// => 1
console.log(200 >> 31 | -200 >>> 31);
```

Opaque Code

It is possible to write obtuse or obfuscated code in any language. There are whole communities dedicated to these pursuits. For example, black hat coders use hard-to-read code as a layer of defense against white hats. Others find sport in writing cryptic code. There is an entire pastime called Programming Golf, in which players attempt to return the desired result of a function (hole) in the shortest number of characters (strokes). What follows are examples of purposely muddy syntax for the sheer sport of it. Many of these examples are what might be considered true *WAT* examples in JavaScript. Many examples were inspired by the site wtfjs.com.

Sneaky eval

As the name implies, this function gives the executing code a back door to access eval. Some sites attempt to give users a sanitized subset of JavaScript to use. This is very hard if not impossible to do with a dynamic language such as JavaScript, as this code demonstrates. This script works by accessing the constructor function of the String.sub method. The JavaScript constructor method accepts a string that is then evaluated in place.

```
// => foo
""["sub"]["constructor"]("console.log('foo')")()
```

All Your Base

Be careful when comparing numbers of different bases. For example, here you compare an octal number and one using scientific notation to a base 10 number. Unless you read it carefully, you might be confused by the results.

```
// comparing against octals
// => false
1 + 064 == 65

// => false
064 > 60

// comparing against scientific notation
// => false
3000000000 > 4e9
```

Unicode for Variables

JavaScript allows Unicode to be used as property descriptors and variable names, which can lead to some spectacularly unreadable code. Consider the following:

```
var \u1000 = {\u1001: function () {
        return 'Unicode';
    }
};
// => 'Unicode'
console.log(\u1000.\u1001());
```

WAT Indeed

Although the Unicode example might be a bit hard to read, it cannot compare to what follows. The fact that this code somehow produces the word 'secret' seems almost magical. This code was generated by a program called jsfuck,[2] which, judging by its name, was inspired by the equally offensively yet aptly titled Brainfuck language.[3] This is truly code to make even the most seasoned developer say **WAT**!?

```
// => 'secret'
console.log((![]+[])[+[[!+[]+!+[]+!+[]]]]+(!![]+[])[+[[!+[]+!+[]+!+[]]]]+([][(![]+[])
[+[[+[]]]]+([][[]]+[])[+[[!+[]+!+[]+!+[]+!+[]+!+[]]]]+(![]+[])[+[[!+[]+!+[]]]]+(!![]+[])
[+[[+[]]]]+(!![]+[])[+[[!+[]+!+[]+!+[]]]]+(!![]+[])[+[[+!+[]]]]+[])[+[[!+[]+!+[]+!+[]]]]+(!![]+[])
[+[[+!+[]]]]+(!![]+[])[+[[!+[]+!+[]+!+[]]]]+(!![]+[])[+[[+![]]]])
```

   To understand how this code ultimately produces the string 'secret', you need to simply figure out the mechanism by which it does its converting. Actually it is easier than it first appears. For the sake of brevity, let's just

---

[2]http://www.jsfuck.com/
[3]http://en.wikipedia.org/wiki/Brainfuck

figure out how to reproduce the letter *s* in the hidden word. In the code, *s* can be found in this expression: (![]+[])
[+[[!+[]+!+[]+!+[]]]]. Knowing what you do about coercion and unary operations, you can begin to step through
this code little by little. First look at the inner arrays:

```
// => [3]
[!+[]+!+[]+!+[]]
```

You know that unary operator converts the empty array into a number; in this case, a zero. Next you see the
logical NOT operator, which you know gives the opposite Boolean value of the operand. In this case, the operand is
coerced into false, which the NOT operator dutifully flips to true. This leaves the equation true + true + true. Next,
the binary operator adds the true values together, which first requires coercing them to numbers. That means true
+ true + true is now 1 + 1 + 1. Adding them all together gives 3. The following code proves what was just stepped
through:

```
// => true
+[[!+[]+!+[]+!+[]]] == [3]
```

To continue you need to understand what is happening inside the parentheses. Again, this is pretty easy to figure
out once you break it down. First consider this:

```
// => true
!+[]
```

Okay, that's clear; you saw the same sequence previously. However, in this version the Boolean false is
concatenated with the empty array. This means the Boolean false becomes the string "false". In essence our code
has been simplified to a string being accessed like an array to get the fourth item, which is the letter *s* you were after.
Success!

```
// => 's'
("false")[3]
```

```
// => true
"s" == (![]+[])[+[[!+[]+!+[]+!+[]]]]
```

I encourage you to look at the source for the jsfuck[4] project because there is some interesting ship-in-a-bottle-
style contortions used to get all the required characters needed to fully encode anything. Some of the encodings are
pretty epic. Here's an example:

```
// => true
'(' == ([][(![]+[])[+[[+[]]]]+([][[]]+[])[+[[!+[]+!+[]+!+[]+!+[]+!+[]]]]+(![]+[])
[+[[!+[]+!+[]]]]+(!![]+[])[+[[+[]]]]+(!![]+[])[+[[!+[]+!+[]+!+[]]]]+(!![]+[])[+[[+!+[]]]]]+[])[+[[+!
+[]]]+[[!+[]+!+[]+!+[]+!+[]+!+[]]]]
```

That's *209* characters to encode a single right parenthesis. ***WAT*** indeed!

---

[4]https://github.com/aemkei/jsfuck

Summary

You just spent an entire chapter learning about coercion, bitwise operations, and logical operators. You now better understand why there is often a disconnection between the actual and expected results when employing these features of JavaScript. Programmers who are adept at exploiting these nuances can often pack very complex behavior into a just a couple of characters. As I mentioned in my introduction, this highly contextual code is what I call *programmatic jargon*, but others derogatorily tag it as *WAT* style programming. Here are a couple of points to remember when trying to use or read jargon in JavaScript.

- Programmatic jargon is a compression of code through the use of highly specific and often technical rules of the language.

- Jargon is neither good nor bad; it depends on whether the speaker and the audience understand the context and point of reference for the expression.

- Coercion is the act of forcing an object or entity of one type into another.

- In JavaScript, coercion is either for simplifying complex objects to a primitive form or converting between two primitive types.

- Logical operators are used to return Boolean values, but under certain conditions they can be used to short-circuit control flows within a statement.

- Bitwise operations can be performed only on integers.

- Bitwise operations are useful to algorithms that require fast execution and/or have limited resources in which to operate.

- Bitwise operations can often be used in place of other math-related functions—for example, using `~~'10'` instead of `parseInt('10',10)`.

Additional References

- http://rocha.la/JavaScript-bitwise-operators-in-practice

- http://sla.ckers.org/forum/read.php?24,32930

- http://javascriptissexy.com/12-simple-yet-powerful-javascript-tips/

- http://codegolf.stackexchange.com/questions/2682/tips-for-golfing-in-javascript

- http://stackoverflow.com/questions/2350718/are-there-any-short-tricks-in-javascript-1-8-that-i-can-use-to-reduce-my-golf

- http://www.benlesh.com/2012/05/javascript-fun-part-6-code-golf.html?m=1

- http://wtfjs.com/

- http://jscoercion.qfox.nl/

■ ■ ■

## CHAPTER 5

Living Asynchronously

Those who pontificate over where the Internet is going have spent much of the last couple of years talking about the rise of the responsive Web. Responsiveness as it relates to web design hinges on the developer's ability to craft a web site that adapts intelligently to the myriad number of devices used to access their content. Ideally, a responsive site does more than just *fit* onto the given screen size; it also shifts the site's features, visual flow, and aesthetics to fit the capabilities of the platform or device.

Responsiveness as it relates to JavaScript is writing code that minimizes a user's sense that the interface has become locked or frozen. Making an interface feel responsive can be tricky to do correctly because modern web applications increasingly require access to external application programming interfaces (APIs) or long-running processes that do not return results immediately. Most languages allow developers to push these extended processes to the so-called background using threading or concurrent operations.

However, JavaScript is single-threaded, which means the developer must handle long-running processes more cleverly. This chapter explains the various mechanisms available through JavaScript or the browser to help properly plan and write responsive code.

Understanding Concurrency in JavaScript

When researching this topic, I realized that many people conflate concurrent execution with the ability to run asynchronous code. Although asynchronous execution is often used to achieve the appearance of concurrency, the two are not the same. Before I discuss specific technical approaches and limitations to writing concurrent and asynchronous code using JavaScript, it will be helpful to discuss a base definition of concurrency.

Concurrency

In a programming context, *concurrency* is the ability for two or more computational procedures to execute simultaneously while sharing resources. These processes (sometimes called *threads*) can either share a single processor or be distributed across a network and synchronized later by an execution manager. Communication between parallel processes is usually explicit, either happening through message passing or by sharing variables. Generally, concurrent processes should be used only for problems that are nondeterministic, meaning that the sequencing of state is not important. Concurrent execution of code provides many advantages and some disadvantages, which I have outlined in the following sections.

Advantages of Concurrency

- Increasing the number of programs that can be run at one time.

- Allowing programs that have resource-independent sequential steps to be processed out of order. This is especially useful if an intermediate step is of an unknown duration.

- Applications do not become unresponsive while long-running tasks complete.

- Tasks that have prerequisites for execution can be queued for later until those dependencies have been met.

Disadvantages of Concurrency

- Two processes that list each other as a prerequisite can wait for each other indefinitely. This is sometimes called a *deadlock*.

- Race conditions can occur when the result of a process is dependent on a specific sequence or timing that cannot be guaranteed due to parallel execution.

- Management and synchronization of concurrent operations is more complex than sequential execution.

- Concurrent programs often are many times more resource-intensive. Multiple processes may be executing in parallel. and there is overhead needed to marshal and synchronize them together.

- Data integrity can be lost when concurrent operations corrupt each other's state due to a failure to be correctly synchronized.

The Hard Truth of Concurrency in JavaScript

With only a single thread, JavaScript cannot have true concurrency. This reality is not a legacy of having to support underpowered browsers of yore. Brendan Eich pointed out that Java added threads to Netscape in 1995, but that in his words "no way was I putting shared-mutable-state preemptive threading in JS." He felt that threads were wrong for the audience.[1] In defense of the decision, though, I would argue that part of JavaScript's popularity is due to the fact that unseasoned programmers can grow into the language. If every JavaScript newbie had to worry about deadlocks and race conditions right out of the gate, the adoption of the language would be much slower. Being single-threaded means that deadlocks are impossible except in conditions in which a sequential process would fail to end. This could happen if a program had cyclic dependencies.

There are obvious downsides to having just one thread. Namely, the programs can hit an arbitrary processing threshold when it maxes out a single core on the computer (even if other cores are available). Additionally, when running in the browser, scripts must periodically yield to the browser's user interface (UI) process in order to keep the web page responsive. A script that takes too long to become idle will most likely be misinterpreted by the browser as a runaway script, at which point the user sees a pop-up like the one shown in Figure 5-1.

---

[1] https://brendaneich.com/2007/02/threads-suck/

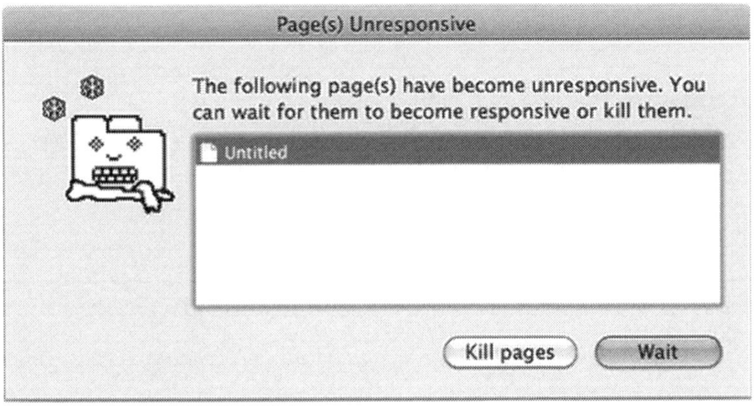

Figure 5-1. *Unresponsive script pop-up*

Over time, the JavaScript community and the language have evolved to maximize the single thread. For example, although JavaScript does not have true concurrency, it is possible to emulate its effects through the strategic use of functions such as setInterval(), setTimeout(), or the asynchronous version of XMLHttpRequest(). When those techniques don't suffice, it is possible to deploy background workers (which I'll cover later in the chapter). To better understand how you can structure your programs to maximize concurrent-like behavior, you have to appreciate how the event loop works in JavaScript.

Understanding JavaScript Event Loop

Now that you understand concurrency in general, you can evaluate JavaScript's approach to running programs, which is to continually look for incoming event messages to process. JavaScript's single thread means there is only one event loop per runtime process. JavaScript's event loop is heavily influenced by two concepts, *run-to-completion* and *non-blocking input/output (I/O)*.

Run-to-Completion

JavaScript's event loop is designed as a run-to-completion environment. Practically, speaking this means that once JavaScript begins to execute a task, it cannot be interrupted until it completes. Without run-to-completion, you could not be certain about an object's state because it could be accessed outside of the normal event loop cycle. Mozilla describes the goals of run-to-completion thusly:

> *Each message is processed completely before any other message is processed. This offers some nice properties when reasoning about your program, including the fact that whenever a function runs, it cannot be pre-empted and will run entirely before any other code runs (and can modify data the function manipulates). This differs from C, for instance, where if a function runs in a thread, it can be stopped at any point to run some other code in another thread.*[2]

---

[2]https://developer.mozilla.org/en-US/docs/Web/JavaScript/Guide/EventLoop

Evented by Design

In JavaScript, running programs create messages for the event loop to process. These messages are created by listeners that are triggered when an event happens. This may seem unremarkable at first, but it hints at a powerful feature of JavaScript's event loop. JavaScript's use of listeners to monitor events means that input can arrive from many places at once. The listeners allow events to unfold in parallel. Mozilla explains the evented design this way:

> *A very interesting property of the event loop model is that JavaScript, unlike a lot of other languages never blocks. Handling I/O is typically performed via events and callbacks, so when the application is waiting for an IndexedDB query to return or an XHR request to return, it can still process other things like user input.*
>
> *Legacy exception exists like alert or synchronous XHR, but it is considered as a good practice to avoid them. Beware, exceptions to the exception do exist (but are usually implementation bugs rather than anything else).*[3]

Non-blocking I/O is the mechanism in JavaScript that allows incoming messages to be sequenced while waiting for results from another operation to complete. Event-based messaging also allows JavaScript to capture actions that happen simultaneously, but ensure they are processed sequentially by the event loop. This capability is how concurrency is emulated in JavaScript, and it allows the effects of operations with slow execution to be mitigated through the clever use of callbacks, closures, or promises.

Inside the Event Loop

In the event loop, incoming messages are extracted into a stack of frames and processed in a specific order. At the point at which a frame is added to the stack, any objects and variables needed by the frame are added or retrieved from a shared memory heap. Any code that is not presently being executed is added to the queue for later. Once an entire stack is complete, unneeded variables are removed from the heap, and the next message in the queue is extracted into a stack. The event loop life cycle is represented in Figure 5-2.

---

[3]https://developer.mozilla.org/en-US/docs/Web/JavaScript/Guide/EventLoop

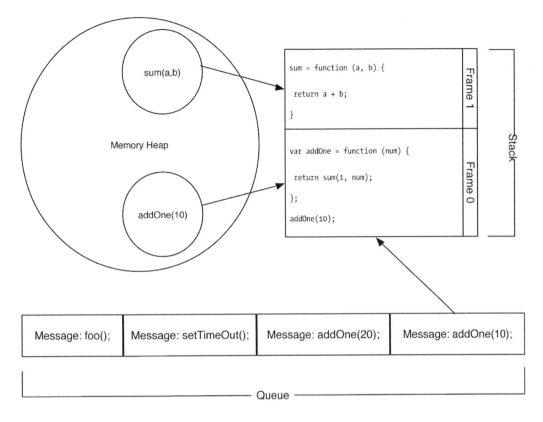

Figure 5-2. *Diagram of the JavaScript event loop*

Heap

The *heap* is an order-agnostic container in memory. The heap is where JavaScript stores variables and objects currently in use, or that the garbage collection process has not reaped.

Frame

The *frame* is a sequential unit of work needing to be performed during the event loop cycle. The frame contains an execution context that links together function objects and variable somewhere in the heap.

Stack

The event loop *stack* contains all the sequential steps (frames) that a message requires to execute. Frames are processed by the event loop from top to bottom. Frames are added to the stack based on their dependency chain. Frames with a dependency have their dependent frame added on top. This process ensures that dependencies are met before being referenced by contingent code. Consider the following example:

```
var sum = function (a, b) {
    return a + b;
}, addOne = function (num) {
```

```
      return sum(1, num);
};

// => 11
addOne(10);
```

At the point where the addOne() message moves from the queue to the stack, it becomes the base frame. I'll call this frame0. Frame0 contains a reference to the addOne() function and the value of the num argument (currently 10). Because addOne() depends on the sum() function, a new frame is created (frame1), which contains a reference to the sum() function and the values of the incoming arguments "a" and "b". In this example, frame1 has no other dependencies that need to be met, so the stack can now be unwound starting with frame1 and working its way down. Once the event loop processes a frame, it is popped off the top of the stack. This continues until the stack is empty, at which point a new item is retrieved from the queue.

Queue

The *queue* is a list of messages waiting to be processed. Each message references a JavaScript function. When a stack is empty, the oldest message in the queue is added to the stack as the next base frame.

Callbacks

The design of JavaScript's event loop forces code to execute sequentially. Knowing this means writing synchronous code will afford developers a great deal of clarity because they can write code in way that it will be run. The intent of the following source is very clear because of the use of the synchronous structure. The flow mirrors what will happen when the event loop processes it:

```
var person = {};
var bank = {
  funds: 0,
  receiveDepositFrom: function(person) {
    this.funds += person.funds;
    person.funds = 0;
  }
};

// => undefined
console.log(person.funds);
person.funds = (function work() {
  return 100;
})();

// => 100
console.log(person.funds);
bank.receiveDepositFrom(person);

// => 0
console.log(person.funds);
```

Writing synchronous code in JavaScript has some definite advantages:

- Code is easier to understand because the program can be read in sequence.

- Synchronous functions return values and throw exceptions in a lexical context, making them easier to debug.

However, most JavaScript programs with any level of complexity should not be written merely as a series of consecutive steps. Doing so will cause problems in both performance and code quality. Let's look at both of these issues individually.

Perceived Performance

Many programs rely on functions that do not immediately return a value. Imagine if the work() function in the previous example took some time to complete instead of immediately returning:

```
person.funds = (function work() {

  // Simulate a long running task.
  var end = Date.now() + 4000;
  while (Date.now() < end){

    //noop
  }
  return 100;
})();
```

The code continues to perform as intended, but the use experience will degrade because the program will seem frozen until the work() function returns a value. Synchronous delay in execution is not the only problem you could face. The code expects that the worker will have money *before* they try and deposit it. It is possible that the work() function instead polls a remote service, which doesn't block until complete like the previous example. In this case, the code would break because person.funds would be undefined at the point it was accessed:

```
var person = {};
var bank = {
  funds: 0,
  receiveDepositFrom: function(person) {

    // Now NaN because person.funds is undefined.
    this.funds += person.funds;
    person.funds = 0;
  }
};

// => undefined
console.log(person.funds);
(function work(person) {

  // Assumes you have jQuery installed
  $.ajax({
    url: "http://some.webservice.com/work.json",
    context: document.body
```

```
  }).done(function() {
    person.funds = 100;
  });
})(person);

// => undefined
console.log(person.funds);
bank.receiveDepositFrom(person);

// => 0
console.log(person.funds);
```

Instead of passing in the person object as an argument to the work() function, you could send a function that *calls back* to the previous context once the AJAX request completes. Callbacks are one of the most popular patterns for controlling data flow. *A callback in JavaScript is the act of passing a function object as an argument to another function, which is to be used on the return value.* In effect, callbacks allow you decouple the current lexical context from the synchronous execution of code. Callbacks are a form of continuation passing style, which you'll learn about in the next section.

Continuation Passing Style

Continuation passing style (CPS) is a concept popular in functional programming paradigms, where a program's state is controlled through the use of continuations. For your purposes, the continuation will be your callbacks. Continuations are very popular for asynchronous programming because the program can wait for the data and then advance the state through the supplied continuation. JavaScript can support continuations because functions are first-class citizens within the language. Using continuations (callbacks), you can defer the deposit actions until the AJAX method returns:

```
var person = {};
var bank = {
  funds: 0,
  receiveDepositFrom: function(person) {
    this.funds += person.funds;
    person.funds = 0;
  }
};

// => undefined
console.log(person.funds);

(function work(callback) {
  $.ajax({
    url: "http://some.webservice.com/work.json",
    context: document.body
  }).done(function() {
    callback(100);
  });
})(function(amount) {
  person.funds = amount;
```

```
// => 100
console.log(person.funds);
bank.receiveDepositFrom(person);

// => 0
console.log(person.funds);
});
```

This style of coding should look familiar because CPS is so heavily used by many of the most popular libraries and runtimes that they are nearly unavoidable. Although the code's execution still mirrors its top-to-bottom layout, it has become noticeably less expressive. The reader now needs to mentally jump back and forth within the code body to make sense of the execution flow. However, now that the code is more responsive, you can work to improve the quality of your approach.

Callback Hell

Synchronous design flattens the code base, which can improve clarity, but over time it reduces your ability to organize and reuse code. CPS can fix this issue, but it is not a panacea. Left unchecked, continuations can become algorithmic Matryoshka dolls, nesting inside one another ad infinitum. Here is a hypothetical example:

```
login('user','password', function(result) {
  if (result.ok) {
    getProfile(function(result) {
      if (result.ok) {
        updateProfile(result.user, function(result) {
          if (result.ok) {
            callback(user);
          }
        });
      }
    });
  }
}, callback);
```

Although this code is responsive, due to the asynchronous structure it is borderline unreadable. This style of coding is sometimes called the *pyramid of doom* or *callback hell*[4] because the code extends to the right faster than it moves downward. Callback hell is aptly named because it does the following:

- Makes code harder to read and maintain

- Makes code less modular and tougher to separate into concerns

- Makes error propagation and exception handling more difficult

- Lacks a formalized API, so callbacks may or may not be returned, and what they yield can be a mixed bag.

Design decisions that lead to callback hell are not a problem unique to JavaScript, of course. In many ways, developers continually reinvent antipatterns of yore using new languages and techniques. In the 1970s and 1980s, many programs suffered through the overuse of the goto statement. The goto statement "performs a one-way transfer of control to another line of code."[5] Just like callbacks, the use of goto to jump somewhere else in code breaks the

---

[4]http://callbackhell.com/
[5]http://en.wikipedia.org/wiki/Goto

linearity of the source. The resulting code often required the programmer to mentally unwind the stack to understand the current context. The most widely cited criticism of goto was written by Edsger Dijkstra:

> *My second remark is that our intellectual powers are rather geared to master static relations and that our powers to visualize processes evolving in time are relatively poorly developed. For that reason we should do (as wise programmers aware of our limitations) our utmost to shorten the conceptual gap between the static program and the dynamic process, to make the correspondence between the program (spread out in text space) and the process (spread out in time) as trivial as possible. Edsger W. Dijkstra (Dijkstra, 1968).*

There is nothing inherently wrong with callbacks or CPS. However, when overused, CPS increases the cognitive dissonance for the programmer between the original intent of the function as written and the context from which it is finally executed. This is because the goal of CPS is *never* to return control to the caller. Instead, continuations use callbacks as stateful hot potatoes always looking to pass it to someone else.

Imagine for a moment if the priorities of a continuation were reversed. Instead of emphasizing the ability to pass the current context along, the process instead immediately returned a token that represented a deferred future state. This forms a kind of computational I.O.U, which affords the same asynchronous execution as CPS while remaining highly declarative. What I am describing is the Promise pattern, which you'll put to the test in the following section.

Promises: Back from the Future

A promise is a token object the represents the future value or exception of a function that has not yet returned. Promises offer a clean and easy-to-read approach for wrangling asynchronous execution back into a visually sequential control flow. Any process that blocks the event loop is a candidate for the promise pattern. Consider this program, written first using CPS and then rewritten using a promise:

```
// CPS style
var user;
login('user', 'password', function(result) {
  if (result.ok) {
    user = result.user;
  }
});

// Promise style and assumes login returns a promise object.
var promise = login('user', 'password');

promise.then(function(result) {
  if (result.ok) {
    user = result.user;
  }
});
```

As you can see from the previous code, promises do not pass the execution state along as a function argument as is the case with CPS. Instead, a placeholder for the future context is immediately returned to the current lexical scope. This allows the code to remain non-blocking like CPS but with the advantage of shortening *the conceptual gap between the static program and the dynamic process*, as Dijkstra implored us to do.

Although I'll refer to promises in the abstract, there are actually several implementations. In this chapter, when I say *promise*, I technically mean Promise A+,[6] which is well-suited for JavaScript. According to the spec, a promise object is composed of the following parts:

- **Promise** is an object or function with a then method whose behavior conforms to this specification.

- **Thenable** is an object or function that defines a then method.

- **Value** is any legal JavaScript value (including undefined, a thenable, or a promise).

- **Exception** is a value that is thrown using the throw statement.

- **Reason** is a value that indicates why a promise was rejected.

Keeping Promises

As in real life, promise objects offer contracts that define expectations around an event. Because promise objects are returned immediately in lieu of the actual value, they afford much better composition than you get with CPS. Specifically, promises can be chained or joined together and executed in a variety of contexts. However, creating these chains require a bit of boilerplate code to get working. Thankfully others have abstracted away these bits into libraries. The following examples leverage Kristopher Kowal's Q[7] library to demonstrate promise chains and joins.

■ **Note**   Before you begin, you need to install Q though npm: npm install q.

Chained and Deferred Execution

One of the primary use cases in which promises improve over CPS is when a program has a series of asynchronous functions that need to be run in a specific order. In the following example, you will see how a sequential chain of promises can be executed in a specific order. During the resolution the computed number is passed along to the next link in the chain. The capability to compare and contrast this sequence is also implemented as a series of nested callbacks:

```
Q = require('q');

// Simulates a long running process
var sleep = function(ms) {
    return function(callback) {
        setTimeout(callback, ms);
    };
};

// Using Continuation Passing Style.
var squareCPS = function(num, callback){
```

[6]http://promises-aplus.github.io/promises-spec/
[7]https://github.com/kriskowal/q

```
  sleep(1000).call(this, function(){
    callback(num * num);
  });
};

// => 100000000
squareCPS(10, function(num){
  squareCPS(num, function(num){
    squareCPS(num, function(num){
        console.log(num);
    });
  });
});

// Using Promises.
var square = function(num) {
    var later = Q.defer();
    sleep(1000).call(this, function() {
      later.resolve(num * num);
    });
    return later.promise;
};

// => 100000000
square(10)
.then(square)
.then(square)
.then(function(total){
  console.log(total);
});
```

Parallel Joins

If you have a series of functions that are nondeterministic, you can use Q to execute your functions in parallel, as the following example demonstrates:

```
Q.allSettled([
    square(10),
    square(20),
    square(30)
]).then(function(results){
  results.forEach(function (result) {

    // => 100
    // => 400
    // => 900
    console.log(result.value);
  });
});
```

This section is meant to be a brief introduction to promise objects, so there are some important topics worth exploring in greater depth if you see the promise in promises. If you're curious, I encourage you to check out the documentation on Q in particular because it offers a more complete introduction to promises than I presented here.

Generators and Coroutines

While this chapter is about asynchronous code and concurrency the soft underbelly of these two topics are actually about controlling flow of execution. As a thought experiment, right now try to distill JavaScript down to its essential ingredients in your mind. What features would you allow to evaporate into the ether, and what, if removed, would break the language completely? I wager that you would leave untouched those components that control the flow of execution. Among other components, control flow mechanisms within JavaScript give your applications the capability to do the following:

- Execute statements when preconditions have been met

- Conditionally branch between statements

- Conditionally continue from one statement to another

- Divert the flow of execution out of one context and then later resume at a predetermined position.

This section is about the last bullet point in the list. Languages—including Python, Lua, and Smalltalk—deal with structured nonlocal control flow[8] through the use of coroutines and generators. *Coroutines and generators allow for the suspension and resumption of the execution of code using predetermined entry and exit points.* ECMAScript 6 is poised to introduce both of these concepts into the language. This section explores how they work and demonstrates how to use them.

Generators

Generators are functions that afford iteration over a collection while maintaining its own internal state. The fact that generators can have their own state and temporarily yield their execution to another process means that they are useful for a variety of tasks like these:

- Shared multitasking

- Sequential processing of elements

- Sequencing multiple processes that have some amount of waiting as part of their design

- Simple state machines

In JavaScript, any function that contains a `yield` operator is considered a generator. Here is a simple example that demonstrates how generators maintain their own internal state:

```
var sequence, sq;

sq = function* (initialValue) {
    var current, num, step;
    num = initialValue || 2;
    step = 0;
```

---

[8]`http://en.wikipedia.org/wiki/Control_flow#Structured_non-local_control_flow`

```
        while (true) {
            current = num * step++;
            yield current
        }
};

sequence = sq(20);

// => 0
console.log(sequence.next().value);

// => 20
console.log(sequence.next().value);

// => 40
console.log(sequence.next().value);

// => 60
console.log(sequence.next().value);
```

■ **Note** According the ECMAScript spec,[9] coroutines/generators are defined by supplying an asterisk after the function keyword: `Function*(){...}`. In V8, you can enable generators using the `--harmony-generators` flag: `$ node --harmony-generators foo.js`. At the time of this writing, only node 0.11.+ supports harmony generators.

The previous generator iterates until it hits the ceiling of the largest number JavaScript can support ($1.7976931348623157e+308$.) Generators can also define a range of possible values. When all the possibilities are exhausted a StopIteration exception can be raised:

```
var a, alphabet, sequence;

alphabet = function*() {
  var charCode = 65;
  while (charCode < 91) {
    yield String.fromCharCode(charCode++);
  }
  throw new Error("StopIteration")
};

sequence = alphabet();

a = 0;

while (a < 27) {
  try {
```

---

[9]http://wiki.ecmascript.org/doku.php?id=harmony:generators

```
    // => a..z
    console.log(sequence.next().value);
  } catch (e) {

    // => [Error: StopIteration]
    console.log(e);
  }
  a++;
}
```

Having to worry about catching an optional out of range error makes your code brittle. As it turns out, generators have a built in Boolean done value that can be checked to determine whether you have reached the end of a sequence. Knowing this, you can rewrite the previous example this way:

```
var letter, alphabet, sequence;

function* alphabet() {
  var charCode = 65;
  while (charCode < 91) {
    yield String.fromCharCode(charCode++);
  }
};
sequence = alphabet(),
letter = sequence.next();

while (!letter.done) {

    // => A..Z
    console.log(letter.value);
    letter = sequence.next();
}
```

Coroutines by Convention

Coroutines are sometimes referred to as cooperatively scheduled threads because they allow for shared execution on a single process. In JavaScript, coroutines are generators used for flow control. Like generators, coroutines are objects that can suspend and resume their execution context though the use of the yield operator. Unlike generators, coroutines can control which execution context to return to after yielding; this capability makes them perfect for controlling a program's flow. Wikipedia delineates this point even further: "Since generators are primarily used to simplify the writing of iterators, the yield statement in a generator does not specify a coroutine to jump to, but rather passes a value back to a parent routine."[10]

In many languages, coroutines are defined explicitly apart from generators. In JavaScript, coroutines are implemented as a pattern, not as a distinct feature of the language. This is possible because JavaScript natively supports continuations, as you learned in the callback section. What follows are a few examples of how to implement coroutines in JavaScript. The most basic coroutine is a binary toggle, which you can write this way:

```
var toggle = (function*(){
  while(true){
    yield true
```

---

[10]http://en.wikipedia.org/wiki/Coroutine#Comparison_with_generators

```
    yield false
  }
})();

for(var x = 0; x < 5; x++){

  // => true, false, true, false, true
  console.log(toggle.next().value)
}
```

This example uses the multiple yield statements as a control flow mechanism to oscillate between true and false states. Notice that this coroutine forms a very basic state machine that handles two positions (on, off) without needing to explicitly define a Boolean variable. You could use this coroutine for toggling a UI element repeatedly. Harold Cooper points out that this "variable can only be avoided because coroutines add an entirely new form of state to the language, namely the state of where the coroutine is currently suspended."[11] Though this example is instructional, it has limited usefulness. Let's look at a more complex use case.

Continuable Generators

Tim Caswell recently released a helpful library called Gen-run[12] that according to Caswell "consumes continuable yielding generators and passes in its own continuations to the continuables so that when they resolve, the generator body will resume with a return value or throw an error." In layman's terms, Gen-run injects control flow rules around the act of yielding and resuming to handle both asynchronous and synchronous functions together. The entire library is small enough to display inline here:

```
function run(generator, callback) {
  // Pass in resume for no-wrap function calls
  var iterator = generator(resume);
  var data = null, yielded = false;

  var next = callback ? nextSafe : nextPlain;

  next();
  check();

  function nextSafe(item) {
    var n;
    try {
      n = iterator.next(item);
      if (!n.done) {
        if (typeof n.value === "function") n.value(resume());
        yielded = true;
        return;
      }
    }
```

[11]http://syzygy.st/javascript-coroutines/
[12]https://github.com/creationix/gen-run

```
    catch (err) {
      return callback(err);
    }
    return callback(null, n.value);
  }

  function nextPlain(item) {
    var cont = iterator.next(item).value;
    // Pass in resume to continuables if one was yielded.
    if (typeof cont === "function") cont(resume());
    yielded = true;
  }

  function resume() {
    var done = false;
    return function () {
      if (done) return;
      done = true;
      data = arguments;
      check();
    };
  }

  function check() {
    while (data && yielded) {
      var err = data[0];
      var item = data[1];
      data = null;
      yielded = false;
      if (err) return iterator.throw(err);
      next(item);
      yielded = true;
    }
  }

}
```

To understand how this library works, consider this simple example that sequences a series of calls to the sleep function:

```
function sleep(ms) {
  return function (callback) {
    setTimeout(callback, ms);
  };
}

// => Prints "Started", "Almost Done", and "Done" on indvidual lines.
run(function* () {
  console.log("Started");
  yield sleep(1000);
  console.log("Almost Done")
```

```
  yield sleep(1000);
  console.log("Done!");
});
```

Without the use of Gen-run, there would be no control flow mechanism, and thus the console statements would immediately spit out to the screen. However, because the generators yield their execution context to the incoming sleep function, you can pause and then resume execution in a synchronous fashion.

Gen-run's design is enhanced due to the fact that generators can themselves delegate their own yield context to other generators. This is accomplished using the yield* syntax. Consider this example, in which the run wrapper delegates to the sub generator:

```
function* sub(n) {
  while (n) {
    console.log(n--);
    yield sleep(10);
  }
}

// => Prints "Start", "[10..1]","End" on individual lines.
run(function* () {
  console.log("Start");
  yield* sub(10);
  console.log("End");
});
```

As you can see from the previous examples, the sweet spot for Gen-run is to control the execution of an arbitrary number of functions where order of execution is essential.

Web Workers

Web workers are JavaScript processes that can be spun up to work in the so-called *background* of the browser. In reality, each new worker gets its own global context that allows it to execute long-running processes without having to yield to update the user interface. It is worth noting that workers are part of the HTML specification,[13] not a part of ECMAScript. From the standpoint of JavaScript, there is nothing special about web workers other than the fact that they can be created on demand by the browser and controlled by the main browser context. This section explores web workers in detail and how they can be used to minimize drag on the user experience when heavy computation is required.

■ **Note**   Do not confuse the worker's global context with being just an operating system thread. The global context is actually a significantly more resource-intensive process.

---

[13]http://www.whatwg.org/specs/web-apps/current-work/multipage/workers.html#workers

Concurrency

It may be tempting to think of web workers as a means to achieve concurrency in the JavaScript, but part of true concurrency is the ability to share an execution context. Although workers do have access to some attributes of the parent browser context, their access is handled as a message-passing API, which is not the same thing as sharing resources. This API ensures that the background workers play in a sandbox and do not clobber the state of the main window's document environment. Mozilla's own documentation expands on this need for thread safety:[14]

> *The Worker interface spawns real OS-level threads, and concurrency can cause interesting effects in your code if you aren't careful. However, in the case of web workers, the carefully controlled communication points with other threads means that it's actually very hard to cause concurrency problems. There's no access to non-thread safe components or the DOM and you have to pass specific data in and out of a thread through serialized objects. So you have to work really hard to cause problems in your code.*

Knowing When to Be a Foreman

Just as in real life, knowing when to hire someone is one of the biggest decisions you can make as a manger. Hiring at the right time can mean the difference between success and failure; unfortunately, the inverse is also true. What follows is a list of pros and cons to consider before using web workers within your program. Web workers are an excellent choice for problems that do not need frequent messages from the UI layer; for example, physic simulations, long-polling network operations, image manipulation, or intense data parsing. They are not a panacea, however, and used in the wrong quantities or for the wrong problem they can actually hurt an application's performance. In certain cases, workers can even crash the browser because their messages back to the main script are not throttled.[15]

Advantages

- They allow for long-running or computationally intense tasks to be decoupled from the UI event loop, which makes the program feel more responsive.

- Workers can be spun up on demand, so it is possible to increase or decrease background resources as needed.

Disadvantages

- Workers are *resource*-intensive to start up, with a high per-instance memory footprint.

- They work independently of the main UI thread, so they do not have access to many parts of the DOM or global variables.

- Not all runtime environments support all types of web workers, so developers must take care in testing cross-platforms.

- Extra attention must be taken when minifying a script to prevent it from breaking references to the workers.

---

[14]https://developer.mozilla.org/en-US/docs/Web/Guide/Performance/Using_web_workers
[15]http://blog.sethladd.com/2011/09/box2d-and-web-workers-for-javascript.html

Hiring Workers

The best way to understand web workers is to see them in action. As it turns out, there are actually two forms of workers described in the spec: *dedicated* and *shared*. These workers are nearly identical; they differ in only a few ways:

- When a dedicated worker is created, it has access only to the parent that created it. However, shared workers can have multiple concerns.

- Dedicated workers also persist only as long as their parent does, while the shared worker must be explicitly terminated.

Basics

All workers are created through the use of the Worker constructor:

```
worker = new Worker("worker.js");
```

Once created, workers are managed through a simple message-passing API. The message passing is facilitated through a basic handshake using two methods: postMessage() and onmessage(). A simple ping pong example would require only two files and look like this:

```
// ping.html
<!DOCTYPE HTML>
<html>
<body>
<script type="text/javascript" charset="utf-8">
addEventListener("DOMContentLoaded", (function() {
  worker = new Worker("pong.js");
  worker.onmessage = function(e) {
    console.log(e.data);
  };
  console.log('ping');
  worker.postMessage();
}), false);
</script>
</body>
</html>

// pong.js
onmessage = function(event) {
  postMessage('pong');
};
```

Once this program runs, you will see "ping" and then "pong" written out to the developer console. Because this simple example is a dedicated worker, it will automatically end as soon as the web browser is closed.

Dedicated Workers

Dedicated web workers are background processes that are available only to the script that invoked them. Due to their isolated nature, they are less complicated than shared web workers, and therefore have the widest browser support. Again, the goal of web workers is to give the developer the capacity to push computationally intense or long-running processes to the background. Without web workers, these processes would normally block the event loop, making the program feel frozen.

The following code example demonstrates how web workers might speed up image-manipulation programs, which are notoriously resource-hungry. This example creates highly detailed canvas animation using a stand-alone worker that accepts a collection of canvas pixels and then modifies and returns them to the parent script. This entire process happens using the requestAnimationFrame function, which allows the updates to occur only when the host platform is ready for a new frame. This approach scales the animation fluidity and seamlessly because the worker is called only when the computer has available resources. A still frame of the animation is shown in Figure 5-3.

Figure 5-3. *Still frame of the canvas animation*

```
// index.html
<html>
<head>
<title>index</title>
</head>
<body>
<script type="text/javascript" charset="utf-8">
addEventListener("DOMContentLoaded", (function() {
  var canvas, ctx, imageData, requestAnimationFrame, worker;

  // get the correct animationFrame handler
  requestAnimationFrame = window.requestAnimationFrame || window.mozRequestAnimationFrame ||
window.webkitRequestAnimationFrame || window.msRequestAnimationFrame;
  window.requestAnimationFrame = requestAnimationFrame;

  // add a canvas element and create a rendering context
  canvas = document.createElement("canvas");
  document.getElementsByTagName("body")[0].appendChild(canvas);
```

```
  canvas.height = canvas.width = 400;
  ctx = canvas.getContext("2d");
  imageData = ctx.createImageData(canvas.width, canvas.height);

  // create a new web worker instance
  worker = new Worker("worker.js");
  worker.onmessage = function(e) {
    ctx.putImageData(e.data.pixels, 0, 0);

    // once the canvas is ready for another frame request it from the worker
    window.requestAnimationFrame(function() {
      worker.postMessage({
        pixels: ctx.getImageData(0, 0, canvas.width, canvas.height),
        seed: e.data.seed
      });
    });
  };

  // seed the worker process.
  worker.postMessage({
    pixels: ctx.getImageData(0, 0, canvas.width, canvas.height),
    seed: +new Date()
  });
}), false);
</script>
</body>
</html>

// worker.js
setPixel = function() {
  var index;
  index = (x + y * imageData.width) * 4;
  imageData.data[index + 0] = r;
  imageData.data[index + 1] = g;
  imageData.data[index + 2] = b;
  imageData.data[index + 3] = 255;
};

onmessage = function(event) {
  var b, d, g, height, imageData, pos, r, seed, t, width, x, x2, xoff, y, y2, yoff;
  pos = 0;
  imageData = event.data.pixels;
  seed = event.data.seed;
  width = imageData.width;
  height = imageData.height;
  xoff = width / 2;
  yoff = height / 2;
  y = 0;
  while (y < height) {
    x = 0;
```

```
  while (x < width) {
    x2 = x - xoff;
    y2 = y - yoff;
    d = Math.sqrt(x2 * x2 + y2 * y2);
    t = Math.sin(d / 6.0 * (+new Date() - seed) / 5000);
    r = t * 200 + y;
    g = t * 200 - y;
    b = t * 255 - x / height;
    imageData.data[pos++] = Math.max(0, Math.min(255, r));
    imageData.data[pos++] = Math.max(0, Math.min(255, g));
    imageData.data[pos++] = Math.max(0, Math.min(255, b));
    imageData.data[pos++] = 255;
    x++;
  }
  y++;
}
postMessage({
  pixels: imageData,
  seed: seed
});
};
```

■ **Note**   The URI where the worker file resides must not violate the browser's same-origin policy.[16]

Shared workers

Unlike a dedicated worker whose scope is limited to that of the parent document, shared workers can be pooled across many browser contexts. Communication is handled by passing messages over a unique port that is assigned when the constructor is invoked. What follows is a simple public/private chat application that demonstrates how shared workers function.

■ **Note**   Shared workers are not as well supported by browsers as dedicated workers.[17]

```
// chat.html
<!DOCTYPE HTML>
<html>
 <head>
  <title>Chat Room</title>
  <script>
  var configure, name, sendMessage, update, updateChannel, updatePrivateChannel,
updatePublicChannel, worker;
```

---

[16]https://developer.mozilla.org/en-US/docs/Web/JavaScript/Same_origin_policy_for_JavaScript
[17]http://caniuse.com/#feat=sharedworkers

```
configure = function(event) {
  var name;
  name = event.data.envelope.from;
  return document.getElementById("guest_name").textContent += " " + name;
};

updatePublicChannel = function(event) {
  return updateChannel(document.getElementById("public_channel"), event);
};

updatePrivateChannel = function(event) {
  return updateChannel(document.getElementById("private_channel"), event);
};

updateChannel = function(channel, event) {
  var div, from, m, message, n;
  from = event.data.envelope.from;
  message = event.data.envelope.body;
  div = document.createElement("div");
  n = document.createElement("button");
  n.textContent = from;
  n.onclick = function() {
    return worker.port.postMessage({
      action: "msg",
      envelope: {
        from: name,
        to: from,
        body: document.getElementById("message").value
      }
    });
  };
  div.appendChild(n);
  m = document.createElement("span");
  m.textContent = message;
  div.appendChild(m);
  return channel.appendChild(div);
};

update = function(event) {
  switch (event.data.action) {
    case "cfg":
      return configure(event);
    case "txt":
      return updatePublicChannel(event);
    case "msg":
      return updatePrivateChannel(event);
  }
};

sendMessage = function(message) {
  return worker.port.postMessage({
    action: "txt",
```

```
        envelope: {
          from: name,
          body: message
        }
      });
  };

  worker = new SharedWorker("chat_worker.js", "core");

  name = void 0;

  worker.port.addEventListener("message", update, false);

  worker.port.start();

</script>
</head>
<body>
 <h2>Public Chat</h2>
 <h1>Welcome <span id="guest_name"></span></h1>
 <h4>public</h4>
 <div id="public_channel"></div>
 <h4>private</h4>
 <div id="private_channel"></div>
 <form onsubmit="sendMessage(message.value);message.value = ''; return false;">
   <p>
    <input id='message' type="text" name="message" size="50">
    <button>Post</button>
   </p>
 </form>
</body>
</html>

// chat_worker.js
/*
  Simplified example from:
  http://www.whatwg.org/specs/web-apps/current-work/multipage/workers.html
*/
var getMessage, getNextName, nextName, onconnect, viewers;

getNextName = function() {
  nextName++;
  return "Guest" + nextName;
};

getMessage = function(event) {
  var channel, from, to, viewer, _results;
  switch (event.data.action) {
  case "txt":
    _results = [];
```

```
    for (viewer in viewers) {
      _results.push(viewers[viewer].port.postMessage({
        action: "txt",
        envelope: {
          from: event.target.session.name,
          body: event.data.envelope.body
        }
      }));
    }
    return _results;
    break;
  case "msg":
    from = event.target.session;
    to = viewers[event.data.envelope.to];
    if (to) {
      channel = new MessageChannel();
      from.port.postMessage({
        action: "msg",
        envelope: {
          to: to.name,
          from: from.name,
          body: "private message sent to: " + event.data.envelope.to
        }
      }, [channel.port1]);
      return to.port.postMessage({
        action: "msg",
        envelope: {
          to: from.name,
          from: to.name,
          body: "private message: " + event.data.envelope.body
        }
      }, [channel.port2]);
    }
  }
};

nextName = 0;

viewers = {};

onconnect = function(event) {
  var name;
  name = getNextName();
  event.ports[0].session = {
    port: event.ports[0],
    name: name
  };
  viewers[name] = event.ports[0].session;
  event.ports[0].postMessage({
    action: "cfg",
```

```
    envelope: {
      from: name,
      body: "connected"
    }
  });
  return event.ports[0].onmessage = getMessage;
};
```

Subworkers

The main document context is not the only element that can spawn workers. Web workers can delegate gnarly processing tasks to a set of their own minions that are referred to as *subworkers*. Just like web workers, subworkers must not violate the browser's same-origin policy, although the subworker's origin is based off the instantiating worker's location, not the master document. Unfortunately, support for subworkers is extremely thin, so I won't give an example use case. I have included this topic mainly as a matter of completeness.

Blob the Builder

Modern workflows often minify and concatenate individual scripts into a single master file as part of a deploy process. Doing this would break the reference to the worker source file in the previous example because the worker file would not exist on the production environment. One way around this problem is to write your worker code so that it executes inline with the rest of your application. This process can be mostly painless using the Blob API.[18] Let's look at an example:

```
var blobTheBuilder, winUrl, worker;

winUrl = window.URL || window.webkitURL;

blobTheBuilder = new Blob(["self.onmessage=function(e){postMessage(Math.round(Math.sqrt(e.data)))}"]);

worker = new Worker(winUrl.createObjectURL(blobTheBuilder));

worker.onmessage = function (e) {
    return console.log(e.data);
};

// Find the closest square root of a number
// => 6
worker.postMessage(42);
```

Summary

The following section aggregates concepts from this chapter into a series of key points:

- Concurrency in programming is the capability for two or more computational procedures to execute simultaneously while sharing resources.

- Concurrent processes should be used only for problems that are nondeterministic, meaning that the sequencing of state is not important.

---

[18]https://developer.mozilla.org/en-US/docs/Web/API/Blob

- JavaScript is a single-threaded language, which means concurrency is often faked using other means.

- JavaScript's event loop is designed to be non-blocking for I/O operations.

- A callback in JavaScript is the act of passing a function object as an argument to another function that is to be used on the return value.

- A promise is a token object the represents the future value or exception of a function that has not yet returned.

- Coroutines and generators allow for the suspension and resumption of the execution of code using predetermined entry and exit points.

- Web workers are JavaScript processes that can be spun up to work in the so-called *background* of the browser.

Additional Resources

What follows are a list of useful posts and essays on the various topics discussed in this chapter.

Callbacks

- http://docs.nodejitsu.com/articles/getting-started/control-flow/what-are-callbacks
- http://matt.might.net/articles/by-example-continuation-passing-style/

Generators

- http://devsmash.com/blog/whats-the-big-deal-with-generators
- http://jlongster.com/A-Study-on-Solving-Callbacks-with-JavaScript-Generators

Coroutines

- http://syzygy.st/javascript-coroutines/
- http://www.dabeaz.com/coroutines/Coroutines.pdf
- http://calculist.org/blog/2011/12/14/why-coroutines-wont-work-on-the-web/

Promises

- http://promises-aplus.github.io/promises-spec/
- https://github.com/kriskowal/q

Web Workers

- http://www.html5rocks.com/en/tutorials/workers/basics/
- https://developer.mozilla.org/en-US/docs/Web/Guide/Performance/Using_web_workers

■ ■ ■

## CHAPTER 6

JavaScript IRL

"A mind is a simulation that simulates itself."

—Erol Ozan

Get excited; this chapter is about robots, JavaScript and, well, nothing else. But seriously, robots and JavaScript should be enough. In this chapter, I will quickly survey the field of physical computing and how robots written in JavaScript fit in. The bulk of this chapter covers the ways in which you can interact with the world around you using machines that listen to JavaScript.

Diary of a Hardware Wannabe

When I was growing up, my little brother Matt got all the hand-me-down tech. Anytime our family upgraded a piece of consumer electronics, the old version went to Matt, who would almost immediately curl up with it on the carpet of his room, wrapping his legs around to secure his kill. Then, like a vulture with OCD, he would begin methodically picking apart the plastic carcass with his kid-sized screwdriver set. Eventually the machine would give up the ghost, and small plastic gears, wires, and circuit boards would spill out. Then sometimes he would try and put it back together or save the parts for later. Matt was interested in a whole different kind of machine learning.

Hardware hacking was not a phase that he outgrew. He was becoming a boy wizard with a right–angle Makita screw gun instead of a wand. When he was 15, he landed a job installing car audio systems for a company called Dashboard Stereo. He badgered the owner Darrell until he relented and gave Matt a job. Matt was the youngest technician by at least a decade, but he was already better than most of them would ever be. He was the youngest-ever Mobile Electronics Certified Professional (MECP) installer at the age of 15. He worked at the stereo shop until college and then went off to Virginia Tech. Not surprisingly, Matt became an electrical engineer and is now a member of the research staff at MIT.

Fire Hoses

As a high school student, I was accepted into the North Carolina School of the Arts, which meant I lived about two hours away from home. At the start of the year, Matt lent me his powered subwoofer to take with me back to my dorm. Unfortunately, once I arrived at school, I realized I'd left the plug for the speaker at home. I went down to Radio Shack and bought a universal power adapter, which looked like a shuriken but with plugs of various sizes instead of metal points. I returned to school and plugged the shuriken into the back of the speaker and stood with the other side of the cord in my hand looking at the wall.

Growing up I dreamed of unlocking hardware the way Matt could, but here I was petrified by even plugging something in. I realized I had no idea what I was doing, so I called my dad. This, as it turns out, was a bad idea. My father is another gifted machine whisperer; at times when my brother and he had nothing else in common they at least spoke the common language of watts and ohms. I explained my problem about not knowing which plug to use, and this is what he told me:

> *The problem you have here is that you don't know the correct voltage or amperage to power the speaker. Think of it is as if your speaker runs on water, and so you hook it to a fire hose. The water then flows through the hose is the voltage, the velocity at which it travels is the amperage.*

I know he felt he'd explained it in such a way that a first grader would have understood it. But I stood there with the pay phone receiver pressed against my ear, trying to visualize what he just said. I might as well have called China, though, because he lost me at *fire hose*. I returned to my dorm room and again picked up the end of the cord. How bad could it be, I thought?

I chose a power setting in the middle of the available options and plugged the cord into the wall outlet. Instantly I heard a faint buzzing coming from the speaker, then a loud *pop*, and then absolutely nothing. I quickly realized that I'd nuked my brother's speaker, and any illusions I harbored that the ability to commune with hardware somehow ran in our family evaporated. Gray smoke slowly wafted out of the port hole of the speaker. Matt, of course, was furious when he found out, maybe because I didn't ask him, and maybe because he couldn't fathom how someone could be so ignorant about the basics of electricity. After that, I was too chicken to try again—that is, until as an adult I discovered the Arduino.

Hardware for Everyone Else

I was attending a presentation at UCLA and I went to hear Casey Reas speak about his project "Processing." Processing is a program he and Ben Fry created to enable artists to sketch with code. Reas had recently joined the Design Media Arts department at UCLA, and I was interested to meet him in person having followed his work from afar when he was a student at MIT. As part of the presentations that night, someone else spoke about a new effort to create a cheap microcontroller that would fit on a single board. The board and the project were going by the name of Arduino, and it sought to make hardware accessible to the uninitiated in the same way Processing had done for programming. The goal was to liberate physical computing devices through the production of open-source hardware.

I casually followed the project as an interested observer and finally purchased my own board sometime later. When the board arrived, it went up on a shelf in my office and sat there like a trophy for a sport I didn't play. I looked at the Arduino from time to time, taking it off the shelf during conference calls, running my fingers around the edge of the PCB, and pressing my thumb against the jumper pins as if they were a mini bed of nails. This little piece of metal and silicone contained both promise and peril of hardware to me. I wanted desperately to interact with the world though hardware of my own design, but all that I could envision was that gray smoke wafting from my brother's speakers.

Let's Get Physical

One of the great qualities about software programming is that it is *very* hard to screw up the computer's hardware. Sure, you can inadvertently wipe your hard drive by writing `rm -rf /` instead of `rm -rf ./` (I am speaking from experience here), but the drive still functions fine. Software is more forgiving and allows for more trial and error. Hardware can be like a trial by fire (literally). There is the possibility that you can fry your Arduino or your computer (or both) with an inadvertently misplaced wire. Yet hardware beckons me with an undeniable siren song played through a Piezo buzzer. The potential for a blinking LED under my control is more rewarding than it has any right to be.

Much of this first section was dedicated to my own personal frustrations and fears when it comes to hardware. I included the section as a means of encouragement to those of you who are sitting on the concrete lip of the hardware pool with your JavaScript floaty wings on. If I can learn to swim here, so can you. Come on in; the *water* (I mean *voltage*) is fine.

Physical Computing

I know I promised robots, and I'll get there, but much of what you will be learning about in this chapter is lumped into the category of physical computing. The name itself sounds so spectacularly vague that it borders on meaninglessness. Starting with a definition will help you get your bearings. Wikipedia defines physical computing this way:

> *Physical computing, in the broadest sense, means building interactive physical systems by the use of software and hardware that can sense and respond to the analog world. While this definition is broad enough to encompass things such as smart automotive traffic control systems or factory automation processes, it is not commonly used to describe them. In the broad sense, physical computing is a creative framework for understanding human beings' relationship to the digital world. In practical use, the term most often describes handmade art, design or DIY hobby projects that use sensors and microcontrollers to translate analog input to a software system, and/or control electro-mechanical devices such as motors, servos, lighting or other hardware.*[1]

In popular culture, physical computing is typically associated with engineering outsiders or new media artists who orbit outside the gravitational pull of *professional engineering*. Many of the most interesting examples of physical computing take one of two approaches:

- They interweave the computer into an existing analog physical process in an unexpected way.

- They map rules, tropes, or artifacts of the virtual world into physical space.

Even though the Wikipedia definition infers a DIY quality to physical computing, that is not to say that the field has no place for consumer-grade, mass market electronics. The Microsoft Kinect is a perfect example of such a device.

The name *Kinect* cleverly alludes to its purpose, which is to use its camera to read a player's body gestures as the means to control a game. The name is the amalgamation of *kinetics* (movement) and *connect* (data transmission), two key facets of physical computing. The Kinect is a great example of a finely polished and extremely sophisticated physical computing device.

You may be asking yourself this question: what is the line in the silicone that divides devices that are and are not for physical computing? Consider the differences between the Kinect and a digital video camera. The important distinction between the two is not the asymmetry in technical complexity, but rather that the Kinect uses video capture as part of a larger feedback processing loop involving the player, the game system, and potentially remote servers. Alternatively, the video camera merely stores all available input *indiscriminately* and waits for further instruction.

The point of physical computing is not to make more *things*. The goal is to make new pathways between the physical and virtual worlds, which allow users to read, remix, and rebroadcast the world around them.

An Internet of Things

Physical computing devices are often referred to as being part of the "Internet of Things." Kevin Ashton is credited with coining this term, which he used to theorize a world in which all devices would be persistently connected together through omnipresent networks and low-powered, cheap, and promiscuous sensors. He was interested in how these devices might track and categorize themselves or speak up when needed by the user. Much of his emphasis was on the emerging field of radio frequency identification (RFID) tags, which are small circuits that can be read from and written to when energized by external power. RFID tags are now incredibly pervasive in daily life. They are

---

[1]http://en.wikipedia.org/wiki/Physical_computing

embedded in everything from credit cards to the scruff of the neck of a family pet. Ashton explained his concept in the July 2009 edition of the RFID journal:

> Today computers—and, therefore, the Internet—are almost wholly dependent on human beings for information. Nearly all of the roughly 50 petabytes (a petabyte is 1,024 terabytes) of data available on the Internet were first captured and created by human beings—by typing, pressing a record button, taking a digital picture or scanning a bar code. Conventional diagrams of the Internet . . . leave out the most numerous and important routers of all - people. The problem is, people have limited time, attention and accuracy—all of which means they are not very good at capturing data about things in the real world. And that's a big deal. We're physical, and so is our environment . . . You can't eat bits, burn them to stay warm or put them in your gas tank. Ideas and information are important, but things matter much more. Yet today's information technology is so dependent on data originated by people that our computers know more about ideas than things. If we had computers that knew everything there was to know about things—using data they gathered without any help from us—we would be able to track and count everything, and greatly reduce waste, loss and cost. We would know when things needed replacing, repairing or recalling, and whether they were fresh or past their best. The Internet of Things has the potential to change the world, just as the Internet did. Maybe even more so.[2]

—Kevin Ashton

Today, this term has been co-opted by several other fields. Depending on who you are talking to, the Internet of Things now simultaneously describes:

- Inventory and fulfillment systems as in Ashton's definition

- Physical computing devices like the Kinect

- Augmented reality devices that overlay virtual objects into a specific real spaces, which can be viewed only through virtual portholes (i.e., a smartphone)

- Virtual objects that exist as patterns to be produced using rapid prototyping tools like 3D printers.

Because this is a chapter about JavaScript robots, I'll be using the second definition.

Why JavaScript

As discussed earlier, physical computing is not a hardware-only affair. It is actually a carefully choreographed dance of I/O cycles between the physical and virtual. The language you choose determines how effortlessly the dance appears to the user. JavaScript, as it turns out, allows these two partners to embrace one another almost effortlessly, but not for the reasons you might expect. JavaScript has both technical and semantic characteristics that lend themselves to physical computing, and a growing collection of libraries that make hardware less hard. This section explains why JavaScript is a great choice for physical computing.

Building Bridges

Chris Williams, the creator of NodeBots (which I'll discuss later), has thought a lot about the how JavaScript empowers robotics. While working on a project to enable sensors to communicate over various wireless spectrums he became dissatisfied with the methods used in other libraries. He felt that the approach, although technically adept,

---

[2]http://en.wikipedia.org/wiki/Internet_of_Things

was semantically awkward.[3] In his mind, these libraries suffered a disconnection between how the library expected the world to behave and how it actually worked. Sometime later, Williams reviewed a proposal for a presentation by Nikolai Onken and Jörn Zaefferer on "Robotic JavaScript." Their proposal asserted that JavaScript could be used to control devices in the real world. This piqued his imagination and he formulated a minimal yet expressive syntax:

```
$("livingroom").bind("motion", function() {
  $(this).find("lights").brightness("75%").dimAfter("120s");
});
```

The beauty of this simple code snippet is that in Williams' words: "modeling real world objects and actions as chainable, evented processes felt almost natural." This proposed syntax inspired Williams to write node-serialport, which he saw as the "gateway to hardware."

Reactive Programming Paradigm

Williams' living room light example alludes to a fundamental quality of the real world, which is that it is a collection of asynchronous operations that execute over a variety of durations. In his model, the living room object bound an event listener to any motion that occurred within it. Once triggered, the bound function invoked a method to turn on the lights. The lights in turn had their own reactive task chain to complete, first turning on and then dimming after a given timeframe.

This event observer pattern, as referenced in the previous snippet, is very common in many JavaScript libraries like jQuery. This familiarity is one of the reasons Williams felt JavaScript could be a good choice for controlling hardware because even developers with no hardware experience can still leverage their knowledge of building interactive web pages.

The snippet also implies that the framework needs to be written to handle a world where events streams from many inputs at once. The goal of a reactive system is to respond to state changes on watched objects and propagate those changes to any other dependent objects. The classic example of a reactive system is a spreadsheet where a sum in column "c" depends on adding columns "a" and "b" together. Normally, this computation would occur only once. If the values of "a" or "b" changed, "c" would no longer be correct. Unless "c" was told about the change, it would never update and thus be perpetually out of sync. In a reactive system, however, "c" would observe "a" and "b" for changes. Once a change was detected, it would sum "a" and "b" again. The process of recalculating its value would in turn trigger objects dependent on "c" higher in the event stream to react as well.

When programming robots, it is possible that a bot will be simultaneously tracking many different environment variables using a variety of different sensors. These sensors, however, may return results at different intervals. Therefore, a reactive system would be useful to aggregate, reprocess, and potentially invalidate input long before the hardware has to respond. The goal of a reactive programming system as it relates to robotics is to handle the asynchronous nature of the real world and reformulate it into a series of sequential steps that the hardware can perform. In the next section, you will begin to build your reactive system using the NodeBots software stack.

NodeBots: Fast, Cheap, and Servo-controlled

NodeBots are robots controlled using an invisible JavaScript tether. This tether is composed of a Node server and a collection of libraries that abstract much of the drudgery of communicating with hardware. The NodeBots you will build leverage the Arduino board to control the output peripherals. Before you can properly begin to build your bot, though, you must first understand how all these technologies work together. Consider the following diagram shown in Figure 6-1. It explains the anatomy of the Nodebot you will ultimately build.

---

[3]http://voodootikigod.com/nodebots-the-rise-of-js-robotics/

Anatomy of a Nodebot

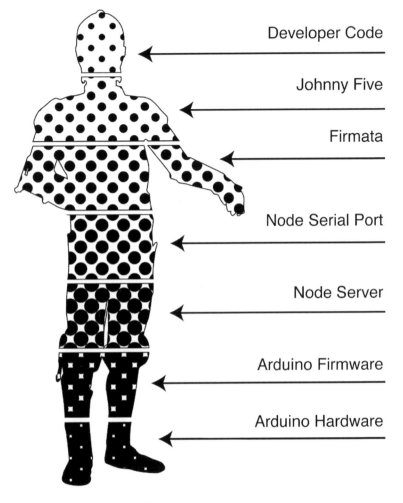

Figure 6-1. *Anatomy of a Nodebot*

Thankfully, you will spend most of your time in this chapter writing code designated from the shoulders up. This is because as you move lower on your bot diagram, the code required to make the magic happen becomes more machine-specific, less expressive, and ostensibly no fun to write. However, just so you know how well you have it, and to ensure that you fully understand how the individual parts of the stack work together, you will begin writing code below the knees working your way upward. The process will be to repeatedly write the code needed to make an LED blink, which is the hardware equivalent of "Hello world".

You will begin by first writing directly for the Arduino using the native IDE and then transition to writing a firmware that handshakes with the Node serial port. Finally, you'll move on to Firmata and then Johnny-Five.

REPL

I mentioned earlier that the machines will be linked to a host computer using JavaScript. This is much different from the typical approach, which is to edit the source files and then compile it down into byte code so that it can be stored directly on the chip of the Arduino. Only then can the program be run. This development cycle is called edit-compile-run-debug (ECRD), and is how most Arduino bots are built. In contrast, NodeBots keep the robot's brains on the host computer and use a read-eval-print-loop (REPL) environment. This approach has certain advantages and disadvantages that I'll enumerate here.

Advantages

- Encourages experimentation because of the real-time interaction between the host computer and hardware.

- Reduces complexity in debugging because the code remains accessible on the host computer and is not compiled down into a different form, which may introduce inconsistencies.

- Affords a clear separation of concerns between the low-level control of the hardware and high-level business logic.

- Programs can be more complex due to the additional resources available from the host computer.

Disadvantages

- Requires a persistent tether, which may limit the autonomy of the robot.

- Increases dependencies needed to make the robot run.

- May incur a delay in responsiveness between the host computer and the bot due to the time it takes for messages to be sent over the tether.

Why Bother?

For years when I would badger my brother Matt for advice over the phone about my newest pie-in-the-sky hardware idea, he would typically respond the same way, "Why would you want to do that?" His verbal pin always popped my mental bubble, and I'd deflate back down to earth, feeling dejected that real engineers would think my idea was dumb. The couple of times that he did try to answer my question, I was quickly lost in concepts and minutiae that I had no frame of reference to understand. I know he was not out to hurt my feelings, and maybe in his mind he was saving me time and effort in pursuing what he knew to be a naive approach. As I began to get excited about JavaScript robots I asked myself this question: *would real robotic engineers thumb their noses at NodeBots as being without merit*? To find out, I asked a real robotics engineer.

Raquel Vélez is a mechanical engineer who trained at Caltech and has since worked in the robotics field for nearly a decade. She also happens to be very active in the NodeBots community. Because Vélez is an insider in both the professional and hobbyist robotics communities I felt she could answer the "why bother" question. When I posed it to her, she said this:

> It's true that NodeBots are still in their infancy; we're not going to be running a self-driving car with node anytime soon. But the point isn't that node is going to replace C++/Python—rather, by opening the robotics community to the JavaScript community, we're enabling a whole world of people to robotics that didn't exist before. This influx, in turn, increases the diversity of people trying to solve hard problems, and thereby pushes all technology (the web, robotics) forward.

She continued to compare and contrast the two communities this way:

> *Basically, having the ability to be truly open source, with a super fast turn-around time is something you can't get in the "traditional" robotics industry. When I worked in academia/industry, you had to have lots of money, experience, and time to get any significant work done. With NodeBots, you don't need any of those things—you can just get started.*

I was sold on the idea even before Vélez gave it the expert's thumbs up for all the reasons that she mentioned, but also because I didn't need to ask anyone's permission to get started. There is literally no barrier to entry, provided you can cobble together less than a hundred dollars in parts and tools, which I'll cover next.

Prerequisites

This chapter has a variety of external and system-specific prerequisites that need to be met to be able to follow along step-by-step. Please ensure that you have taken the necessary time to confirm that your environment meets the following preconditions before attempting to replicate the Nodebot examples.

General

Before installing anything, *make sure that your system has the ability to compile any and all native modules for Node.* At the time of this writing, Python 2.x is required; using version 3.x will result in failure because `node-serialport` depends on `node-gyp`, which requires Python 2.x

Windows

You must have Visual Studio 2010+ installed (Express edition is fine). If you will use the Arduino, ensure that you install the necessary drivers.[4]

Mac OS X

You must ensure that you have the xCode command line tools[5] installed (at a minimum).

Linux

Most likely, no special dependencies exist for your system above and beyond the general prerequisites.

Shopping List

Before you can build your robot army, you must get a basic kit of parts and a small selection of tools together. What follows is the minimum shopping list required to replicate the examples in this chapter. If you think JavaScript robots might be something that will hold your interest for some time, you might consider buying a pre-bundled kit. These packs include your required parts and a few other nice-to-have components. Many times these kits are marketed under names such as *explorer, inventor* or *introductory*; and are available through a variety of local and online electronics retailers.

---

[4]`http://arduino.cc/en/Main/Software`
[5]`https://developer.apple.com/xcode/`

- An Arduino Uno R3 Board[6]
- 10 ft. USB 2.0 Certified 480Mbps Type A Male to B Male Cable
- A few basic Red 5mm LEDs
- A package of breadboard jumper wires
- Micro servo motor
- Safety glasses

Arduino IDE

In this section, you will make an Arduino blink using the native IDE. You will write a trivial script, which must then be uploaded to the Arduino board. This two-step process is needed only when using the IDE; as soon as you add a Node serial port to your stack, you will have the means for creating a persistent connection to your Arduino board.

Setup

You will first need to download the Arduino IDE[7] and get it successfully installed. Once you install it, you will want to place the longer leg (positive) of your LED in pin slot 13 and the shorter leg (negative) in the ground slot. The reason you use pin 13 is because it has a resistor already built in. Once installed, your board should look something like Figure 6-2.

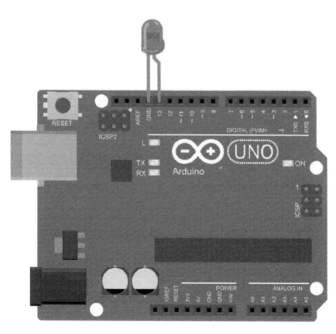

Figure 6-2. *Board layout for the blink example*

---

[6]http://arduino.cc/en/Main/arduinoBoardUno
[7]http://arduino.cc/en/Main/Software

Smoke Test

To perform this test, you will need to follow a series of steps to get your LED to blink.

Step 1: Connect the Board

Connect the USB cord to the Arduino and the computer. You should see a small LED on the board light and remain lit. This LED indicates power is flowing to the board.

■ **Note** On a Windows machine, you may be prompted by the hardware wizard to install drivers for the Arduino. You will need to unzip FTDI USB Drivers.zip, which can be found in the drivers folder of the Arduino distribution you downloaded with the IDE. Point the wizard to these drivers from the (Advanced) menu option.

Step 2: Select the Correct Board

Ensure that you have the correct board selected inside the IDE. You can do this by picking the board from the Tools ➤ Board submenu, as shown in Figure 6-3.

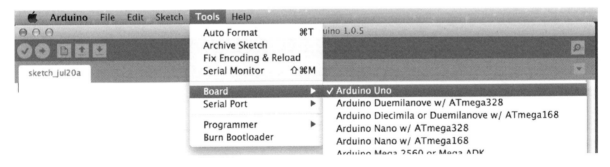

Figure 6-3. *Arduino IDE board selection menu*

■ **Note** This chapter assumes that you are using the Arduino Uno. If you are using another kind of board, the preceding screenshot will not be 100 percent accurate.

Step 3: Write Firmware

The Arduino IDE uses the metaphor of a sketch book in which every page is a sketch that can be loaded into the Arduino. Sketches are saved with the .ino file extension. Below is the sketch that you will upload to your Arduino. Fortunately you will not need to transcribe it because this code can be found in the examples folder inside the IDE (see Figure 6-4).

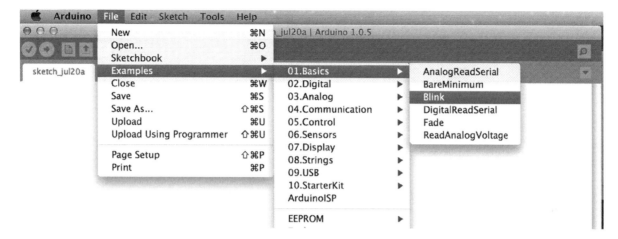

Figure 6-4. *Arduino IDE example selection menu*

```
/*
  Blink
  Turns on an LED on for one second, then off for one second, repeatedly.

  This example code is in the public domain.
 */

// Pin 13 has an LED connected on most Arduino boards.
// give it a name:
int led = 13;

// the setup routine runs once when you press reset:
void setup() {
  // initialize the digital pin as an output.
  pinMode(led, OUTPUT);
}

// the loop routine runs over and over again forever:
void loop() {
  digitalWrite(led, HIGH);   // turn the LED on (HIGH is the voltage level)
  delay(1000);               // wait for a second
  digitalWrite(led, LOW);    // turn the LED off by making the voltage LOW
  delay(1000);               // wait for a second
}
```

This code should be pretty self-explanatory; it just initializes the board and then begins to loop repeatedly. During each loop, the code issues a call to write either a high or low value to pin 13 of the Arduino. One aspect of this code that is hard to understand is what the constants OUTPUT, HIGH, and LOW actually do.

Step 4: Compile and Upload a Firmware

Once the blink tutorial is selected, a new sketch window will appear. This new window has several icons running along the top. Locate the check mark icon and press it. This action tells the IDE to verify and compile the code into a format suitable for upload to the Arduino board. If everything works, you should see a Done Compiling message near the bottom of the interface.

Click the right-arrow icon in the top menu, which will upload the code to the Arduino. You will see a progress indicator near the bottom appear that updates as the code is transferred to the board. Once you see Done Uploading, you should see your Arduino rhythmically blinking an LED for you.

Step 5: Unplug Arduino

Once you have successfully completed this test, unplug the USB cable from your computer, which should cut power to the Arduino.

Node Serial Port

The node serial port is the base of the NodeBot layer cake. Every other library covered in this chapter will depend on this library in one way or another. However, before you can communicate with the Arduino using the Node serial port, you need to create the custom `.ino` firmware, which allows handshaking between the Node code and the Arduino.

Smoke Test

Step 1: Connect the Board

Reconnect your board to the computer using the USB cable. You should see the onboard LED become lit, designating the board has power.

■ **Note** If you skipped the previous Arduino example, please refer to that section to ensure that you have installed all the requisite drivers.

Step 2: Select the Correct Board

Ensure that you have the correct board selected inside the IDE just as you did in the previous Arduino IDE example.

Step 3: Write Firmware

Open a new sketch file in the Arduino IDE and transcribe the following code:

```
int bytesRead = 0;
boolean isPinSet;
byte stored[2];

void setup()
{
  Serial.begin(57600);
}
```

```
void loop()
{
  while (Serial.available()) {
    int data = Serial.read();

    stored[bytesRead] = data;
    bytesRead++;

    if (bytesRead == 2) {
      if (isPinSet == false) {
        isPinSet = true;
        pinMode(stored[0], OUTPUT);
      } else {
        digitalWrite(stored[0], stored[1]);
      }
      bytesRead = 0;
    }
  }
}
```

Step 4: Compile and Upload Firmware

Once you have transcribed the previous code into your sketch file, click the check mark icon to verify and compile the source. If you have typed everything correctly, you should see the message "Done compiling" toward the bottom of the interface. Next, click the right arrow to upload the compiled code to the Arduino. You should see a progress indicator appear as it transfers the code. Once everything completes, you should see the message "Done uploading" toward the bottom of the interface.

Step 5: Install Node Serial Port

Provided that you already have node and npm installed on your computer, you can install node-serial port like this:

npm install serialport

Step 6: Write a Program

Create a new file from within your favorite text editor, and type the following code. Once transcribed, save it as serial-blinky.js to the same folder you installed node serial port.

```
var serial = require("serialport"),
    raddress = /usb|acm|com/i,
    pin = 13;

serial.list(function(err, result) {
  var read = new Buffer(0),
      address, port, bite;

  if (result.length) {
    address = result.filter(function(val) {
```

```
      // Match only address that Arduino cares about
      // ttyUSB#, cu.usbmodem#, COM#
      if (raddress.test(val.comName)) {
        return val;
      }
    }).map(function(val) {
      return val.comName;
    })[0];

    port = new serial.SerialPort(address, {
      baudrate: 57600,
      buffersize: 1
    });

    port.on("open", function() {
      var bite;

      function loop() {
        port.write([pin, (bite ^= 0x01)]);
      }

      setInterval(loop, 500);
    });
  } else {
    console.log("No valid port found");
  }
});
```

Now run your code from the command line using this:

node serial-blinky.js

If everything works, the LED should begin to blink for you.

■ **Caution**   If you get a "Cannot find module 'serialport'" error, you will need to save this sketch beside the 'node_modules' folder that contains the node serial-port library.

Step 7: Unplug Arduino

Once you have successfully completed this test, unplug the USB cable from your computer. Doing so should cut power to the Arduino.

Too Close for Comfort

This approach actually feels more cumbersome than writing just for the Arduino because it requires two tightly coupled files to work. If you made substantial changes to your JavaScript file, you would need to reflect those changes in your .ino file. This is because Node serial port is a low-level library meant just for communicating over the serial port, nothing more; nothing less. Thankfully, you will be moving one layer higher in abstraction as you move on to Firmata.

Firmata

Firmata is a generic protocol for communicating between an Arduino and host computer. In this example, you will be working with two forms of Firmata. The first will be a firmware .ino file that you will load directly onto the Arduino. The second Firmata is a Node library that handshakes with the firmware. In this section, you will re-create the blinking example, but this time using Firmata as a bridge.

Smoke Test

Step 1: Connect the Board

Reconnect your board to the computer using the USB cable. You should see the onboard LED become lit, designating that the board has power.

■ **Note**　If you skipped the previous Arduino example, please refer to that section to ensure that you have installed all the requisite drivers.

Step 2: Select the Correct Board

Ensure that you have the correct board selected inside the IDE just as you did in the Arduino IDE example.

Step 3: Locate the Serial Port

Node serial port needs to know which port the Arduino is connected to. To find the path to the port, look under the Tools ➤ Serial Port submenu, as shown in Figure 6-5. The Arduino will be connected to the port with the check mark. Jot down this reference so that you can use it later.

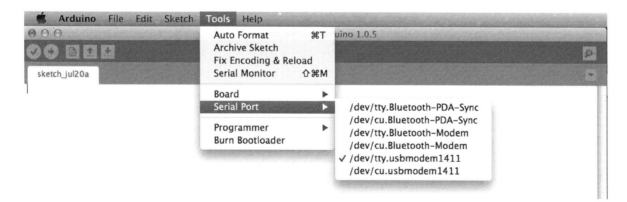

Figure 6-5. *Arduino IDE serial port selection menu*

Step 4: Install Firmata Firmware

To set up the REPL development environment, you must install the StandardFirmata firmware onto your Arduino. Fortunately, this code comes bundled with the IDE. Simply choose File ➤ Examples ➤ Firmata ➤ StandardFirmata, as seen in Figure 6-6. This will open a new sketch window with the required code already present. Now click the right arrow and upload the compiled code to the board.

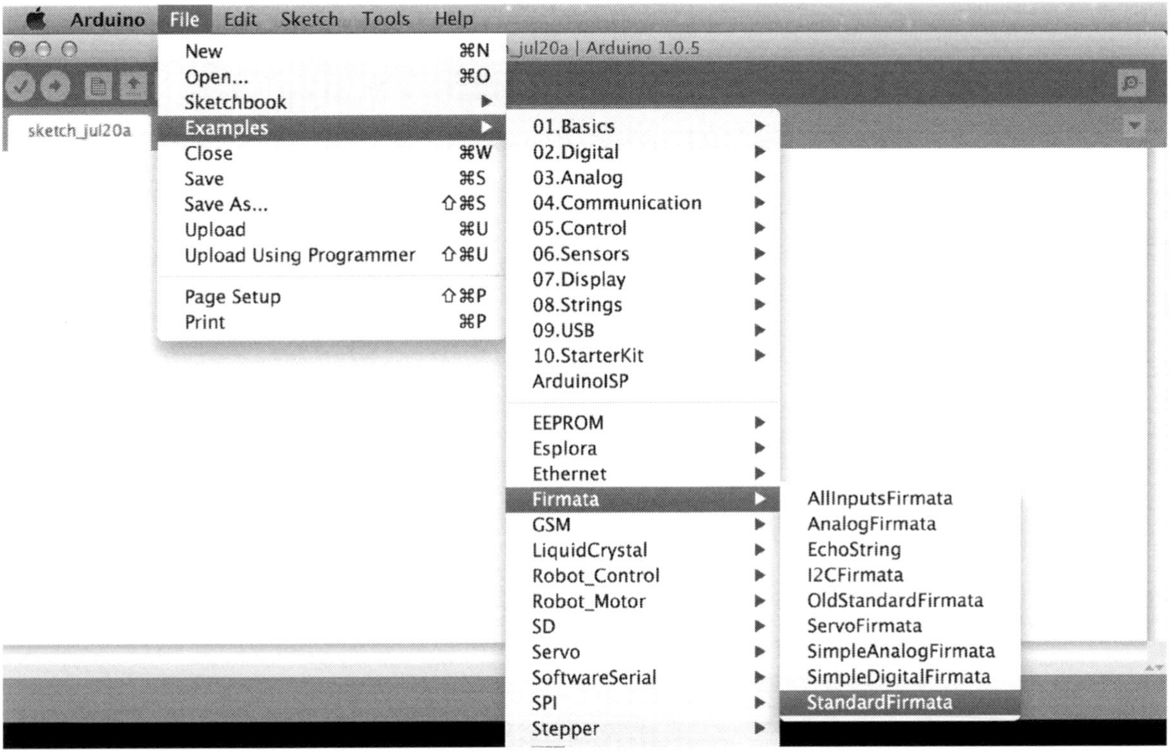

Figure 6-6. Arduino IDE Firmata selection menu

Once the upload completes, your REPL environment is good to go. At this point, you can close native Arduino IDE; you will not need it again for the rest of the chapter.

Step 5: Install the Firmata Library

Now that you have loaded the standard Firmata firmware onto your board,, you need to install the Firmata Node library that understands how to communicate with it. From within the same directory that you installed node-serialport, type the following:

```
npm install firmata
```

Step 6: Write a Program

Provided that Firmata installed correctly, you are ready to rewrite your blinking program. In a text editor, transcribe the following code and save it as 'firmata-blinky.js' in the same folder in which you used to store your previous examples:

```
/**
 * Sample script to blink LED 13
 */

console.log('blink start ...');

var pin = 13;

var firmata = require('firmata');
var board = new firmata.Board('/dev/cu.usbmodem1411', function(err) {
  var bite;

  board.pinMode(pin, board.MODES.OUTPUT);

  function loop() {
    board.digitalWrite([pin, (bite ^= 0x01)]);
  }

  setInterval(loop, 500);
});
```

Now run your code from the command line using the following:

node firmata-blinky.js

If everything works, you should see the LED begin to blink for you.

Step 7: Unplug Arduino

Once you have successfully completed this test unplug the USB cable from your computer, which should cut power to the Arduino.

REPL for Real

Now that you have the Firmata firmware installed and communicating with the Firmata library on your host computer, you have a true REPL development environment setup. This means that (unlike in your Node serial port version) you would not be forced to update the firmware each time you changed your source code on the host computer. Unfortunately, as great as Firmata is, the JavaScript code that you have to write is still very domain-specific. Just as in the Arduino IDE example, there are several obtuse constants and modes that you need to understand before your code will work correctly. To write code that is even more hardware-agnostic, you need to climb one more layer up the stack. Onward to Johnny-Five!

Johnny-Five

Rick Waldron is serious about robots, so much so that he built his own to propose to his wife. Not being an engineer and with no robot emissary of her own, she instead gave Waldron the happy news in her best robot voice. Personally, I think of Waldron as a *Crash Override* figure in the JavaScript community—one who happily exploits his own intellect for fun over profit, yet is serious in his commitment to pushing the community and the language forward.

Waldron created Johnny-Five, which is an open-source Arduino programming framework that sits on top of the Firmata and Node serial port stack. Johnny-Five has a clean expressive API that feels like the JavaScript most developers are used to writing in other contexts. It is the closest to the platonic ideal that Chris Williams proposed in his hypothetical living room example. I asked Waldron about Johnny-Five and why he, like others, felt a JavaScript REPL environment would be ideal for programming robots. He responded this way:

> *All hardware is implicitly synchronous; it exists in the real world. If you tell something to move, it takes actual time to move. This means any program written to interact with hardware must be aware of these temporal constraints and capable of providing efficient control mechanisms. Traditionally, this achieved with multi-threaded, interrupt based programming models; I believe that a single threaded, turn based execution model can provide the same level of efficient control.*

> *Consider a simple sensor attached to an Arduino; traditionally, you'd have some function that is called repeatedly to read and process the value of an analog sensor and conditionally executing some other part of the program based on a change in the value. When writing the same program within JavaScript, using the Johnny-Five framework, the programming model changes to an observer in the form of an event bus. A sensor's value changes, and listeners are notified.*

> *When programming output, the ideas are the same but have much more impact. Let's say we want our program to move a servo from 0 to 180 degrees and back; using the datasheet for our servo, we calculate that it takes 1000ms to travel the full 180 degrees. If you wrote this in Arduino C, it would require a delay(1000) after the first move, which blocks the execution process for entire second. If this is in a loop, then each loop suffers a 1 second hold. If the program must also read sensors for some conditional execution, those sensors are also blocked for 1000ms. In JavaScript on Node.js, using Johnny-Five, tasks that require a "delay" or "loop" will not block execution. Instead, they are scheduled tasks that will be invoked in a later execution turn, allowing the rest of the program to continue as normal.*

> *The turn based execution model is actually not part of the JavaScript language; it's a paradigm of the embedded environment, e.g. a browser, or in this case Node.js. Node.js's turn based execution is implemented in the form of libuv, which provides an asynchronous, event based execution environment. This model is an implicit analog to the explicit loop() in Arduino C.*

> —Rick Waldron

Waldron's approach is very much in the spirit of the Reactive Programming paradigm that was covered earlier in the chapter. The way state changes propagate throughout the framework means that you can write much less code to efficiently model an analog for the real world. In the next section, you will re-create the blinking LED. Then you will explore Johnny-Five's REPL environment by creating a more advanced example.

Smoke Test

Step 1: Connect the Board

Reconnect your board to the computer using the USB cable. You should see the onboard LED become lit, designating that the board has power.

Step 2: Install Johnny-Five

This step assumes that you have already flashed the StandardFirmata firmware onto your Arduino. If you have not completed this step, consult the Firmata section earlier in the chapter. From within the same directory that you installed node-serialport and Firmata, type the following:

```
npm install johnny-five
```

Step 3: Write a Program

Assuming that Johnny-Five installed correctly, you are ready to rewrite your blinking LED example. In a text editor, transcribe the following code and save it as 'johnny-blinky.js' in the same folder you used to store your previous examples:

```
var five = require("johnny-five"),
    board = new five.Board();

board.on("ready", function() {
    (new five.Led(13)).strobe();

});
```

Now run your code from the command line using the following:

```
node johnny-blinky.js
```

If everything works, the LED should begin to blink for you.

Step 4: Unplug Arduino

Once you have successfully completed this test, unplug the USB cable from your computer, which should cut power to the Arduino.

Fiddling with Johnny-Five

It should be clear by simply looking at the number of lines that Johnny-Five requires to blink the LED that this framework really does make writing for the Arduino much easier. However, you are just getting started! In the next example, you will control a micro server motor in real-time using the REPL console. Through this process, you'll understand more about how Johnny-Five models hardware internally and how you can use this knowledge to improve your own programs.

Step 1: Prepare the Board

In this example, you will be controlling a micro servo using Johnny-Five. Provided you have your motor available, plug the data wire into pin 10 and the power wire into the 5 volt pin. Finally, plug the ground wire into one of the available ground pins (see Figure 6-7).

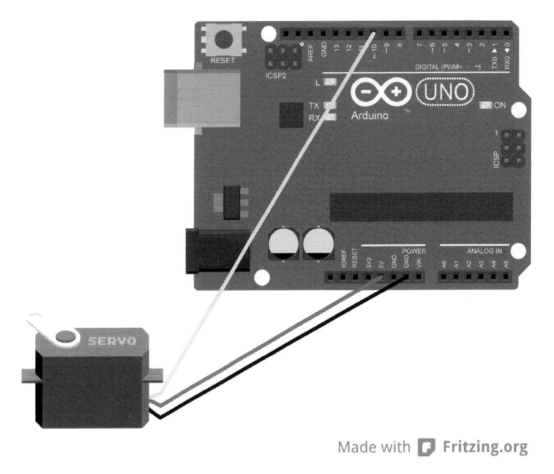

Figure 6-7. *Wiring diagram for servo example*

> **Note** This diagram shows wires connecting directly to the Arduino's pin slots. However, in reality you will probably need to use jumper wires to connect your servo to the Arduino.

Step 2: Connect the Board

Reconnect your board to the computer using the USB cable. You should see the onboard LED become lit designating the board has power.

Step 3: Write a Program

You will now write a simple program to interact with your servo. In a text editor, transcribe the following code into a file. Save the file as 'servo.js' in the same directory that you have been using for your examples.

```
var five = require("johnny-five"),
    board = new five.Board();
```

```
board.on("ready", function() {
  var servo = new five.Servo(10);

  this.repl.inject({
    servo: servo
  });

  servo.center();
  servo.on("move", function(err, degrees) {
    console.log("move", degrees);
  });
});
```

Now run your code from the command line using the following:

node servo.js

If everything works, you should see the servo center and the following output in the terminal window:

```
1374513199929 Board Connecting...
1374513199933 Serial Found possible serial port /dev/cu.usbmodem1411
1374513199934 Board -> Serialport connected /dev/cu.usbmodem1411
1374513203157 Board <- Serialport ready /dev/cu.usbmodem1411
1374513203158 Repl Initialized
>>
```

From within the REPL console, type this:

this.servo.move(90)

Two things should happen: you should see the servo rotate 90 degrees and see Johnny-Five's representation of the hardware state rendered to the console (which you'll explore in detail in the next section).

Step 4: Unplug Arduino

Once you have successfully completed this test, unplug the USB cable from your computer, which should cut power to the Arduino.

Number Five Is Alive

As you issue commands to Johnny-Five's REPL instance, it returns a JavaScript object presenting the current environment state. In your servo example, after you issued a move command, Johnny-Five returned an object that looked a bit like this:

```
{
  board: {
    ready: true,
    firmata: {...},
    register: [ [Circular] ],
    id: '98880E34-5D9E-49A9-8BA0-89496E54F765',
    debug: true,
    pins: { '0': [Object], '1': [Object], '2': [Object], '3': [Object], '4': [Object], '5':
```

127

```
[Object], '6': [Object], '7': [Object], '8': [Object], '9': [Object], '10': [Object], '11':
[Object], '12': [Object], '13': [Object], '14': [Object], '15': [Object], '16': [Object],'17':
[Object], '18': [Object], '19': [Object] },
    repl: {
      context: [Object],
      ready: false,
      _events: {}
    },
    _events: { ready: [Function] },
    port: '/dev/cu.usbmodem1411'
  },
  firmata: {...},
    _maxListeners: 10,
    MODES: {
      INPUT: 0,
      OUTPUT: 1,
      ANALOG: 2,
      PWM: 3,
      SERVO: 4
    },
    I2C_MODES: {
      WRITE: 0,
      READ: 1,
      CONTINUOUS_READ: 2,
      STOP_READING: 3
    },
    STEPPER: {
      TYPE: [Object],
      RUNSTATE: [Object],
      DIRECTION: [Object]
    },
    HIGH: 1,
    LOW: 0,
    pins: [ [Object], [Object], [Object], [Object], [Object], [Object], [Object], [Object],
[Object], [Object], [Object], [Object], [Object], [Object], [Object], [Object], [Object],
[Object], [Object], [Object]],
    analogPins: [14, 15, 16, 17, 18, 19],
    version: { major: 2, minor: 3 },
    firmware: { version: [Object], name: 'StandardFirmata.ino'},
    currentBuffer: [],
    versionReceived: true,
    sp: {
      domain: null,
      _events: [Object],
      _maxListeners: 10,
      options: [Object],
      path: '/dev/cu.usbmodem1411',
      fd: 11,
      readStream: [Object]
    }
  },
  id: '946C9829-5DB0-4EA2-8283-6249CC8E25F6',
```

```
  pin: 10,
  mode: 4,
  range: [0, 180],
  type: 'standard',
  specs: {
    speed: 0.17
  },
  history: [{ timestamp: 1374513576399, degrees: 90 }],
  interval: null,
  isMoving: true,
  _events: {
    move: [Function]
  }
}
```

In this object, you can see not only a representation of the Arduino's hardware in terms of pins and ports but you also see Firmata described and the capabilities of your attached servo. In addition to the current state of the board, there is also a history array that contains a list of changes over time. This, of course, is invaluable when you try to debug a complex interaction between multiple inputs and outputs over time.

I cannot oversell how fantastic the ability to fiddle on the fly with the Johnny Five REPL environment is. Just as Raquel Vélez pointed out earlier, part of her excitement with NodeBots is that you can prototype quickly. Using the REPL environment, you can test a hardware hunch interactively in the console, sketching in broad strokes before you refine things into a precisely composed program.

Fauxbots

Although you did get a servo to spin under your control, I would be hard pressed to call this a robot. Practically speaking you could spend an entire book explaining and building NodeBots. Therefore I limited the scope of this chapter to explaining just enough to give you the necessary context to explore them on your own. Here are a couple of key concepts about programming robots using this approach:

- There is the potential for fire or other real-world mishaps when programming hardware, but it doesn't mean it will happen.

- Interesting things happen when you interweave the computer into an existing analog physical process in an unexpected way.

- Interesting things happen when you map qualities of the virtual world into physical space.

- Network-aware objects can be considered part of the Internet of Things.

- The Reactive Programming paradigm handles state change by observing data flows between objects in the aggregate.

- Reactive programming is particularly appropriate for converting an asynchronous world into a series of chainable evented processes.

- Much of traditional hardware development uses the edit-compile-run-debug (ECRD) process, which allows hardware to run in a stand-alone context, but can be slow to develop and debug.

- NodeBots use a read-eval-print-loop (REPL) environment, which allows for faster development and real-time coding. However, this approach requires the hardware to be persistently tethered.

The interest in JavaScript robots is palpable among a subset of the JS community. So much so that NodeBot developers have spawned their own web sites, meet-ups, and conferences; and even created an international NodeBots day in which nerds huddle together and solder among themselves. If you are fascinated, like me, with the potentials this has to offer, I encourage you to seek others with similar interests and get building!

Additional Resources

The Arduino diagrams in this chapter were produced using Fritzing, which is an open-source hardware initiative to support designers, artists, researchers, and hobbyists to work creatively with interactive electronics. It has a wonderful set of tools and tutorials to help hardware novices plan and ultimately produce their own designs. Find out more here: *http://fritzing.org/*.

CHAPTER 7

■ ■ ■

Style

Style is the substance of the subject called unceasingly to the surface.

—Victor Hugo

My goal is to make you a better JavaScript programmer. To that end, I am going to teach you about style in this chapter. I am not talking about fashion because I think most programmers would flunk that test—unless comic-con couture is a thing. I will explain the importance of style, how it forms, how it spreads, and what signs to look for when you need to kill it. Specifically, I'll look at style as it applies to writing JavaScript. Once there is a context for evaluating good technique, I will introduce you to elements of programmatic style that have served me well over the years as a professional software developer.

What Is Style?

Style is often used as a measurement of quality. When someone is described as having style or being stylish, it is almost universally meant as a complement. If anyone's style ever comes into question, it is usually in comparison with another's style. "My style's the best, and so I challenge you," screams the 1970s-era martial arts star.

Stylishness is a fresh approach, a unique perspective, or insight into a subject. The application of a style can become so prominent that it expands the activity itself, for example, by saying that a house is built in a Frank Lloyd Wright style. What starts as a personal style in painting can become an art movement almost overnight. Style spreads like a rumor. It is the original meme, a mind virus that changes the way you see the subject matter forever. Style is the conduit in which new ideas travel.

How does style affect programmers? I have good news for those who are algorithmically inclined. No matter how personal a style may seem, for it to exist it all, it must be repeatable. Style must be codified into a series of steps or combinations of rules that can be followed, and then recognized by others. If style is a measurement of quality and at the same time repeatable, it can be taught. Just ask Strunk and White.

William Strunk Jr. wrote *The Elements of Style* while he was a professor at Cornell. He began with 7 rules for the usage of language, and 11 principles of composition. His student, E.B. White, revised the book nearly 40 years later and added an additional 4 rules. The goal of the book was to give aspiring writers and grammarians a framework from which to evaluate their own work.

According to White, Strunk decided to write the "little book" out of sympathy for those afflicted with reading the writer's ill-composed dreck: "Will felt that the reader was in serious trouble most of the time, floundering in a swamp and that it was the duty of anyone attempting to write English to drain the swap quickly and get the reader up on dry ground, or at least throw a rope."

Over the years, the book has remained popular for those learning to write efficiently, and it is affectionately now referred to as simply "Strunk and White." That is not to say the book has been universally loved or followed. Dorothy Parker is quoted in *The New York Times*[1] as saying, "If you have any young friends who aspire to become writers, the second-greatest favor you can do them is to present them with copies of 'The Elements of Style.' The first-greatest, of course, is to shoot them now, while they're happy."

Many found the rules too restrictive and opinionated. White said Strunk believed "it was worse to be irresolute than to be wrong." Strunk's assertion is that it is not only passion to be stylish, but also the ability to draw boundaries, to allow one idea to flourish while forcing another to die. Style is like a sine wave attracting some while repelling others.

What Is Programmatic Style?

As mentioned previously, Stunk and White wrote their book not only to empower and train writers but also to save readers from slogging through what was, in their minds, a textual tar pit. So, too, good programmatic style services two audiences: the developer and the processor. Code should be well-written, both syntactically and technically. The following sections describe qualities I consider essential in the application of programmatic style.

Consistency

By repeatedly applying rules to the codebase, you can ensure consistency. Consistency mitigates noise in the source code and brings the intent of the coder into clearer focus. If a developer is trying to piece together how to read your code, you have prevented him from understanding what it does. Consistency is concerned with how the code looks, for example, naming conventions, use of whitespace, and method signatures. It is also concerned with how the code is written (e.g., ensuring that all functions return predictable results in all contexts).

Expressiveness

Code is by nature a symbolic language, in which variability and abstractness is implicit. Therefore, the developer must find a way to make the code meaningful and relevant to the reader. Relevancy can be achieved through naming variables and functions precisely. When reviewing a class, method, or variable, the reader should understand the roles and responsibilities of the code by reading the code. If a function can be understood only by reading the comments left by the writer, it should be a clue that the code is not expressive.

Succinctness

Strive to do just enough. Good programming, like good writing, is about clarity of purpose, not merely compactness. It should be about reducing the complexity of a function, not its usefulness.

Restraint

Style should never overpower the subject. At that point, style becomes the subject and it is then a facile artifice, a dish ruined by too much flourish. I am reminded of a minimalist chess set I saw in college. Every piece was either a white or black cube, and all were the same size. The pieces differed only in their weight; the more important pieces

---

[1] http://www.nytimes.com/2009/04/22/books/22elem.html?_r=0

weighed more. This chess set was simultaneously aesthetically beautiful and unplayable. In programming, cleverness kills. Programmers must restrain themselves from using the equivalent of inside jokes in the language that make code hipsters happy, but leave the source hard to understand and maintain.

JavaScript Style Guide

Style guides are just that, guides. They are meant to point you in the right direction, but they are, at best, a mutable truth. Coding theory changes constantly and it is important not to lock yourself into a dogmatic approach to the application of these rules. As my professor Clyde Fowler told me in my studio drawing class, "You must think with your hands." What he meant by that was you must think through doing, while maintaining the ability to get critical distance from your work.

This style guide was created by compiling, reviewing, and considering choices I have made in my own work over the years, and by evaluating coding practices of individuals and development teams I admire in the JavaScript community. This style guide should be seen as an amalgamation of inputs and influences rather than the creative output of a single individual. You can find a list of additional resources at the end of this chapter, which contains other guides and documents I considered when composing this one. This guide is broken down into two sections: "Rules for Visual Clarity" and "Rules for Computational Effectiveness."

Rules for Visual Clarity

- *Write clearly and expressively*: While thinking about good guidelines for visual clarity in your code, it's important to keep this rule in mind. When naming variables and functions, or organizing code, remember that you are writing for humans, not compilers.

- *Follow existing conventions*: If you work on a team or are hired to write code, you are not writing for yourself. Therefore, you should conform your style to co-exist in the existing ecosystem, but without sacrificing quality.

- *Write in only one language*: Where possible, don't use JavaScript as a transport for other languages. This means resisting the urge to write inline HTML or CSS. Clear code enforces a separation of concerns.

- *Enforce a uniform column width*: Strive for consistent line lengths in source code. Long lines tire the eyes, which reduces comprehension. Long lines also cause needless horizontal scrolling. An industry standard is 80 characters per line.

Document Formatting

Understanding a program's source often requires the reader to mentally compile the code. This process needs sustained focus from readers, and any distraction can eject readers from their mental flow. Improperly or inconsistently formatted sources act as visual noise to the source's signal. This section offers conventions and guides that allows the formatting to support the source instead of weighing it down.

Naming Conventions

JavaScript is a terse language of brackets numbers and letters. One of the only ways to make your code expressive to humans is through naming your variables, functions, and properties meaningfully. When choosing a name, it should describe the role and responsibilities of that object. Using vague or obtuse names such as `doStuff` or `item1` is like telling the reader to figure it out, which they often won't.

Choose variables and functions with meaningful, expressive, and descriptive names. Write for the reader, not the compiler.

```
// Bad
var a = 1,
    aa = function(aaa) {
        return '' + aaa;
    };

// Good
var count = 1,
    toString = function(num) {
        return '' + num;
    };
```

Constants

Constants should be declared using the const keyword where supported by the runtime engine. When the const keyword is unavailable, the constant should belong to a namespace or object. Doing so helps organize elements and prevent naming collisions. In both cases, a constant should be written in uppercase with spaces replaced with underscores.

```
// Bad
MEANING_OF_LIFE = 43;

// Good
const MEANING_OF_LIFE = 43;

// Good
com.humansized.MEANING_OF_LIFE = 42;

// Good
Math.PI
```

Additional Naming Conventions

Naming conventions should imbue the variables or objects with extra meaning. Doing so as a means to allude to their functionality and semantic purpose. For example, there are no formal classes in JavaScript, yet classes are a common pattern for organizing code. Therefore, functions that are meant to be classes should differentiate themselves through the use of naming conventions from *normal* functions, even though the runtime process will treat them identically. This naming convention is sometimes called Hungarian notation.

Variables should be CamelCase:

```
myVariableName
```

Classes should be PascalCase:

```
MyAwesomeClass
```

Functions should be CamelCase:

```
isLie(cake)
```

Namespaces should be CamelCase and use periods as delimiters:

```
com.site.namespace
```

Hungarian notation is not required, but can be used to convey that objects are constructed through or dependent on a library or framework.

```
// jQuery infused variable
var $listItem = $("li:first");

// Angular.js uses the dollar sign to refer to angular-dependent variables
$scope, $watch, $filter
```

Constants and Variables

Variables and constants definitions always go at the top of the scope because when the code is processed by the runtime engine, variables are hoisted to the top. Therefore, declaring variables at the top better matches what will happen when the source is parsed:

```
// Bad
function iterate() {
    var limit = 10;
    for (var x = 0; x < limit; x++) {
        console.log(x);
    }
}

// Good
function iterate() {
    var limit = 10,
        x = 0;

    for (x = 0; x < limit; x++) {
        console.log(x);
    }
}
```

Avoid polluting the global namespace by always declaring variables using var, let, or const:

```
// Bad
foo = 'bar';

// Good
var foo = 'bar';
let foo = 'bar';
const foo = 'bar';
```

Declare multiple variables using a single var declaration, but separate each variable with a newline. This reduces unneeded characters while keeping the source readable:

```
// Bad
var foo = "foo";
var note = makeNote('Huge Success');

// Good
var foo = "foo",
    note = makeNote('Huge Success');
```

Declare unassigned variables last. This allows the reader to know they are needed but have delayed initialization:

```
var  foo = "foo",
     baz;
```

Do not assign variables inside a conditional statement because that often masks errors:

```
// Bad because it is easily misread as an equality test.
if (foo = bar) {...}
```

Do not clobber function arguments with variables names because that makes the code harder to debug:

```
// Bad
function addByOne(num) {
    var num = num + 1;
    return num;
}

// Good
function addByOne(num) {
    var newNum = num + 1;
    return newNum;
}
```

Blank Lines

A blank line should always precede the start of a comment because it allows the comment to be visually grouped with the code it refers to:

```
var foo = "foo";
// Too compressed
function bar(){
// Hard to know here things are.
return true;
}

// Cleanly delineated
function baz() {

// Now return true
return true;
}
```

Blank lines should be used to separate logically related code because the reader can process associated code in visual chunks:

```
// Bad
var = wheels;

wheels.clean()

car.apply(wheels);

truck.drive();

// Good
var = wheels;
wheels.clean()
car.apply(wheels);

truck.drive();
```

Commas

Remove trailing commas in object declarations because they break some runtime environments:

```
// Bad
var foo = {
    bar: 'baz',
    foo: 'bar',
};

// Good
var foo = {
    bar: 'baz',
    foo: 'bar'
};
```

Do not use comma first formatting. Some people feel that comma first formatting provides superior readability because it places an emphasis on the comma and therefore affords visual separation of elements in a collection:

```
var fruits = [ 'grapes'
             , 'apples'
             , 'oranges'
             , 'crackers'
             , 'cheese'
             , 'espresso'
             ];
```

However, most of the JavaScript development world uses comma last formatting, and, as Brendan Eich pointed out,[2] the two styles do not mix well and it's easy to miss an errant comma when the two styles are combined:

```
var fruits = [ 'grapes',
             , 'apples'
             , 'oranges'
             , 'crackers'
             , 'cheese'
             , 'espresso'
             ];
```

Semicolons

JavaScript determines semicolons to be optional in certain contexts, but requires them in others. To make the waters even more muddied, the ECMAScript spec has rules for how semicolons can be automatically inserted:

> *Certain ECMAScript statements (empty statement, variable statement, expression statement, do-while statement, continue statement, break statement, return statement, and throw statement) must be terminated with semicolons. Such semicolons may always appear explicitly in the source text. For convenience, however, such semicolons may be omitted from the source text in certain situations. These situations are described by saying that semicolons are automatically inserted into the source code token stream in those situations.*

You should not add meaningless semicolons, but they should be used to clearly delineate the end of a logical statement, even if they are a candidate for automatic insertion.

Whitespace

Whitespace should be removed from the end of a line and from a blank line. Developers should not mix spaces and tabs, and whitespace should appear after each comma in a function declaration. All these rules help to ensure a consistent visual presentation of the source across the wide spectrum of development environments available:

```
// Bad
findUser(foo,bar,baz)
makeSoup( );
var foo = { };
var arr = [ ];

// Good
findUser(foo, bar, baz)
```

Whitespace should not appear inside empty functions or object literals because it reduces readability:

```
makeSoup();
var foo = {};
var arr = [];
```

---

[2]https://mail.mozilla.org/pipermail/es-discuss/2011-September/016802.html

Brackets and Braces

Use brackets and braces only where the compiler calls for them or where the use helps delineate the inner content from the outer source. Brackets should appear on the line that requires them:

```
// Bad
if (hidden)
{
...
}

// Good
if (hidden) {

}
```

Readability should trump succinctness. Let the automatic code compressors worry about making your code smaller:

```
// Bad
if (condition) goTo(10);

// Good
if (condition) {
    goTo(10);
}
```

Whitespace Use with Brackets and Braces

Add whitespace in front and between brackets to aid readability:

```
// Less Readable
if(foo,bar,baz){}

// More readable
if (foo, bar, baz) {
}
```

There are a couple of exceptions to the previous rule:

```
// No whitespace needed when there is a single argument
if (foo) ...

// No whitespace when a parenthesis is used to form a closure
;(function () {...})

// No whitespace when brackets are used as a function argument
function sortThis([2, 3, 4, 1])
```

Strings

Strings should be constructed using single quotes for consistency, but also to help differentiate between object literals and JSON, which requires double quotes.

```
// Bad
var foo = "Bar";

// Good
var foo = 'Bar';
```

Strings longer than the predetermined character line limit should be reconsidered. And, if required, they should instead be concatenated.

Functions

Method signatures must be consistent. If a function returns a variable in one context, it should return a variable in all contexts:

```
// Bad
var findFoo(isFoo){
    if ( isFoo === 'Bar' ) {
        return true;
    }
}

// Good
var findFoo(isFoo) {
    if ( isFoo === 'Bar' ) {
        return true;
    }
    return false;
}
```

Although not a requirement, returning early from a function can make the intent more clear:

```
// Good
var findFoo = function(isFoo) {
    if ( isFoo === 'Bar' ) {
        return true;
    }
    return false;
}
```

Comments

Comments should never trail a statement:

```
var findFoo = function(isFoo); // Do not do this
```

Comments should be used sparingly; overuse of comments should suggest to the writer that their code is unexpressive. Comments should always be written as a complete thought. Multiline comments should always use the multiline syntax because it enables you to treat comments written using the single line syntax as individual items, not a continuation from the previous line.

```
// Some really
// bad multiline comment

/**
* A well-formed multiline comment
* so there...
*/
```

Rules for Computational Effectiveness

Computational effectiveness is important to consider as well as visual clarity. Keep the following examples in mind:

- *Write for concatenation*: Modern applications often munge the JavaScript source into a streamlined file for production. You should defensively program your scripts to protect from switches in operation context and scope corruption.

- *Keep your code browser agnostic*: Keep your business logic free of browser-specific code by abstracting them into interfaces. This will keep your code on a clean upgrade path as browsers fall in and out of fashion.

- *Resist the use of* eval(): It can often be an injection point for malicious code execution.

- *Resist the use of* with(): It can make the implications of the code hard to understand.[3]

- *Keep prototype pristine*: Never modify the prototype of a built-in such as Array.prototype because it can silently break other's code, which expects standard behavior.

Equality Comparisons and Conditional Evaluation

Use === instead of == and use !== instead of != because the dynamic nature of JavaScript means that it is sometimes overly loose when testing equality.

When just testing for "truthiness," you can coerce the values:

```
if (foo) {...}
if (!foo) {...}
```

When testing for emptiness:

```
if (!arr.length) { ... }
```

---

[3]http://yuiblog.com/blog/2006/04/11/with-statement-considered-harmful/

You must be explicit when testing for truth:

```
// Bad because all of these will be coerced into true
var zero = 0,
empty = "",
knull = null,
notANumber = NaN,
notDefined;

if (!zero || !empty || !knull || !notANumber || !notDefined ) ...

// Bad
var truth = "foo",
alsoTrue = 1

if (truth && alsoTrue) ...

// Good
if (foo === true) ...
```

Constants and Variables

When deleting a variable, set it to null instead of calling #delete or setting it to undefined:

```
// Bad because undefined means the variable is useful but as yet has no value
this.unwanted = undefined;

/**
 * Bad because calling delete is much slower than reassigning a value.
 * Use delete if you want to remove the attribute from an objects list of keys.
 */
delete this.unwanted;

// Good
this.unwanted = null;
```

Function Expressions

Function expressions are function objects that are linked to variables. As such, they can be written more ways than a function declaration:

```
// Anonymous Function
var anon = function () {
    return true;
}

// Named Function
var named = function named() {
    return true;
};
```

```
// Immediately-invoked function, hides its contents from the executing scope.
(function main() {
    return true;
})();
```

Function expressions are defined at parse-time. Therefore, do not have their names hoisted to the top of the scope. However, function expressions are preferred over function declarations because of certain bugs in older browsers.

```
// Bad - Runtime Error
iGoBoom();

var iGoBoom = function () {
    alert('boom');
}

// Good
iGoBoom();
function iGoBoom() {
    alert('boom');
}
```

Do not use function declarations within block statements; they are not part of ECMAScript. Use a function expression instead:

```
// Bad
if (ball.is(round)) {
    function bounce(){

        // Statements Continue
    }
    return bounce()
}

// Good
if (ball.is(round)) {
  var bounce = function () {

        // Statements Continue
    }
}
```

Break chained methods where it enhances clarity:

```
// Bad
jQuery.map([1,3,2,5,0], function(a) { return a + a; }).sort(function(a, b) { return a - b;});

// Good
jQuery.map([1,3,2,5,0], function(a) { return a + a; })
.sort(function(a, b) { return a - b;});
```

Do not hide the native arguments object by using the same name in a function:

```
// Bad
var foo = function(arguments) {
    alert(arguments.join(' '));
}

// Good
var foo = function(args) {
    alert(args.join(' '));
}
```

Objects

Object literal notation should be favored over a new `Object()` when creating an empty object because the object literals scope does not need to be first resolved and therefore performs better. Additionally, the object literal syntax is less verbose:

```
// Ok
var person = new Object();
person.firstName = "John";
person.lastName = "Doe";

// Better
var person = {
  firstName: "John",
  lastName: "Doe"
}
```

Don't overwrite reserved words as keys because doing so obscures access to those attributes, which might have unintended consequences:

```
// Bad
var person = { class : "Person" };

// Good
var person = { klass : "Person" };
```

Arrays

For clarity and succinctness, use literal syntax to create a new `Array()`.

```
// Verbose
var arr = new Array();

// Succinct
var arr = [];
```

Separation of Concerns

Write only code that is the responsibility of the program. Keep your code free of view layer and template code:

```
var view = {
    title: "Joe",
    calc: function () {
        return 2 + 4;
    }
}, output;

// Bad
output = '<div><h5>' + title + '</h5><p>' + calc() + '</div>';

// Good
var output = Mustache.compilePartial('my-template', view);
```

Keep JavaScript out of the HTML:

```
// Bad
<button onclick="doSomething()" id="something-btn">Click Here</button>

// Good
var element = document.getElementById("something-btn");
element.addEventListener("click", doSomething, false);
```

■ **Note**   There are many templating libraries in JavaScript, such as mustache.js,[4] which can help extract HTML from your JavaScript.

Operating Context and Scope

Where possible, wrap your code inside an immediately invoked function expression (IIFE). It insulates your code from pollution by others and makes it easier to abstract into reusable modules.

```
// Good
;(function( window, document, undefined) {

  // My Awesome Library
  ...

})(this, document);
```

Design for duration-agnostic execution of code, which prevents your code from building up a backlog of requests that may no longer be relevant.

---

[4]https://github.com/ja/nl/mustache.js/

```
// Bad because this might take longer than 100 milliseconds to complete.
setInterval(function () {
  findFoo();
}, 100);

// Good this will only be called again once findFoo has completed.
;(function main() {
    findFoo();
    setTimeout(main, 100);
})();
```

To prevent breaking, community code declaring an operating context (e.g., use strict) should be wrapped inside an IIFE for modules or inside a function when needed:

```
// Bad
var bar = findLooseyGoosey();

"use strict";

var foo = findStrictly();

// Good
var bar = findLooseyGoosey();

;(function () {
  "use strict";
  var foo = findStrictly();
})();

var findStrictly = function() {
  "use strict";
}
```

Coercion

Use explicit conversion over implicit coercion because it makes the code base more declarative:

```
var num = '1';

// Bad implicit coercion
num = +num;

// Good expressive conversion
num = Number(num);
```

Enforcing Style

As I discussed earlier, for style to exist it must be codified into a series or rules that can be repeated. One of the biggest challenges when writing code in a team environment is maintaining uniform style between developers. Fortunately, there are several ways for individuals and teams to ensure style compliance.

Beautifiers

Beautifiers are programs that process code by using a series of formatting conventions to apply style uniformly to the source code. Often beautifiers are hooked into a workflow process where they are run automatically when a watched file is saved. Beautifiers are also used to unpack or remove obfuscation from a source file (coincidentally, the code packing is sometimes called uglification). Two popular beautifiers are JS Beautify and CodePainter, which draws its inspiration from Microsoft Word's format painter. Many beautifiers allow you to manually specify formatting rules using configuration objects or command-line arguments.

Let's take a quick look at the JS Beautify interface and options. First, you must install JS Beautify by downloading it from NPM. In this example, a -g flag is supplied, which installs JS Beautify globally:

```
npm -g install js-beautify
```

Once installed, you can beautify straight from the command line like so:

```
js-beautify jquery.min.js
```

What follows is a list of the command-line and beautifier options that JS Beautify supports.

CLI options:

```
-f, --file                 Input file(s) (Pass '-' for stdin). Can also be passed directly.
-r, --replace              Write output in-place, replacing input
-o, --outfile              Write output to file (default stdout)
--config                   Path to config file
--type                     [js|css|html] ["js"]
-q, --quiet                Suppress logging to stdout
-v, --version              Show the version
-h, --help                 Show this help
```

Beautifier options:

```
-s, --indent-size          Indentation size [4]
-c, --indent-char          Indentation character [" "]
-l, --indent-level         Initial indentation level [0]
-t, --indent-with-tabs     Indent with tabs, overrides -s and -c
-p, --preserve-newlines    Preserve existing line-breaks (--no-preserve-newlines disables)
-m, --max-preserve-newlines Maximum number of line-breaks to be preserved in one chunk [10]
-j, --jslint-happy         Enable jslint-stricter mode
-b, --brace-style          [collapse|expand|end-expand] ["collapse"]
-B, --break-chained-methods Break chained method calls across subsequent lines
-k, --keep-array-indentation Preserve array indentation
-x, --unescape-strings     Decode printable characters encoded in xNN notation
-w, --wrap-line-length     Wrap lines at next opportunity after N characters [0]
--good-stuff               Warm the cockles of Crockford's heart
```

Enforcing through the IDE

Many popular integrated development environments (IDEs) come with a multitude of ways to tune and configure their functionality to support an individual's formatting needs. Through macros and formatting engines, these editors enable the developer to automatically handle decisions around the use of whitespaces, line endings, or tab characters, among others. Theoretically, these tools should give the developer a way to handle some of the low-hanging formatting fruit in the style guide. However, as mentioned earlier, there are many factors, such as team preference, language requirements, and personal choice that go into defining style. These variabilities make it unlikely that any developers would maintain their sanity having to manually configure their IDEs to support each new project's styling requirements.

In an attempt to solve the need for a flexible project-level configuration system, developers have begun to embrace tools that allow them to specify style rules as part of the project's configuration setup. One of the most popular projects is the Editor Config project. The maintainers of the project describe the goals this way:

> *EditorConfig helps developers define and maintain consistent coding styles between different editors and IDEs. The EditorConfig project consists of a file format for defining coding styles and a collection of text editor plugins that enable editors to read the file format and adhere to defined styles. EditorConfig files are easily readable and they work nicely with version control systems.*

Once installed into a supported IDE, the EditorConfig plug-in scans for a hidden configuration file named .editorconfig and then adjusts formatting settings accordingly.

In the following section, I describe some of the attributes that EditorConfig can control and how a developer can enforce a baseline of coding style. Consider the following example, in which .editorconfig config is placed in the root of a JavaScript application:

```
# EditorConfig helps developers define and maintain consistent
# coding styles between different editors and IDEs
# editorconfig.org

# Top most config file
root = true

# Base style guide to apply to all files unless overridden by lower rules.
[*]

# Define end of line options
# Available options are  "lf", "cr", or "crlf"
end_of_line = lf

# Define character set options
# "latin1", "utf-8", "utf-8-bom", "utf-16be" or "utf-16le"
# Note: Use of "utf-8-bom" is discouraged.
charset = utf-8

trim_trailing_whitespace = true
insert_final_newline = true

# Commonly user-defined settings
indent_style = space
indent_size = 2

# Indentation override for all JS under lib directory
[lib/**.js]
indent_size = 4

# Markdown file configurations
[*.md]
trim_trailing_whitespace = false
```

As you can see from the preceding configuration file, the EditorConfig file gives the developer an easy-to-use tool to enforce certain amount of high-level formatting tasks. Unfortunately, this tool was never intended to enforce some of the semantic best practices defined earlier. To uniformly enforce a JavaScript style, a tool designed specifically for this job is needed. Enter JSHint.

Enforcing Style Through JSHint

JSHint, which was originally written by Anton Kovalyov, is another great option for enforcing code style. JSHint started as a fork of Douglas Crockford's JSLint project. The two programs work essentially the same way: by iterating over a source file line by line and making a list of notes of potential problems or deviations from acceptable style.

Many felt that JSLint was too opinionated and that although the goal of JSLint was to detect potential errors and oversights in a JavaScript program, it also forced developers into writing JavaScript in an arbitrary form that was not necessarily an improvement over their existing approach. The source of JSLint hints at this tension:

```
"WARNING: JSLint will hurt your feelings."
```

Kovalyov loosened the thumbscrews of JSLint and attempted to separate the opinions about style from the need for static code analysis. In doing so, JSHint became a kinder and gentler version of the original. The JSHint web site alludes to this when describing its goal:

> *Our goal is to help JavaScript developers write complex programs without worrying about typos and language gotchas. We believe that static code analysis programs—as well as other code quality tools–are important and beneficial to the JavaScript community and, thus, should not alienate their users.*

As mentioned previously, one of the goals of JSHint was to provide a means to configure the linter in such a way that it enforced only the coding conventions a team or individual sought to promote. Generally, JSHint's options are divided into four main categories: Legacy, Enforceable, Relaxable, and Environment options. Each category contains many different options—too many, in fact, to enumerate here. I'll give just a few canonical examples of each category to make the point, but if you are interested, I encourage you to read the documentation in detail.

- *Enforceable options*: As the name suggests, these extra options can be enforced by jsHint. Here are a few examples:

```
camelcase (true | false) // This option allows you to enforce camelCase style for all variable names.
undef (true | false) // Prevents you from defining variables which are initially undefined.
Often times when this happens it is because a variable was declared but never used at all.
```

- *Relaxable options*: Some rules that are best practices for one person are just annoying to another. JSHint knows this, and offers a collection of options that reduces the number of things that trigger a warning by the linter by default. For example:

```
evil (true | false) // It is almost universally agreed that the use of eval is a bad idea because
it exposes a conduit for a third-party to inject malicious code and have the host application
execute it.
debug (true | false) // This option allows you to suppress warnings about any use of the debugger
statement in the code.
```

- *Environment options*: The options in this category define any global variables that are exposed by other libraries such as jQuery or Nodejs.

```
jquery (true | false) // whether or not to expose the global $ or jQuery variables.
```

▓ **Caution**   A word of warning before you proceed. Static code analysis tools such as JSHint validate only the syntactic structure of the code. This is a huge asset for catching small bugs or inconsistencies in style that might otherwise slip through the cracks of day-to-day development. However, these tools cannot tell you whether the code that is written actually does what it was intended to do. For that, developers need to test code under a variety of contexts to assert that it performs as expected.

Summary

In this chapter, you learned that style is a unique approach for a process. For style to exist, it must be codified into a series of repeatable steps. Style, as it relates to JavaScript, is designed to make the code more expressive, easier to read and understand, and written in ways that also minimize potential pitfalls that might introduce bugs.

There are a few rules that programmers should keep in mind of when plying their trade. Be consistent in your formatting and naming conventions. Be expressive by using names for variables and functions that describe their purpose. Be succinct by writing modular code that embraces a separation of concerns, in which functions and variables have a single task. Use restraint and embrace JavaScript's terseness, but not at the expense of readability.

You can find out more about beautifiers here:

- *JS Beautify*: https://github.com/einars/js-beautify

- *Code Painter*: https://github.com/fawek/codepainter

You can find out more on style guides here:

- *"Principles of Writing Consistent, Idiomatic JavaScript"*:
  https://github.com/rwldrn/idiomatic.js/

- *Google JavaScript Style Guide*:
  http://google-styleguide.googlecode.com/svn/trunk/javascriptguide.xml

- *Airbnb JavaScript Style Guide*: https://github.com/airbnb/javascript

- *jQuery Style Guide*: http://contribute.jquery.org/style-guide/js/

CHAPTER 8

■ ■ ■

Workflow

A freak snowstorm provided me with insights on how I could make JavaScript application development faster, more enjoyable, and ostensibly more profitable by improving my workflow. The goal of this chapter is to teach others how to do the same.

Don't Shovel Snow

Don't mistake activity with achievement.

—John Wooden

We had a huge snowstorm in Kansas that people were affectionately calling, "The Blizzard of Oz." Like many people with school-age children, ours was a house divided. Our children looked forward to a day off from school, frolicking outside and returning to cups of warm cocoa while cozying up next to the fire. My wife and I were dreading the virtual avalanche of work this snowstorm would bury us under.

Like all good Kansans, the day of the storm, I dutifully got ready for my battle with Mother Nature. I dressed myself several times over, padding my limbs in layers of warmth. I then waddled into the garage and unhooked my plastic red snow shovel from the peg board where it hung. I imagined myself to be a Viking unlatching his blood-stained battle axe from above the stone fireplace. I raised the garage door and headed out into the pristine white alien landscape of my driveway.

A few minutes into shoveling, the novelty of "honest labor" had already worn off. It was replaced by the numbing realization that I would be stuck with the drudgery of excavating my driveway for most of the morning. Like many other people who are not professional snow shovelers, I was doing this work instead of what pays my bills, namely designing and developing software. I then began to calculate how many snow blowers I could have purchased in the amount of billable hours I had already wasted, knee deep in frozen frustration.

At this point, I had an epiphany about my situation and how it related to software development. What I had was a workflow problem. I was engaged in a task that was temporarily essential but worthless in the long run. I spent much of the morning relocating snow from my driveway into impressive minimountains of white along the edges of my yard. This process took me hours, but soon the sun would erase all evidence of this hard work.

I began to wonder what tasks in my daily development process were like shoveling snow. These tasks seemed essential and unavoidable, but ultimately could be done faster with better tools or a clearer perspective.

What Is Workflow

When developing a project in JavaScript or any language, there are distinct stages each project goes through as it is produced. Managers find it useful to give names to these stages (e.g., "planning," "development," "testing," and "deployment"). Then they organize the day-to-day tasks into one stage or another. As they do this, they are employing a workflow, which put simply is the process for defining and applying rules to govern how and when tasks, data, and collateral are passed from one person to another.

Workflows are often tightly coupled with the larger development methodology that a team follows. For example, an Agile team would likely follow a workflow that emphasizes tight iterations and smaller development phases. Whereas a Waterfall team might enforce a workflow rule that ensures nothing can be built without a complete specification first. The goal of a workflow is to maximize productivity and minimize complexity.

This aspiration is easier said than deployed, though. Often a proper implementation of a workflow is a balancing act, achieved only by defining rules that are precise enough to be completely followed, without restricting innovation or improvements in the process or product that is being developed. The moment a workflow slows the pace of development is the moment that it needs to be reevaluated.

A Sensible JavaScript Development Workflow

Although I previously stated that workflows are often dictated by the team or the development methodology, developers also have personal workflows. This section describes a sensible personal workflow for JavaScript development, which is divided into six phases: Tool Choice, Bootstrapping, Development, Testing, Building, and Support. Figure 8-1 visualizes this workflow.

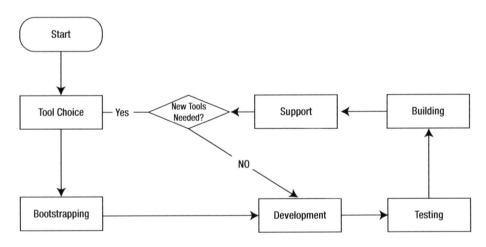

Figure 8-1. *A diagram that visualizes the workflow process*

Tool Choice

Before you can build anything, you must choose the right tools for the job. During this stage, developers lay the groundwork for the application by making crucial choices about what the coding environment will be and by identifying any external resources (e.g., libraries or application frameworks) that are needed. The choice of tools has a lasting impact on the application, even after the person who chose the tool moves on. You are not only choosing the development stack for yourself but also for other developers that come after. This section is dedicated to knowing how to choose the right tool, where to get it, and how to keep it current.

In my youth, I trained to be an artist. My drawing professor, Clyde Fowler, lectured his students as we drew. We arranged our easels as a haphazard circle around the model or still life in the center of the room. Clyde would then slowly orbit around the outer ring of the studio, stopping to offer feedback to a particular student; but usually just pontificating aloud. One day, while I was obsessing over correctly rendering the shadows that formed in the wrinkles of a bag, he said to the class that people who knew little about art would say things like this: "I don't know art, but I know what I like." In reality, he asserted that they were really saying, "I don't know art, but I like what I know." I didn't truly understand this concept until later in life. The mindset that you like what you know is a precarious position to be in when choosing the correct tools. This is especially true if you are under the gun to show progress as quickly as possible. At this stage, the goal should be to pick a tool that is right for the project, not right for the developer.

I know it is tempting for developers to choose the tool that they are most familiar or expert with. This makes intuitive sense because if you are proficient with a tool, then you will be more efficient when using it. While this might be true, it also allows the developer to fall prey to a mindset called the "Law of the Instrument." This means you always pick the tool you favor most, even when it is the wrong choice for the task at hand.

Abraham Maslow summed it up perfectly when he said, "I suppose it is tempting, if the only tool you have is a hammer, to treat everything as if it were a nail." Put another way, you may be an expert with a hammer, but no one wants to live in a house built only with a hammer.

Ordering Tools

Until recently, if you wanted to add external JavaScript to your application, you either copied the code and pasted into your existing script file, or downloaded a copy of the source and included it into your page using a script tag. Before I discuss the actual integration of the tools, let me quickly digress into how to order them in the first place.

After you pick your tool, you need to know where to buy it. As a thought experiment, imagine how you might buy a hammer in real life. Most likely, you would pick a store to purchase it from. To choose the store, you consider several factors about the store itself—possibly price, convenience, and return policy. Now imagine that we took those three aspects and cast them back onto a software tool.

Price

The price is what it will cost you (time, effort, sanity) to integrate this tool into your project codebase. When evaluating the price of a software tool, you want to know how well it's written, supported, and tested. Think of price as a factor of the risk you assume by using the tool. The goal is to get the most value for the smallest price. Consider the price of using jQuery, one of the world's most popular JavaScript libraries. It has a large user base (support) and is written by experts in the field (code quality). Finally, developers have integrated it into just about every conceivable platform that can run JavaScript (tested). Therefore, jQuery most likely has a lower price than a library you wrote by yourself over a weekend, for example.

Convenience

Buying a hammer online is much more convenient for me than driving down to my local big box store. Unless I need it immediately; then the local store wins hands down. Imagine that the software tool I want is jQuery. It may seem convenient to just go to its web site and download my own copy and place it directly into my application's source folder. Doing so is the equivalent of going down to the neighborhood hardware store and buying a hammer. However, what happens if I later want to change the version of jQuery? Do I need to go back to the site and download it all over again? How do I know if there is even a new version in the first place? Do I need to go to its site again and again waiting for the new release? Suddenly, this doesn't seem very convenient. In the software world, this task is typically handled by a package manager, which I will explain in detail later.

Return Policy

What if I hate the hammer after I get it? If the store I bought it from doesn't accept returns, I've effectively added the price of this hammer to the next one I buy because I can't return this one. This is also true in development. If it takes a ton of effort to integrate a tool into your codebase, it will most likely take an equal amount (or more) of effort to extract it later. For a software tool to have a good return policy, it means that it is mostly painless to extract it from your codebase. This is where package managers come in.

JavaScript Package Managers

Package managers are applications that curate collections of software tools and implement methods to automatically install, configure, update, and remove them from various platforms. Package managers solve three main problems in workflow development: dependency management, upgrade path protection, and software tool management. Package management is nothing new. Many programming languages such as Perl or Ruby have enjoyed sophisticated package managers for years.

Until recently, there was very little perceived need for a similar solution for JavaScript. Many felt that a scripting language didn't need the overhead, and that the best way to handle this was just to copy and paste your way into a working application. As the popularity and uses of JavaScript have grown, so too have the needs and choices for package management. Here is just a sample of the popular choices for JavaScript package management: NPM, Bower, Ender, and Component!

To illustrate why package managers are worth the effort when it comes to integration in your JavaScript development workflow, I'll explore implicit problems they solve one at a time. I am going to use Bower as an example.

Bower to the People

I chose Bower as the package manager to demonstrate, not only because of the perfect pun it provided but also because Bower focuses on the front end. For many JavaScript developers, the front end is where they spend most of their time. Bower supports many different package types, and it even boasts a powerful API, which developers can interact with and program against. Let's take a look at how to get Bower up and running. Ironically, Bower is distributed through another package manager (npm). So first you'll want to install npm. After npm is ready, Bower can be installed in a single line:

```
npm install -g bower
```

To install the latest greatest jQuery, you can simply write this:

```
bower install jquery
```

This command causes Bower to clone the appropriate repository from the remote server. Bower maintains its own catalog of components in a local cache on the developer's system. Once cached locally, Bower makes a copy of the software and places it in a bower_components/ directory relative to the path in which the install command was run.

You can just as easily check out a specific version of jQuery:

```
bower install jquery#1.6.0
```

If you inspect the checked-out code, you'll find a jquery directory. Inside that, you'll find only two files: component.json and jquery.js. Using the component.json file is how Bower handles one of the most important tasks of package management: management of dependencies.

Bower Beware

Before proceeding any further, it must be said that Bower does not do any validation or verification of the packages uploaded to its repositories. It is easy to think that these collections of tools are vetted or are official offerings in some way. They are not. You would not eat something just because it fits in your mouth. Neither should you install a random package just because Bower has it available.

Dependency Management

Thus far, I have been using a hammer as metaphor for a software tool. This mental image is admittedly a bit contrived, but it is also misleading. The great thing about a hammer is that after you understand how it works, it behaves the same way every time you use it. You don't have to worry about how your choice of screwdrivers affects the hammer's function. Unfortunately, this is not the case in development. Most software tools depend on a series of other programs. This layering is inherent in the nature of programming and means that these tools form chains of dependencies between one another. These chains often wind their way through the guts of your computer. If another program modifies a link of the shared chain, it can wreak havoc on your system. And as a bonus, it often does this silently.

Package managers try to protect these chains by using config files that they follow like a recipe. Each attribute in the configuration tells the package manager how the software is to be installed and what, if any, programs it depends on. There is a convention among package managers of placing a recipe in the root of the source tree. Bower calls these config files bower.json files. Here is an example of a jQuery's bower.json file:

```
{
  "name": "jquery",
  "version": "1.8.0",
  "main": "./jquery.js",
  "ignore": [],
  "dependencies": {},
  "devDependencies": {},
  "gitHead": "a81132c96b530736a14a48aad3916b676d102368",
  "_id": "jquery@1.8.0",
  "repository": {
    "type": "git",
    "url": "git://github.com/components/jquery.git"
  }
}
```

The structure of this object is pretty straightforward:

- **name**: This is required. And it is, of course, the name of your project.

- **version**: This is a semantic version number.

- **main**: This is a string or array of endpoints in which the software can be found.

- **ignore**: Some applications generate files periodically as a developer aid, such as logging exceptions to a file or creating hidden resource folders. Often, these files are important only to the creator of the tool and can be ignored by the developer who is installing the package. This directive allows you to specify a variety of paths to ignore.

- **dependencies**: This is where Bower starts to do the heavy lifting for you. This directive is a JavaScript hash that defines a list of other tools and their particulars, such as version numbers that the software needs to function in production. Bower either checks a local cache for a compatible version or downloads it from a remote location.

- **devDependencies**: Some tools specify dependencies needed only during development. Many well-written tools also come with unit tests that verify the functionality. The creator can add the test framework to this list of dependencies and then Bower will include it during development, ignoring it when compiling the code for a production.

- **gitHead**: As projects evolve, newer code replaces older code. Git assigns a unique hash to each commit, which allows Bower to reference an exact moment in the lifetime of a software project. In this way, Bower can check out a specific version of jQuery or any other project.

- **_id**: An internal id used to reference the specific component.

- **repository**: A hash that describes the location and type of source control used to store the software tool.

Protecting the Upgrade Path

Many package managers, such as Homebrew, install packages system-wide. This typically means that you cannot have more than one version of a tool installed at any one time.

As mentioned earlier, Bower takes a different approach. Bower attempts to manage just the software needed by the front end and for just one application at a time. By compartmentalizing the dependencies per application, the developer doesn't have to worry about how specifying the newest version of jQuery will affect previous applications that used older versions. Earlier, Bower checked out an old copy of jQuery. If you later decided to check out jQueryUI, you could do so like this:

```
bower install jquery-ui
```

Upon inspecting the bower_components directory, you see that Bower added a new folder: jquery-ui. Wait; there is more! If you reinvestigate the jQuery folder, notice that Bower automatically updated it to a newer build because in the bower.json file of jquery-ui, it lists a specific dependency for jQuery:

```
"dependencies": {
    "jquery": ">= 1.8"
},
```

As you can see, it requires a newer version of jQuery. Any version newer than 1.8 does work. Bower checks out the latest version of jQuery and replaces the older version.

The final benefit that package managers provide over the do-it-yourself approach is that they offer a way to easily handle common tasks around finding, integrating, and removing tools. You already saw how easy it is to install a tool. It is just as easy to uninstall one:

```
bower uninstall jquery
conflict jquery-ui depends on jquery
bower warn To proceed, run uninstall with the --force flag
```

See uninstalled... oh wait, actually the command failed because jQuery-ui depends on jQuery. If you uninstalled jQuery now, one of jQuery-ui's dependencies would no longer be met. If you still wanted to watch the world burn, you could force the uninstall by supplying the --force flag to the end of the command.

In addition to Bower being able to save your bacon, it also has some time-saving features that allow you to find and install software more easily. Bower offers a powerful interface to search and find packages relevant to your interests. For example, if you wanted to see what jQuery or related plug-ins are available, you could first search Bower like this:

```
bower search jque
Search results:
- jquery git://github.com/components/jquery.git
- jquery-ui git://github.com/components/jqueryui
jquery.cookie git://github.com/carhartl/jquery-cookie.git
... results continue...
```

If you wanted to see what packages you already have installed locally, you could have Bower list them for you:

```
bower ls
/Users/heavysixer/Desktop/bower
    ├── jquery#1.9.1
    └─┬ jquery-ui#1.10.2
      └── jquery#1.9.1
```

Notice that Bower not only lists the packages you have installed but also lists the dependencies for each one.

Earlier you attempted to uninstall jQuery, but you were stopped by Bower's dependency manager. If this command had succeeded, Bower would still have a hidden local cache of the package, which you could use to reinstall later. If you wanted to clear out the local cache, you could do so like this:

```
bower cache-clean
```

Bower strives to solve a narrow slice of the overall package management problem: control of components for front-end development. The developers of Bower understood that although this was an open problem ready to be solved, part of their success hinged on Bower's capability to integrate with other processes in the build stack.

Many apps these days go through a tiered deployment process, in which code is sent down a programmatic conveyor belt to be sanitized, minified, obfuscated, packaged, and deployed. For Bower to be adopted by developers, it must find a way to coexist with these other external processes. Bower's solution is to expose a simple high-level API, which allows programmers to script against. And wouldn't you know, it is written in JavaScript! Here is an example of how it works:

```
var bower = require('bower');
bower.commands
  .search('jquery', {})
  .on('packages', function(packages) {
    /* `packages` is a list of packages returned by searching for 'jquery' */
  });
```

In this snippet, you see Bower being required by some external script. Once defined, the Bower instance is issued a command whereby it is told to search for any available packages with "jquery" in the name. Bower's API is designed to optionally emit events in response to commands that are issued. The calling script can register a listener for these emitted events.

In the toy script, you are listening for the "packages" event that, when called, allows you to loop over the list of jQuery packages returned by Bower. Some other common events that Bower emits are data, end, result, and error.

In this section, you learned how to choose tools, where to get them, and how to offload much of the drudgery of managing these tools to package managers such as Bower.

In the next section, you'll explore how to use tools to generate code, which gives you a leg up on development. Onward to bootstrapping!

Bootstrapping

Before Douglas Engelbart popularized the concept of "bootstrapping" with his Bootstrap Alliance, the term described the wildly unreasonable attempt to accomplish a task alone that would normally require multiple people. Visualize the absurdity of actually pulling yourself up by your own bootstraps. Over time, the term came to reflect the indomitable inner spirit of the entrepreneur who starts up quickly while making use of limited resources. A bootstrapped endeavor is like building a ladder to heaven that is primarily held together with duct tape.

Bootstrapping, as it relates to development, involves programmers trying to jumpstart the codebase with code generators, plug-ins, frameworks, and existing code. Custom code is not written at this stage. Instead, developers leverage anything they can get off the shelf to solve the generic features of their project.

Bootstrapping is not only about solving the generic problems by snapping a kit of parts together but also about using code to write code. Frameworks such as Ruby on Rails have the concept of code generation baked into their DNA. They have generators that accept custom parameters that allow the developer to quickly create tailored blocks of code. JavaScript, because of its cut-and-paste culture, was slow to catch on to this concept. Instead, bootstrapping in JavaScript typically involved dumping copious libraries into a folder and wiring them into the HTML page. Within the last two years, the JavaScript community has gotten charged up over generators.

Nowhere is this embrace of generators more evident than in Yeoman, which is an opinionated workflow tool written by developers from Google. Like Rails, Yeoman emphasizes the concept of code writing code. Historically, a yeoman was a kind of clerical attendant of a royal household. As the name implies, the Yeoman project attempts to lift some of the mundane drudgery of managing the development workflow off the developer.

Just as I used Bower to explain the salient issues around tool choice, I will similarly use Yeoman to explain bootstrapping and task automation as it relates to JavaScript development workflow. This demonstration takes you through the process of installing and configuring Yeoman, and scaffolding a basic AngularJS application.

Using Yeoman

Before you can put Yeoman to work, you have to install it. With npm already in place, you simply type this command into the console:

```
npm install -g yo grunt-cli bower
```

■ **Note**   If you used Yeoman before 1.0 it is possible you will need to clear your npm cache before this command will work. Previously, you could not use the -g flag to specify a global installation. You can force npm to clear the cache and update Yeoman like this: npm cache clean && npm update -g yo

---

This code installs Yeoman, the grunt command-line interface (CLI) and the Bower package manager (which you should already have installed if you are following along). As you can tell by the install command alone, Yeoman aids the developer by wiring together a series of related technologies. Yeoman uses these programs towards the service of four main goals, discussed in the following sections.

Scaffolding

Yeoman gives the developer the opportunity to use a variety of predefined templates as the basis from which to build. Many of these templates are built off of well-known projects, such as HTML5 Boilerplate, Twitter Bootstrap, or AngularJS.

Out-of-the-box Yeoman officially supports several generators: webapp, angular, backbone, bbb, ember, chromeapp, chrome-extension, bootstrap, mocha, and karma. I leave it as an exercise to the reader to explore each one.

Yeoman offers a mechanism for downloading and installing new generators directly from npm. Before you can scaffold the AngularJS application, you must ensure that you have the AngularJS generator installed:

```
npm install generator-angular
```

Once installed, you can scaffold the AngularJS app using this:

```
yo angular
```

This code invokes the AngularJS generators. Once running, the program prompts the developer through a series of yes or no questions as it tries to identify more about your project's basic needs. I answered no (N) for all these questions to keep things simple for now. Once completed, Yeoman generates output similar to this:

```
create app/styles/bootstrap.css
   create app/index.html
   create component.json
   create package.json
   create Gruntfile.js
   invoke    angular:common:/Users/heavysixer/Desktop/yeomanapp/node_modules/generator-angular/app/
index.js
   create    .bowerrc
   create    .editorconfig
   create    .gitattributes
   create    .jshintrc
   create    app/.buildignore
   create    app/.htaccess
   create    app/404.html
   create    app/favicon.ico
   create    app/robots.txt
   create    app/styles/main.css
   create    app/views/main.html
   create    test/runner.html
   create    .gitignore
   invoke    angular:main:/Users/heavysixer/Desktop/yeomanapp/node_modules/generator-angular/app/
index.js
   create    app/scripts/app.js
   invoke    angular:controller:/Users/heavysixer/Desktop/yeomanapp/node_modules/generator-angular/
app/index.js
   create    app/scripts/controllers/main.js
   create    test/spec/controllers/main.js
```

This is a great start! Yeoman has created a sensible application structure and wired in all the AngularJS dependencies. As the man on the TV says, though, "But wait; there's more!"

Although this generator created an entire AngularJS app, there are also smaller generators that can be used to create individual facets of the AngularJS framework. Here are some examples:

```
yo angular:controller myController
yo angular:directive myDirective
yo angular:filter myFilter
```

Package Management

If you need to add a new dependency to the project, it is a snap using Yeoman because it integrates with Bower. Let's add the Angular-UI project to the app. This code adds a collection of helpful AngularJS filters and directives:

```
bower install angular-ui
```

Again, if everything worked, you should see something like this output to the terminal window:

```
bower cloning git://github.com/angular-ui/angular-ui.git
bower caching git://github.com/angular-ui/angular-ui.git
bower fetching angular-ui
bower checking out angular-ui#v0.4.0
bower copying /Users/heavysixer/.bower/cache/angular-ui/bd4cf7fc7bfe2a2118a7705a22201834
bower installing angular-ui#0.4.0
```

After Bower caches the angular-ui source for its own purposes, it then places a copy in a bower_components folder inside the app directory that Yeoman created. Bower makes this shallow copy as part of the dependency management process.

Built-in Server

The purpose of the Yeoman AngularJS generator is to quickly scaffold out a basic AngularJS app, which developers can begin to modify to suit their own needs. Like many modern JavaScript frameworks, AngularJS is meant to be data-driven. That typically means connecting to a server to pull back resources to display to the user. Unfortunately, security restrictions in your browser prevent you from dragging your local file into a browser and then making a remote AJAX request. Luckily, Yeoman has a great server built right in.

From the root folder of the project, you can quickly start up your AngularJS app by typing the following command into the console:

```
grunt server
```

■ **Note** If you do not have Ruby or the Compass gem installed, you might get a warning message trying to run the server. You can either install Ruby and the Compass gem or force the server to start without them using the -- force environment flag: `grunt server --force`.

What you should see is that Grunt starts a server running as a process on your computer and then opens your default browser with your application already loaded. The capability to quickly spin up a server without first having to deploy your site to the web is a huge timesaver, but this isn't even the coolest part. The Yeoman server is actually a LiveReload server. This means that along with serving your site's local files, the server also watches them for changes. When it spots that you changed a file, it automatically reloads the browser.

Although this may seem like a trivial addition, just imagine how many little increments of time you waste, leaving your IDE moving to your browser and hitting Reload. Killing this kind of repetitive task really adds up in the long run. Now that our newly minted app is bootstrapped and humming along in our browser, it is time to move on to the next phase of the workflow: development.

Development

During the Development phase, programmers write code, test product assertions, and chase down bugs. Many of these tasks involve a large amount of repetitive manual labor. In this way, the developers become the bottleneck because they can do only one task at a time. Just as you saw in the Bootstrapping phase, task automation plays a big role in improving the velocity and quality of production during Development.

It improves velocity in two ways: It can often do these tasks faster than the developer can and many of these tasks can be run in parallel, which improves what was once a series of sequential steps.

The Bootstrapping section focused on code that wrote code. In the Development phase, you explore tools that improve the quality of code the developer writes by catching simple errors or enforcing best practices.

A case of CoffeeScript

CoffeeScript is a boutique language that compiles to JavaScript. CoffeeScript is heavily influenced by Ruby and borrows much of its terse syntax from it. Unlike Ruby, indentation of code matters in CoffeeScript. This is because CoffeeScript uses indentation to help define the lexical scope for the code during the compilation process.

CoffeeScript is sometimes dismissed by serious JavaScript programmers as an unnecessary abstraction that just muddies the development waters with yet another microlanguage to learn. In their mind, JavaScript as a language is already easy to write and read. Therefore, there is no benefit to having another language do it for them. Let me take the next section to make my argument in favor of CoffeeScript.

■ **Note** The following examples assume that you have CoffeeScript already installed. More information on installing CoffeeScript can be found here: `http://coffeescript.org/`

Write Less

If writing code is the process that takes the most time, writing less code and getting the same result is a good thing, right? CoffeeScript has a very succinct grammar, which allows you to write something like this:

```
square = (x) -> x * x
```

Depending on your CoffeeScript compiler settings, it compiles the previous line to something like this:

```
(function() {
    var square;
    square = function(x) {
      return x * x;
    };
}).call(this)
```

The purpose of this section is to explain why you should use CoffeeScript, not how to write it. For now, all I am going to say is that in CoffeeScript, the single arrow defines a function, and the parentheses define the arguments that the function can accept. The important takeaway is that CoffeeScript can take a very terse statement and extrapolate it into a JavaScript source file that any JavaScript developer should be able to read.

Opinionated Translations

As you can see in the previous example, the CoffeeScript compiler did more than just create a one-to-one translation of our function. CoffeeScript tries to follow common best practices in JavaScript and, where possible, enforces them for you. When training a new developer on my team, I often have them start with CoffeeScript before moving on to JavaScript. This way, I can talk about the reasoning behind CoffeeScript's alterations to its code. There are several crucial modifications that CoffeeScript made to this simple method and they are worth covering one at a time.

The first modification is that the CoffeeScript compiler wrapped the function into an immediately invoked function expression (IIFE). By sealing the function into a closure, CoffeeScript protects the code from other scripts overwriting the function accidentally.

The IIFE also prepares the code for concatenation with other source files. Concatenation and minifying of files is a common task used in automated build systems. By joining all the files into a single file, the browser has to make fewer requests, which speeds up the rendering of the site. Unfortunately, sometimes concatenation can break code. This can occur for a variety of reasons, but one common error is that one or more of the files do not have line breaks at the start or end. This can cause code to run together, which can produce errors.

The next enhancement that CoffeeScript makes to our code is more subtle because it is an opinion on how to write code. In the original function, you used a function expression instead of a function declaration. CoffeeScript makes it nearly impossible to write a function declaration, but it does this for a very good reason.

Earlier versions of Internet Explorer (version 8 and lower) had a scoping problem whereby a named function could be treated simultaneously as a declaration and an expression.

CoffeeScript sidesteps the whole issue by using function expressions almost exclusively. In fact, the only place in which CoffeeScript allows for function declarations is when defining a class.

Along with enforcing function expressions, CoffeeScript also defined the variable as a local variable and moved its declaration to the top of the function block. By doing so, CoffeeScript protects you against any unforeseen variable hoisting issues that might arise from calling a function before it is defined.

Last but not least, CoffeeScript returns a value from the function, even if you did not explicitly request it. Just as in Ruby, CoffeeScript assumes that the last element in a function body should be the return value. Because CoffeeScript enforces this convention, all function signatures benefit from a base level of uniformity.

Fail Fast

It may seem counterintuitive at first, but the fact that CoffeeScript fails to compile to JavaScript can actually be a blessing. As its name implies, JavaScript is a scripting language that the browser does not need to compile before it can be executed.

CoffeeScript compiles to JavaScript only if it is syntactically correct. Now, this doesn't mean the code will do what you want, but at least it will be valid JavaScript by the time the browser executes it.

Uniform Team Code

Most professional developers write code in groups as part of a team. Typically, teams have a style guide that they follow to keep the code readable and uniform. These conventions can run the gamut from how to name your variables to how many spaces to indent your code. Using CoffeeScript will not solve all of these issues, but it will at least guarantee some level of uniformity in the compiled JavaScript.

One reason why I promote CoffeeScript is that it adheres to a collection of best practices that aim to improve the quality of your code for you. CoffeeScript enforces its set of best practices by controlling the final form of the source code (as when it wrapped our code in an IIFE) or by restricting the kind of code you can write in the first place (as when they made it hard to write a function declaration).

CoffeeScript is often cast as a love-it-or-hate-it technology. Unfortunately, many people make up their minds about it even before they have tried it. Sometimes I feel like I am talking to my children when cajoling an obstinate developer, "You don't have to like it, but you do have to try it."

Regardless of your personal feelings about CoffeeScript, the popularity of the language is undeniable, and the ecosystem of tools that support it is growing. By default, Yeoman automatically watches for CoffeeScript files and compiles them for you, and now many of the generators have recently added support for CoffeeScript, too. For example, if you wanted to generate the AngularJS project using CoffeeScript instead of vanilla JavaScript, you could have supplied the optional "--coffee" parameter. The full command would look like this:

```
yo angular --coffee
```

Lint Traps

CoffeeScript's automatic enforcement of code style provides a layer of *de facto* code analysis to the source code. It is as if someone were looking over your shoulder saying, "You don't really want to write it that way; let me fix it for you." This approach alienates some people. Fortunately for those developers, there are other tools that can provide static code analysis without writing the code for you.

JSHint, which was originally written by Anton Kovalyov, is another great option for the code analysis task. JSHint started as a fork of Douglas Crockford's JSLint project. The two programs work essentially the same way: by iterating over a source file line by line and making a list of notes of potential problems or deviations from acceptable style.

Many felt that JSLint was too opinionated. And although the goal of JSLint was to detect potential errors and oversights in a JavaScript program, it also forced developers into writing JavaScript in an arbitrary form that was not necessarily an improvement over their existing approach. The source of JSLint hints at this tension:

```
"WARNING: JSLint will hurt your feelings."
```

Kovalyov loosened the thumbscrews of JSLint and attempted to separate the opinions about style from the need for static code analysis. In doing so, JSHint became a kinder and gentler version of the original. JSHint's web site alludes to this when describing the goal:

> *Our goal is to help JavaScript developers write complex programs without worrying about typos and language gotchas. I believe that static code analysis programs—as well as other code quality tools—are important and beneficial to the JavaScript community and, thus, should not alienate their users.*

One of the goals of JSHint was to provide a means to configure the linter so that it enforced only the coding conventions that a team or individual sought to promote. JSHint's options are divided into three main categories: Enforceable, Relaxable, and Environment options.

Each category contains many different options; too many, in fact, to enumerate here. Instead, I'll furnish just a few canonical examples of each category to make the point, but I encourage those who are interested to read the documentation in detail.

Enforceable Options

As the name suggests, these extra options can be enforced by JSHint. Here are two examples:

- **camelcase (true | false) //**: This option allows you to enforce camelCase style for all variable names.

- **undef (true | false) //**: Prevents you from defining variables that are initially undefined. This often happens a variable was declared but never used at all

Relaxable Options

Rules that are best practices for one person are just annoying to another. JSHint knows this and offers a collection of options that reduces the number of things that trigger a warning by the linter by default. Here are two examples:

- **evil (true | false) //**: It is almost universally agreed that the use of eval is a bad idea because it exposes a conduit for a third party to inject malicious code and have the host application execute it.

- **debug (true | false) //**: This option allows you to suppress warnings about any use of the debugger statement in the code.

Environment Options

The options in this category define any global variables that are exposed by other libraries such as jQuery or Nodejs. Here's an example:

- **jquery (true | false) //**: Whether to expose the global $ or jQuery variables.

Fortunately, Yeoman is automatically configured to lint any JavaScript as part of the automated build process, which I'll cover later. You can modify the default JSHint settings by editing the JSHint resource file, which is located in the root of the application directory. The file is named .jshintrc.

A word of warning before you proceed: static code analysis tools such as JSHint only validate the syntactic structure of the code. This is a huge asset for catching small bugs or inconsistencies in style that might otherwise slip through the cracks of day-to-day development. However, these tools cannot tell you if the code that is written actually does what it was intended to do. For that, the developer needs to test code under a variety of contexts to assert that it performs as expected.

Testing

Testing can mean anything from asserting that the application performs the task it was designed for to whether it looks correct on various platforms such as desktops, phones, or tablets. Writing efficient tests and knowing what to test in the first place improve this stage of the workflow. Here again, automation is key, not only when running tests for the developer but also when distributing the testing cases across multiple platforms.

I should also mention that tests do not always follow the development process. Methodologies that embrace Test Driven Development (TDD) or Behavior Driven Development (BDD) follow a test-first paradigm. These developers begin by writing tests that describe the functionality that needs to be written. The tests are then run to ensure that they fail. Once a test has been written, only then does the coding begin.

Many methodologies also state that the developer should write only enough code to make the test pass. The hope is that the codebase can be leaner because unneeded functionality is not added. I placed tests after development in this chapter mainly because I believe that it is the order most people think of the processes flowing together. In reality, the development and testing can be tightly coupled phases that oscillate together.

In this section, I introduce several testing-related tools and demonstrate how they can be efficiently integrated into your workflow.

How to Test

I could make a pretty safe bet that most professional developers in languages other than JavaScript write tests as part of their normal workflow. The reason why JavaScript still lags behind in this regard has less to do with the quality of the typical JavaScript developers and more to do with the fact that JavaScript can be run across so many different platforms and contexts. In most languages, writing tests is the hard part, but in JavaScript it is running them.

Fortunately, many smart developers have been hard at work, slowly chipping away at this problem. There are several viable options for running JavaScript test reliably in an automated fashion.

JavaScript test runners usually fall into one of two camps: those that test using stand-alone engines such as V8 or Rhino, and those that run in the browser. I will demonstrate two test runners: Karma and PhantomJS.

Karma

Karma is a test runner originally developed in parallel by the AngularJS team as it was writing AngularJS. It is test framework–agnostic, meaning that you can use whatever JavaScript testing library you are most comfortable with. It has a built-in file watcher that developers can configure to automatically run the related tests when the watcher sees a source file change.

Karma is designed to run tests on actual devices and browsers, which means that the tests get a true representation of how the code will perform on the target device/platform. Karma is built with the larger workflow process in mind, and offers a variety of entry points for continuous integration tools such as Jenkins, Travis, and Teamcity.

Karma's only dependency is Node.js, which you should already have installed. The Karma team recommends that you install the project globally through npm, which can be done like this:

```
$ npm install -g karma

# Start Karma
$ karma start
```

Running the start command should open a browser with Karma running in the active tab. You should see something like this in your console:

```
INFO [karma]: Karma server started at http://localhost:8080/
INFO [launcher]: Starting browser Chrome
INFO [Chrome 26.0 (Mac)]: Connected on socket id TPVQXqXCvrM2XhRwABfC
```

So far, Karma is not that helpful; it just sits there idling in the open browser because there is no test to run—or is there? If you look inside the directory structure that Yeoman generated, you should see a main.js file. It is located inside the /test/spec/controllers/ directory. Now that you have a test to run, you just need to configure Karma to run it, which takes a tiny bit of configuration.

As part of the bootstrapping process, Yeoman already generated a configuration file for you. If you look in the root directory you should see a file named karma.conf.js. By default, Karma looks for this file and uses it to determine the test runner preferences. Fortunately, the file is well annotated by the developers, and the options are pretty easy to understand.

By default, Karma is set to run in integration mode but if you manually change singleRun to true in the Karma configuration file, you can instruct Karma to run the tests on demand:

```
// Karma configuration

// base path, that will be used to resolve files and exclude
basePath = '';

// list of files / patterns to load in the browser
files = [
  JASMINE,
  JASMINE_ADAPTER,
  'app/components/angular/angular.js',
```

```
    'app/components/angular-mocks/angular-mocks.js',
    'app/scripts/*.js',
    'app/scripts/**/*.js',
    'test/mock/**/*.js',
    'test/spec/**/*.js'
];

// list of files to exclude
exclude = [];

// test results reporter to use
// possible values: dots || progress || growl
reporters = ['progress'];

// web server port
port = 8080;

// cli runner port
runnerPort = 9100;

// enable / disable colors in the output (reporters and logs)
colors = true;
// level of logging
// possible values: LOG_DISABLE || LOG_ERROR || LOG_WARN || LOG_INFO || LOG_DEBUG

logLevel = LOG_INFO;
// enable / disable watching file and executing tests whenever any file changes
autoWatch = false;

// Start these browsers, currently available:
// - Chrome
// - ChromeCanary
// - Firefox
// - Opera
// - Safari (only Mac)
// - PhantomJS
// - IE (only Windows)
browsers = ['Chrome'];

// If browser does not capture in given timeout [ms], kill it
captureTimeout = 5000;

// Continuous Integration mode
// if true, it capture browsers, run tests and exit
singleRun = false;
```

After you save your changes, when you rerun the Karma start command, you should see a different result:

```
karma start
```

The browser should appear for a split second and then disappear again. And checking the console, you should see the relevant bits should be at the bottom, and it should look a little something like this:

```
INFO [karma]: Karma server started at http://localhost:8080/
INFO [launcher]: Starting browser Chrome
INFO [Chrome 26.0 (Mac)]: Connected on socket id UpRyiPnI-M9x4d35NiqQ
Chrome 26.0 (Mac): Executed 1 of 1 SUCCESS (0.084 secs / 0.013 secs)
```

As you can see, you started Karma, which in turn launched Chrome, which finally ran your Jasmine tests for you. Do you see what I mean about dependency management? At the end of the console output, you can see that your single test ran in a fraction of a second.

The Ghost with the Most

PhantomJS is the next test runner you will investigate. Unlike Karma, which is stickily a test runner, PhantomJS seeks to replicate the entire web stack (DOM traversal, CSS selection, JSON parsing, Canvas and SVG processing) in an invisible interface. This is sometimes called a headless browser. PhantomJS augments the normal browser features by layering a powerful JavaScript API on top.

Developers can use the API to do all sorts of helpful tasks such as programmatically capturing screenshots, monitoring web site performance, or simulating a user interacting with web sites. The PhantomJS API also lets developers use familiar libraries such as jQuery to script the API, which makes getting up and running much faster.

Under the sheets, PhantomJS is just Webkit. This means that when writing tests, the programmer must be aware that the results may not truly reflect how the code will behave on other browsers (for example, Internet Explorer). Unlike Karma, which is only a test runner, PhantomJS considers test running just one of many use cases it is good for.

The test running infrastructure is not as easy to access as in Karma. Thankfully, PhantomJS has a vibrant user base and several bolt-on projects have been written to get the phantom to run the tests with little hassle. There are several testing projects in the PhantomJS ecosystem worth mentioning, including casperJS, Poltergeist, and GhostDriver.

Unfortunately, getting them up and running is too far outside the scope of this chapter. Instead, let's focus on integrating PhantomJS into Karma. When Karma ran the tests previously, the browser popped up for a split second to run the tests and then automatically closed.

By switching to PhantomJS, you can avoid this altogether because the tests will run in an invisible headless browser. Fortunately, this integration is straightforward to get working. You just need to reopen the karma.conf.js file and change the single entry in the browsers array to read PhantomJS.

Once you save and close the file, you should again trigger the Karma start command. This time, no browser window appears and you should see a slightly different result in the console output:

```
INFO [karma]: Karma server started at http://localhost:8080/
INFO [launcher]: Starting browser PhantomJS
INFO [PhantomJS 1.7 (Mac)]: Connected on socket id 2WUOvjjU9KSbb442Kkt9
PhantomJS 1.7 (Mac): Executed 1 of 1 SUCCESS (0.034 secs / 0.007 secs)
```

Karma used PhantomJS this time, and as a bonus ran the tests in nearly half the time! Now that you have an idea of how to reliably run tests as part of a JavaScript development workflow, let's take a minute to explore the types of tests that can and should be written.

What to Test

To properly test an application, you must attack it from a variety of different vectors. You want to test the code both in isolation and then again once it has been integrated into the final deployed environment. Simultaneously, you can also focus another stream of tests to see how well the code performs.

Typically, tests fall into one of four testing categories: units, integration, performance, and compatibility. I will use the remainder of this section to introduce tools for each one of these categories.

Unit Tests

Unit tests test a single unit of code, for example, a specific function of a larger class. Unit tests enable you to test in isolation to ensure that your function does what it is intended to do at the most basic level. There are several excellent test frameworks for JavaScript: Mocha, QUnit, and Jasmine, to name just three. Here is the same test written in each framework:

```
/* Written in Mocha */
var assert = require("assert")
describe('truth test', function(){
  it('should know that true is equal to true', function(){
    assert.equal(true, true);
  })
})

/* Written in QUnit */
test( "truth test", function() {
  ok( true === true, "is true!" );
});

/* Written In Jasmine */
describe("truth test", function() {
  it("should know true is equal to true", function() {
    expect(true).toBe(true);
  });
});
```

Integration Tests

Integration tests are sometimes called end-to-end tests because they test a collection of smaller features together to ensure that a larger tasks works as planned. Integration tests are primarily used to perform a scenario that represents a potential use case for how the software might be used. These tests often need access to extra resources, such as external APIs or browser cookies. Hitting these external elements can cause tests to slow down, so they are often mocked out and replaced with a virtual object that represents the expected result.

What follows next is the source code for the MainController of the AngularJS application. This code is followed by a Jasmine test that Yeoman also automatically created. Coincidentally, this test is the same test you ran repeatedly when examining the various test runners.

```
'use strict';

/* app/scripts/controllers/main.js */
angular.module('DesktopApp')
  .controller('MainCtrl', function ($scope) {
```

```
    $scope.awesomeThings = [
      'HTML5 Boilerplate',
      'AngularJS',
      'Karma'
    ];
  });
```

```
/* /test/spec/controllers/main.js */
'use strict';
describe('Controller: MainCtrl', function () {
  // load the controller's module
  beforeEach(module('DesktopApp'));
  var MainCtrl,
    scope;
  // Initialize the controller and a mock scope
  beforeEach(inject(function ($controller, $rootScope) {
    scope = $rootScope.$new();
    MainCtrl = $controller('MainCtrl', {
      $scope: scope
    });
  }));
  it('should attach a list of awesomeThings to the scope', function () {
    expect(scope.awesomeThings.length).toBe(3);
  });
});
```

Notice that much of the code in this test is actually concerned with emulating a state in which the application would be if it were actually running. This is what I meant about mocking out aspects of the larger environment.

Once an instance of the Main controller was created, the test verified the expectations that an array containing three elements was bound to the $scope variable. The test framework counts this toward the passing tests and ultimately reports those results to the test runner.

Performance Tests

Performance tests ensure that code that works does it as efficiently as possible. As mentioned earlier, PhantomJS can be used to automate network monitoring of web sites. The typical use case is to measure the duration of the request and response cycle using the onResourceRequested and onResourceReceived attributes. However, this is less useful to a programmer than it is someone in devOps.

When I think of performance testing at the developer level, it typically involves isolating a single function as you would in a unit test and measuring the performance across a variety of different browsers. This kind of test doesn't need to be run again with each iteration because once you have established the result, it doesn't change (unless you change your function). For this reason, I typically just use the jsPerf web site, which takes a code snippet, runs it in a variety of different browsers, and returns a report to you.

Compatibility Tests

JavaScript applications are deployed to a diverse ecosystem of platforms and host applications. Compatibility tests are where the often-unreasonable desire to develop once and deploy everywhere is put on trial. Through compatibility testing, the developer can see how the same code performs on a variety of different devices, browsers, and so on. These tests mostly focus on the differences between the various platforms, which often mean how the applications render visually and what affordances the platform offers or restricts. Therefore, these tests often rely on visual reports over simple pass-fail statistics spit out to a console window.

Collecting (not to mention buying and maintaining) the ever-growing list of devices and browsers under one roof and testing them individually would be the furthest thing from productive. Fortunately, several technologies have sprung up to service this need. Unfortunately, however, you may need to bring your credit card. Here is a quick rundown of some products offering compatibility tests.

Browserstack

According to its web site, this company offers "Instant access to all desktop and mobile browsers." Its pay service gives developers access to a variety of virtual machines, from which they can test their product under development. Browserstack also offers a screenshot service in which developers can provide a URL, and Browserstack in turn creates a screenshot of the resulting page across many different browsers.

Bunyip

This tool can be used to automate multibrowser device testing. Bunyip can be used to corral browsers on your own device farm, but it also offers integration with other tools such as Browserstack.

Adobe Inspect

Inspect is a freemium service that allows you to synchronize various devices together. Using Inspect, as a developer you can make code changes, save the result, and then watch as all your connected devices and browsers update. Just like Browserstack, Adobe Inspect offers screenshot services and also offers a remote inspection tool that can be used to dynamically change HTML, CSS, and JavaScript on a remote device.

You might be wondering why I have not mentioned PhantomJS, especially because it's free and open source. It is true that PhantomJS does offer screenshot capabilities, and because it can capture them programmatically, they could even be strung together into a video. However, PhantomJS is just Webkit and therefore not a true compatibility testing tool.

Building

Once developers complete a feature and are ready to share it with the world, they deploy the code into production. The art of shipping code could be the topic of an entire book and is well outside this book and JavaScript in general. Instead, this section will focus on creating a local build, which means preparing the source code into a form suitable for upload to the Web or inclusion into a larger deployment stream.

As you have seen, much of JavaScript workflow is about writing code in a form that makes development as easy as possible for the programmer. This can mean using local package managers to marshal dependencies or high-level languages such as CoffeeScript as a proxy for JavaScript. Often, other tools such as HAML are used in place of HTML, and SASS is used in place of CSS. These tools exist to make development more enjoyable, efficient, and less error-prone.

There is one huge drawback to these technologies, however: no browser can make heads or tails of them. Therefore, much of the build stage is dedicated to converting code that is easy to read by humans into source that machines can understand. There are several common steps in the typical build process: compilation, analysis, concatenation, optimization, testing, and notification. As usual, I will explain each step in detail in the following sections.

Compilation

JavaScript is compiled only when it starts in some other form such as CoffeeScript. The builder process typically loops through the CoffeeScript files and sends them to the compiler. The results are then typically saved to a temporary build directory.

Analysis

As mentioned earlier, static code analysis plays an important role in ensuring that the code that is delivered meets or exceeds a predetermined quality threshold, and that it conforms to conventions of style defined by the larger team. This analysis is typically performed by tools such as JSHint, which I covered earlier. Failures at this stage can either halt the build or simply warn the developer at the notification stage by writing a report to the console or a log file.

In addition to the static analysis of the code, this process can also use tools such as Istanbul, which is a test coverage tool for JavaScript. Istanbul can report on any areas of code that are not invoked during testing.

Concatenation

Much of the perceived slowness of applications is due to the number of requests needed to download all the relevant source files that an application depends on. By concatenating the entire source into a single file, the site's performance will improve.

Often, framework code and libraries are skipped from this step because many of them are already hosted on content distribution networks (CDNs) elsewhere. Web browsers allow for parallel downloads across multiple domains, which means that leveraging a CDN has at least two benefits. It can speed up the initial download through parallel browser requests and reduce the file size of the remaining concatenated code.

Optimization

Once the raw JavaScript is compiled into a single file, the builder process looks to reduce the file size as much as possible. Typically, this means using a program such as UglifyJS or Google's closure compiler. Some of these compressors are more aggressive than others. For example, the closure compiler attempts to make the source "better" during the conversion process. This can mean rewriting aspects of the code or removing code that it thinks is unused.

Testing

It is possible that all this compressing, optimizing, and beautifying of the source code might unintentionally break something. Therefore, before shipping the code out, it is a good idea to run the code through the tests one last time. Most build processes are designed to stop if the tests fail, thereby mitigating the risk of overwriting code in production with the faulty version.

Notification

There are several audiences interested in the result of the build process. The first is the developer, and the second are any external processes waiting to loop the compiled code into a larger deployment cycle. For the interested humans, notification can mean creating a report that describes the results of the build, which can be as simple as whether it failed or passed.

The report could also outline the findings about code quality and test coverage. Once the code is clean, it can be committed back to the source code repository, at which point any postcommit hooks can be triggered. Any continuous integration tools such as Travis or Cruise Control listening for those triggers now know that a new build is ready to be picked up.

Continuing with Yeoman, you now learn how it handles the build process. Yeoman actually delegates this task to something else—again, the tool of choice is Grunt. During the bootstrapping process, Yeoman created a configuration file for Grunt, named (unsurprisingly) Gruntfile.js. Inside the file, Yeoman defines a series of tasks that the developer or other process can invoke. You have already tried two of them: grunt server and grunt test. The default task, however, is the build process. You can kick off the build process by typing this into the console:

```
grunt
```

Your console begins to scroll by as the various tasks are invoked individually, and at the end of the process you should see the message "Done, without errors." in the console. There should now be a new folder called Dist in the application directory. This folder contains all the freshly compiled files JavaScript otherwise needed to run the AngularJS application.

Congratulations! You have almost reached the end of the development workflow. The last bit that remains is how to support the code once it leaves the nest.

Support

The sad fact of a developer's life is that at some point software will be released into the wild that has an unintended malfunction nestled somewhere in the bowels of the source code. This chapter looked at various ways to integrate checks and safeguards against these errors into a development workflow.

However, sometimes these techniques are not enough, and supporting the deployed code must thus be part of the workflow. In this phase, the developer uses tools and techniques to track down and eliminate any errors as quickly as possible.

Support comes in two stages: being notified when an exception occurs and re-creating the bug on demand, so the problematic source can be isolated. First, I'll discuss a tool for triggering exception notifications and then I'll briefly touch on how to map the bug in production to the development source code.

Error Reporting in JavaScript

Many modern application frameworks have exception notifications built right in. Typically, when an error occurs, the exception is trapped by a block of code so that the stack trace and environment variables can be wrapped up into a report that is typically mailed to the developer. From this report, the developer has a better chance of piecing together what went wrong. There are entire products, such as errorCeption, that are dedicated to parsing, graphing, and reporting this for you. The basics of an error reporter are pretty easy to wire together. Essentially, you just want to bind a listener to the onerror event of the window object.

What follows is an overly simplified example, just to give you the general idea:

```
window.onerror = function(msg, url, lineNum) {
  $.ajax({
    url: "http://someserver.com/exception-notifier",
    type: "get",
    data: {
      message: msg,
      url: url
      lineNumber: lineNum
    },
    success: function(data) {
      alert("Error Reported");
    }
  });
}
```

Unravelling the Sweater

Unfortunately, this approach is not entirely foolproof. Remember when the build process modified the JavaScript source? All this compressing, obfuscating, and concatenation can make trying to debug production code like pulling on a loose thread of a sweater. Before long, you are left with a pile of yarn and not much else. This is because the compressor often shortens variable names and removes newlines from the source. Therefore, the variables, method names, and line numbers returned by the notifier will not match the uncompressed JavaScript. As you can imagine, this makes it harder for the developer to trace the reason for the error back to the original code. Fortunately, in recent years developers, and more importantly browsers, have begun to embrace a concept called source maps.

Source maps are mappings between the compiled file and the uncompressed JavaScript source. This map is generated at the time of compilation by providing special instructions to the compiler. Once the compiler creates the map, it can be parsed by the developer tools of supporting browsers automatically.

Right now, support for generating source maps is still spotty, but major compilers, including Google's Closure Compiler, can generate them. Another important point is that source maps are not exclusive to JavaScript. They are intended to be a standard for any file type that can be minified; therefore, CSS also supports source maps.

Summary

This chapter dissected in detail a modern development workflow for building JavaScript applications. There are several key points that I hope you will take away.

You should minimize snow shoveling, which means doing work that may be essential in the present, but provides no benefits to the long-term progress of the project.

Choose your technology stack wisely; you are often making the decision for not only yourself but for everyone who comes after you. Choose the tool that is right for the job; not just the one you are most expert with.

Embrace automation; if you find yourself manually stepping through a process several times a day, find a way to mechanize it. Look for tools that enforce community standards in both code quality and programmatic style. Not only do these tools help you find minor bugs but they also offer a baseline of consistency between all team members.

Write tests and run them continuously. Not only do they prove that your software works but they also give you and your team confidence to make future changes without fear that it will silently break existing features. Write for humans, and let the build process worry about how to make it smaller and more efficient.

The developer workflow doesn't stop when the code goes live; there will always be an edge case or platform that was not considered. Therefore, it is important to build in support processes for when these errors occur.

CHAPTER 9

■ ■ ■

Code Quality

Quality is not an act, it is a habit.

—Aristotle

What does it mean to write quality JavaScript? Can quality be measured, or is it a subjective point of view, akin to the platonic ideals of beauty and art? Programmers tend to oscillate between subjective and objective understandings of quality. They elevate concepts such as software craftsmanship, which is the artisanal approach to writing software. Software craftsmen are described as having superior skill and have distilled their trade down to its essential components. The electrified manifestation of the craftsman is the so-called rock star programmer. One whose definition is based on the notion that a person can be so uniquely gifted as an artist, that the work product is somehow greater than the sum of their parts. Yet, much of programming revolves around measuring, refactoring, and improving code through procedural and repeatable processes. This would suggest that quality can be extracted into a series of independent and measureable steps.

If quality can be measured, what are the mechanisms available to JavaScript developers to ensure that they produce superior code? This chapter explores in depth the concept of writing quality JavaScript, first defining quality as it relates to programming and then providing a framework for evaluating and improving your code.

Defining Code Quality

Like many complex disciplines that attract individuals from divergent backgrounds, definitions of programmatic quality often straddle the fence between art and science. The act of programming is often an amalgamation of creative problem solving and applying an engineer's rigor to refine a solution. Programming is a tension between objective observations through codified repeatable steps and subjective evaluations born out of personal experience and insight. In truth, the word *quality* supports both of these positions. Barbara W. Tuchman explained the duplicitous nature of quality this way:

> The word "quality" has, of course, two meanings: first, the nature or essential characteristic of something, as in "His voice has the quality of command"; second, a condition of excellence implying fine quality as distinct from poor quality (Tuchman, 1980).

Tuchman goes on to describe quality as being "self-nourishing," which is a wonderfully evocative image. Quality is also described as a pursuit, which suggests that it's not a destination, but rather a journey. This may be because the definition is not fixed; it belongs to the zeitgeist. For proof, you have to look no farther than the history of art, which is continually repelling or embracing different forms of artistic expression. In the span of a lifetime, the French impressionists went from being scorned by the art establishment to reaching the zenith of the art world years later. Their paintings did not change—just the definition of quality.

In this chapter, I argue that both the subjective and objective positions are needed to evaluate JavaScript source. In fact, I believe that you can't even completely separate one from other. However, before I can make this case, I need to properly present both forms.

Subjective Quality

Subjective quality often describes code that is inspired or essential, or what Truchman calls an "innate excellence." In his article on product quality, David Garvin defined a form of quality that he labeled as transcendent. He defined transcendent quality as

> *...both absolute and universally recognizable, a mark of uncompromising standards and high achievement. Nevertheless, proponents of this view claim that quality cannot be defined precisely; rather, it is a simple, unanalyzable property that we learn to recognize only through experience. This definition borrows heavily from Plato's discussion of beauty. In the Symposium, he argues that beauty is one of the "platonic forms," and, therefore, a term that cannot be defined. Like other such terms that philosophers consider to be "logically primitive," beauty (and perhaps quality as well) can be understood only after one is exposed to a succession of objects that display its characteristics. (Garvin, 1984)*

This definition clearly articulates the idea that subjective quality is dependent on personal experience or the guidance of skilled individuals to recognize and promote excellence within their field. It asserts that subjective quality at its essential level is universally true, not so much created as discovered.

Objective Quality

Objective quality asserts that if genius can be measured, it can be quantified and repeated. The quality of a cake is not dependent on the *innate excellence* of the baker, but instead is a result of the exact choice and measurement of ingredients, and the precision to which the recipe is followed. Objective quality makes, applies, and refines empirical approximations about the subject in a feedback loop. This form of quality lends itself to algorithms, test suites, and software tooling. For the remainder of this chapter, I will present an approach for improving code through objective quality.

How Is Quality Measured?

You are on your way to a usable definition for quality, but first you need to consider its various dimensions as they relate to programming. These facets are commonly expressed as software metrics:

> *A software metric is a measure of some property of a piece of software or its specifications. Since quantitative measurements are essential in all sciences, there is a continuous effort by computer science practitioners and theoreticians to bring similar approaches to software development. The goal is obtaining objective, reproducible and quantifiable measurements, which may have numerous valuable applications in schedule and budget planning, cost estimation, quality assurance testing, software debugging, software performance optimization, and optimal personnel task assignments.*

I have included six metrics in an effort to frame code quality through measurements:

- **Aesthetics:** This metric measures the visual cohesion of the code, but also encompasses the consistency and thoughtfulness of formatting, naming conventions, and document structure. Aesthetics are measured to answer these questions:
  - How readable is the code?
  - How are the individual parts organized on the page?
  - Does it use best practices in terms of programming style?

- **Completeness:** Completeness measures whether the code is "fit for purpose."[1] To be considered complete, a program must meet or exceed the requirements of the specified problem. Completeness can also measure how well the particular implementation conforms to industry standards or ideals. The questions about completeness this measure attempts to answer are these:

  - Does the code solve the problem it was meant to?

  - Does the code produce the desired output given an expected input?

  - Does it meet all the defined use cases?

  - Is it secure?

  - Does it handle edge cases well?

  - Is it well-tested?

- **Performance:** Performance measures an implementation against known benchmarks to determine how successful it is. These metrics may consider attributes such as program size, system resource efficiency, load time, or bugs per line of code. Using performance measures, you can answer the following questions:

  - How efficient is this approach?

  - What load can it handle?

  - What are the limits on capacity with this code?

- **Effort:** This metric measures the development cost incurred to produce and support the code. Effort can be categorized in terms of time, money, or resources used. Measuring effort can help answer these questions:

  - Is the code maintainable?

  - Does it deploy easily?

  - Is it documented?

  - How much did it *cost* to write?

- **Durability:** To be durable, a program's life in production is measured. Durability can also be thought of as a measure of reliability, which is another way to measure longevity. Durability can be measured to answer these questions:

  - Does it perform reliably?

  - How long can it be run before it must be restarted, upgraded, and/or replaced?

  - Is it scalable?

- **Reception:** Reception measures how other programmers evaluate and value the code. Tracking reception allows you to answer these questions:

  - How hard to understand is the code?

  - How well-thought-out are the design decisions?

  - Does the approach leverage established best practices?

  - Is it enjoyable to use?

---

[1]http://en.wikipedia.org/wiki/Quality_assurance

Why Measure Code Quality?

"I can't charge for code quality." This is a direct quote from one of my friends when I asked him for his thoughts on the subject. What he meant was that code quality mainly benefits the programmer, and is an invisible tax to the client. I can understand his point of view; I have had more than one experience in which a potential client's eyes rolled back into their head proportionate to the amount I yammered on about testing methodolgies. My friend went on to say, "Clients pay for a result, not a process. When I buy a ticket on Southwest, I pay to get to my destination, not to ride on a plane." This statement makes a sort of naïve sense but I will argue in this section that measuring code quality doesn't make you lose your competitive advantage; *it is your competitive advantage.*

The management consultant Tom Peters once said, "What gets measured gets done." *Measurement* in this context means to look forward in order to forecast change. Often testing and quality measurement is used only as a post-mortem to be performed after something has gone wrong. When applied continually through the development process, measuring code quality gives you the ability to interpret the health of your project. It can also suggest the likelihood of negative events in the future. Consider the following ways that code quality can improve not only your code but also your project's bottom line:

- Technical debt is a metaphor that describes the increasing cost in terms of time, money, and resources that bad code steals from your project over time. There are many quality metrics, including code complexity analysis, that can identify areas of code debt in your software.

- There are several measures (such as the Halstead metrics, which I'll cover later) that can suggest the amount of future effort that will be required to maintain your codebase. Knowing this can inform your ability to accurately budget for these improvements.

- Many code-quality measures attempt to understand the pathways through your code. These measures can then identify the likelihood that bugs exist, and where they may be potentially hiding. These tools are especially valuable when evaluating another team's code because they can act like mine detectors, which sweep algorithmically through the unknown field of functions.

- Although the ability to find new bugs is important, so too is the skill to know when it is safe to stop writing tests. Many prominent developers have proven that tests aren't free,[2] so knowing when to stop saves money. Many code quality tools can tell you when you have reached an appropriate level of test coverage using simple heuristics.

- Embracing code quality measures is a form of preventative maintenance. I've heard people talk about code quality dismissively, saying it's like brushing your teeth. In a way they are right, the nature of quality is that it is much harder to add later, just as brushing your teeth won't get rid of existing cavities.

Now that there is a baseline for code quality, you have a working definition and you understand not only how quality is measured but also why you should do it at all. In the next section, I will explain the various tools and techniques available to you in your pursuit of quality.

Measuring Code Quality in JavaScript

Objective quality analysis churns through code procedurally, in order that the computational cream will rise to the top. This task is accomplished through the use of programmatic tools, which evaluate the code in a variety of contexts, using metrics to arrive at a final quality score. This section explains static code analysis which is an approach well-suited for accessing the quality of your JavaScript.

---

[2]http://37signals.com/svn/posts/3159-testing-like-the-tsa

Static Code Analysis

Static code analysis is the process of analyzing code without running it. Static analysis works much like a spell checker in a text editor. Spell checkers sweep the document for errors and ambiguities within the text body without the need for understanding the meaning of the writing. Similarly, static analysis of code analyzes the source for functional correctness without having to know what it does. Even though JavaScript is a very dynamic language, it is well-suited for static analysis because it is not compiled into another form. This section will evaluate two methods of static analysis in JavaScript, which include syntax validators and complexity analysis tools.

Syntax Validations

In JavaScript, syntax validation can be approached in two ways. The first is to use a linter such as JSLint[3] or JSHint,[4] which not only checks the functional correctness of your code, but also occasionally offer a bit of *tough love* when your program fails to follow their best practices. Consider this code of suspicious quality:

```
// foo.js
onmessage = function(event) {
  "use strict"
  event = event
  if(event){
    return {"success" : postMessage('pong'), "success" : "ok"}
  }
};
```

I am using JSHint, which you can install as an npm module this way (sudo may be required on your system, depending on your user account privileges):

```
npm install jshint -g
```

Once installed, you can run the linter against the source file from the terminal's command line:

```
jshint foo.js
```

JSHint will report these warnings:

```
foo.js: line 7, col 3, Missing semicolon.
foo.js: line 8, col 16, Missing semicolon.
foo.js: line 10, col 56, Duplicate key 'success'.
foo.js: line 10, col 63, Missing semicolon.
```

Notice that the linter informed you only about the lack of semicolons and the duplicate key. Personally, I would consider the meaningless assignment of event = event worth mentioning, too, but *technically* there is nothing wrong with this code. This ambiguity illustrates the linter's opinion-driven approach, which is that it validates not only the syntax but also your approach.

---

[3]http://www.jslint.com/
[4]http://www.jshint.com/

For those less interested in identifying so-called *bad smells in code*, you can use a simple stand-alone ECMAScript parser such as Esprima,[5] which will spaz out only over invalid code. Esprima can be installed from an npm module like this:

```
npm install -g esprima
```

Similar to JSHint, it can validate the code from the terminal's command line:

```
esvalidate foo.js
```

Once complete, Esprima should output something similar to this to the terminal window:

```
foo.js:6: Duplicate data property in object literal not allowed in strict mode
```

Linters and parsers are excellent tools for establishing a base line for code quality. Many of these tools can and *should* be integrated into the larger development workflow. They are key factors in your ability to improve the aesthetics, effort, and reception quality metrics I covered earlier. However, in most cases, simple syntactic hygiene is not enough to ensure quality code. The next section explores tools that help mitigate complexity creep in the codebase.

Complexity

Antoine de Saint-Exupery could have been talking about code quality when he said, "Perfection is achieved, not when there is nothing left to add, but when there is nothing left to take away." Quality code is not only formally correct but also conceptually clear, and expressive in its ability to illustrate to the reader how the required problem is solved. Unfortunately, there are many reasons why concise code can degrade into a mumbling mess of operands and operators. Teams may change, features may grow or shrink, and stakeholder goals may pivot; and all these events happen while programmers are under the gun to *keep on shipping*.

Anyone who has programmed for any amount of time knows that "code is our enemy."[6] A simple fact of development is that as code increases, quality declines. *Code is syntactic cellulite; easier to add than to remove.* Code bloat, as it is called, leads to a complex program because there is more source for programmers to read, understand, and maintain. Smart programmers fight complexity by leveraging design patterns and application frameworks. They embrace development methodologies that attempt to reduce complexity through a consistent approach to programming.

In addition to these approaches, complexity can also be measured programmatically using quality metrics tuned to find difficult code. This section explores the way in which complex JavaScript can be identified, isolated, and finally removed from a program.

Measuring Complexity Through Code Metrics

No JavaScript is complex to a runtime engine. It may be bug-ridden, inefficient, or incomplete, but complexity as it relates to programming is a purely human conundrum. Therefore, code complexity is the measurement of the mental labor a programmer must endure to completely understand a unit of code.

Over a number of years, programmers have developed metrics that measure complexity. These metrics identify telltale shortcomings in the source, which often lead to complex code. Some of these metrics are the result of empirical observation, and others are algorithmic interpretations about how programmers think about code. Other programmers have harnessed these metrics into tools that can periodically scan the program in an effort to help developers understand where their code needs refactoring or additional tests.

This section demonstrates a selection of these complexity metrics, which are well-suited for JavaScript, as well as a collection of tools that can automate the quality control.

---

[5]https://github.com/ariya/esprima
[6]http://www.skrenta.com/2007/05/code_is_our_enemy.html

Excessive Comments

An obvious result of complex code is that the source is no longer self-documenting to the reader. Often comments are used to enable future programmers to translate a previous developer's approach. For this reason, comments can be a compelling complexity measure because they suggest that there is work yet to be done or that improvements can be made.

Lines of Code

Like the excessive comments metric, counting the lines of code makes intuitive sense. As a function expands, so does the likelihood that a developer will misunderstand some nuance of the implementation. Lines of code can be measured in a variety of ways, including Lines of Code (LOC), Source Lines of Code (SLOC), or Non-Commented Source Lines (NCSL).

When evaluating an LOC metric, ensure that you are analyzing at the correct level of detail. For example, refactoring a function into three functions may increase the LOC metric, but in reality reduce the overall complexity of the source. For this reason, developers sometimes call the LOC a naïve measure. When evaluating JavaScript, I find that a LOC metric works best at the function level because long functions are usually a sign of needless complexity.

Coupling

If an object requires explicit knowledge of another object's implementation to work, the dependent object is said to be *tightly coupled* to the other object. This coupling is to be avoided where possible because it makes the overall source brittle. Moreover, it means that information hiding is failing, and that implementation logic is leaking out into the larger codebase.

When statically analyzing JavaScript for tight coupling, it is possible to count the number of dots used to access properties in an object chain. Where possible, you should keep the calling chain to three dots or fewer. Here is an example:

```
// too tighly coupled
var word = library.shelves[0].books[0].pages[0].words[10];

// loosely coupled
var shelf = library.getShelfAt(0);
var book = shelf.getBookAt(0);
var page = book.getPageAt(0);
var word = page.getWordAt(10);
```

Variables per Function

JavaScript functions with too many local variables may suggest that the function can be improved, either through a separation of concerns or by grouping the variables into a common object. Consider the following example:

```
var race = function () {
    var totalLaps = 10;
    var currentLap = 0;
    var driver1 = "Bob";
    var driver2 = "Bill";
    var car1 = {
        driver: driver1,
        fuel: 100,
        maxMph: 100,
```

```
            miles: 0,
            tires: 4
        };
        var car2 = {
            driver: driver2,
            fuel: 100,
            maxMph: 100,
            miles: 0,
            tires: 4
        };
        var cars = [car1, car2];
        while (currentLap < totalLaps) {
            currentLap++;
            cars.forEach(function (car) {
                car.miles += Math.floor(Math.random() * car.maxMph) + 1;
            });
        }
        if (car1.miles > car2.miles) {
            console.log(car1.driver + " wins!");
        } else {
            console.log(car2.driver + " wins!");
        }
    }

    // => (Bob or Bill) wins!
    race();
```

The race function handles more than just simulating the race, so the function body is littered with local variables. You can reduce the number of variables from seven to two by improving the separation of concerns like this:

```
var addCar = function (driver) {
    return {
        driver: driver,
        fuel: 100,
        maxMph: 100,
        miles: 0,
        tires: 4
    };
};

var race = function (cars) {
    var totalLaps = 10;
    var currentLap = 0;
    while (currentLap < totalLaps) {
        currentLap++;
        cars.forEach(function (car) {
            car.miles += Math.floor(Math.random() * car.maxMph) + 1;
        });
    }
    cars.sort(function (a, b) {
        return a.miles > b.miles ? -1 : 1;
```

```
    });
    console.log(cars[0].driver + " wins!");
};

// => (Bob or Bill) wins!
race([addCar('Bob'), addCar('Bill')]);
```

Arguments per Function

There is no hard and fast rule about the number of arguments that makes a function too complex. However, passing in a laundry list of arguments into a function may be a sign that the purpose of your function is muddled. In some cases, you can reduce the number or arguments that a reader has to remember by logically organizing related arguments together. This can be done by grouping them into an object that you can supply to the function instead:

```
var detectCollision = function (x1, x2, y1, y2, xx1, xx2, yy1, yy2) {
    // more code
}

// Restructure the function to accept logically organized objects.
// rect1 == { x1:0, x2:0, y1:0, y2:0 }
var detectCollision = function (rect1, rect2) {
    // more code
}
```

Nesting Depth

Code that is deeply nested is more complex and harder to test than shallow code. Nesting depth in functions is measured in a variety of ways. For example, each of these functions has a nesting depth of four:

```
// Nesting depth of three
var isRGBA = function (color) {
    if (color != 'red') {
        if (color != 'blue') {
            if (color != 'green') {
                if(color != 'alpha'){
                    return false;
                }
            }
        }
    }
    return true;
};

// Nesting depth of three
var isRGBA = function (color) {
    if (color != 'red' && color != 'blue' && color != 'green' && color != 'alpha') {
        return false;
    }
    return true;
};
```

It may seem incorrect that the second implementation of isRGBA has the same nesting depth as the first version; after all, there is only a single if statement. However, the use of logical operators (&&) are used to nest conditional logic, so they must be mentally unwound by the reader. A function with a total nesting depth of four or more should be rethought.

Cyclomatic Complexity

Cyclomatic complexity has a wonderfully intricate-sounding name. I feel smarter every time I say it out loud. Try it for yourself; you will see what I mean. Fortunately, the concept behind the measure is easier to understand than the name suggests. Cyclomatic complexity was invented by Thomas McCabe (McCabe, 1976) as a means of discovering complexity within a function. He asserted that a function's complexity grows proportionality to the number of control flow decisions that occur within its body.

This measure derives a complexity score in one of two ways:

- It can count all the decision points within a function and then increment it by one.

- It can consider the function as a control flow graph[7] (G) and subtract the number of edges (e) from the total number vertices (n) and connected squared components (p); for example:

```
v(G) = e - n + 2p
```

Basic Example

To better understand this measure, let's see it in action. In the following example, I wrote a hypothetical page router that could benefit from some refactoring. In an effort to aid clarity, I have incremented the complexity score at every decision point in the function. Additionally, the score starts at one rather than adding one at the end.

```
var route;

// score = 1
route = function() {

  // score = 2
  if (request && request.controller) {
    switch (true) {

      // score = 3
      case request.controller === "home":

      // score = 4
      if (request.action) {

        // score = 5
        if (request.action === "search") {
          return goTo("/#home/search");
```

---

[7]http://en.wikipedia.org/wiki/Control_flow_graph

```
      // score = 6
      } else if (request.action === "tour") {
        return goTo("/#home/tour");
      } else {
        return goTo("/#home/index");
      }
    }
    break;

    // score = 7
    case request.controller === "users":

      // score = 8
      if (request.action && request.action === "show") {
        return goTo("/#users/show" + request.id);
      } else {
        return goTo("/#users/index");
      }
    }
  } else {
    return goTo("/#error/404");
  }
};
```

This function has a complexity score of 8, which McCabe would consider highly complex. Ideally, McCabe believed the function should score 4 or less. A score of 8 suggests that this function is doing too much. A cyclomatic score can tell you more than the fact that a function needs pruning; McCabe suggested that there be one test written for each cyclomatic point. Doing so would ensure that all the possible decision paths would be covered. Because lower scores are better, any function with a score of 10 or higher increases the likelihood that bugs have nestled into the function somewhere.

Limitations

One blind spot in the cyclomatic measure is that it focuses exclusively on control flow as the only source of complexity within a function. Any programmer who has spent even a trivial amount of time reading code knows that complexity comes from more than just control flow. For example, these two expressions would receive the same cyclomatic score, even though one is obviously harder to understand:

```
// Cyclomatic score: 2
if(true){
  console.log('true');
}
```

```
// Cyclomatic score: 2
if([+[]]+[] == +false){
    console.log('surprise also true!');
}
```

Additionally, by using McCabe's reasoning a single monolithic program, no matter how long, would always be considered less complex than a program with a single if statement. This just does not square well with reality for developers. That is not to say that this metric has no value; it works very well as a canary in the code mine, acting as an early warning about potential problems that might be lurking inside the function. It is worth considering another metric that uses more than just control flow to measure complexity. For that, you need to discover NPATH.

NPATH Complexity

Brian Nejmeh created the NPATH complexity measure to analyze code quality at the function or unit level. Nejmeh felt that the biggest gains in software quality are achieved at the unit level because they can be isolated from the rest of the source and therefore offer an effective means to objectively measure complexity. According to Nejmeh:

> *NPATH, which counts the acyclic execution paths through a function, is an objective measure of software complexity related to the ease with which software can be comprehensively tested. (Nejmeh, 1988)*

Counting acyclic execution paths is an obtuse way of saying that this metric totals all the various ways a function can execute. NPATH uses this path count to derive a final complexity score for the function. This is similar to the way McCabe's cyclomatic complexity measure works. The difference between the two is where cyclomatic complexity counts control flow decisions, NPATH counts all possible paths. Nejmeh saw NPATH's acyclic counting as an improvement to McCabe's approach. Specifically, Nejmeh felt McCabe's metric failed to measure the full complexity of a function for the following reasons:

- The cyclomatic complexity number does not properly account for the different number of acyclic paths through a linear function as opposed to an exponential one.

- It treats all control flow mechanisms the same way. However, Nejmeh argues that some structures are inherently harder to understand and use properly.

- McCabe's approach does not account for the level of nesting within a function. For example, three sequential if statements receive the same score as three nested if statements. However, Nejmeh argues that a programmer will have a harder time understanding the latter and thus should be considered more complex.

Basic Example

To get a better understanding of how the NPATH measure scores a JavaScript function, consider the following example. As mentioned earlier, NPATH scores the various control flow mechanisms differently. To aid the reader, I added the scoring instructions as comments above each control flow statement.

```javascript
var equalize;
equalize = function(a, b) {

  // NP[(if)] = NP[(if-range)] + NP[(else-range)] + NP[(expr)]
  //               1               + 1               + 0
  // NPATH Score = 2
  if (a < b) {

    // NP[while] = NP[(while-range)] + NP[(expr)] + 1
    //                 1                 + 0         + 1
    // NPATH Score = 2
    while (a <= b) {
      a++;
      console.log("a: " + a + " b: " + b);
    }
  } else {
```

```
  // NP[while] = NP[(while-range)] + NP[(expr)] + 1
  //             1                  + 0          + 1
  // NPATH Score = 2
  while (b <= a) {
    b++;
    console.log("a: " + a + " b: " + b);
  }
}
console.log("now everyone is equal");
};

// Total NPATH Score: 2 * 2 * 2 = 8
equalize(10, 9);
```

▪ **Note**   All the NPATH expression calculations NP[(expr)] received a score of 0. NPATH determines the expression score by counting the number of logical operators (&& , | |). This is because these operators can have complex branching effects on the number of possible control flow paths.

Limitations

As I discussed earlier, quantifying complexity benefits the programmer, not the runtime engine. Therefore these metrics are at a fundamental level based around the creator's own personal definition of complexity. In the case of NPATH, Nejmeh argues that some control flow statements are inherently easier to understand than others. For example, you will receive a lower NPATH score for using a switch statement with two case labels over a pair of sequential if statements. Although the pair of if statements may require more lines of code, I don't believe they are intrinsically harder to understand. This is why it is essential to not blindly apply complexity metrics, but to take time to understand their world view. For another opinionated view on complexity, let's consider the Halstead metrics.

Halstead Metrics

In the late '70s, computer programs were written as single files that, over time, became harder to maintain and enhance due to their monolithic structure. In an effort to improve the quality of these programs, Maurice Halstead developed a series of quantitative measures to determine the complexity of a program's source (Halstead, 1977). The *Halstead metrics*, as they would come to be known, are "among the earliest software metrics, [and] they are a strong indicator of complexity."[8]

Halstead side-stepped the common argument that measuring quality and complexity could be performed *only* by domain experts with intimate knowledge of both the goals of the program and the language. Instead, Halstead's argument is that "software should reflect the implementation or expression of algorithms in different languages, but be independent of their execution on a specific platform. These metrics are therefore computed statically from the code."[9] To measure complexity, Halstead's metrics track how the operators and operands that are used in service of a given algorithm.

Nearly 40 years since their introduction, developers have implemented Halstead's metrics into many different languages, including JavaScript. Although these measures and their underlying assumptions about human cognition are not without their detractors, it is still informative to consider each metric individually and how they derive scores for JavaScript code. By understanding how these metrics work, you expand your own mental framework for evaluating code and, at the very least, have a better grasp on how and why a unit of JavaScript is scored using these metrics.

---

[8]http://www.verifysoft.com/en_halstead_metrics.html
[9]http://en.wikipedia.org/wiki/Halstead_complexity_measures

Inputs

Halstead's metrics tally a function's use of operators and operands as inputs for their various measures. However, before you can collect these inputs, you have to consider what Halstead means by operands and operators in JavaScript.

Operands in JavaScript are the parts of a statement that contain the object or expression that work is to be performed on. In contrast, JavaScript has many forms of operators[10] that perform the work on operands. Here is a basic example:

```
var x = 5 + 4;
```

To clearly see the operators and operands in detail, you can use the Esprima JavaScript parser[11] to extract the statement into a syntax tree:

```
// Syntax tree of: var x = 5 + 4;
{
    "type": "Program",
    "body": [
        {
            "type": "VariableDeclaration",
            "declarations": [
                {
                    "type": "VariableDeclarator",
                    "id": {
                        "type": "Identifier",
                        "name": "x"
                    },
                    "init": {
                        "type": "BinaryExpression",
                        "operator": "+",
                        "left": {
                            "type": "Literal",
                            "value": 5,
                            "raw": "5"
                        },
                        "right": {
                            "type": "Literal",
                            "value": 4,
                            "raw": "4"
                        }
                    }
                }
            ],
            "kind": "var"
        }
    ]
}
```

---

[10]https://developer.mozilla.org/en-US/docs/Web/JavaScript/Reference/Operators
[11]http://esprima.org/demo/parse.html

With this syntax tree, you can count the unique operands (3) and operators (2). For the purposes of this chapter, I use this simple statement as the basis for the calculations used in the Halstead metrics. Now with a working definition of operands and operators in JavaScript, you can derive inputs for the Halstead metrics in the following way:

- **n1** = the number of unique operators

- **n2** = the number of unique operands

- **N1** = the number of total operators

- **N2** = the number of total operands

Using the operators and operands counts from the syntax tree, you get the following values:

```
n1 = 2
n2 = 3
N1 = 2
N2 = 3
```

With values for these inputs, you can now feed them into the various metrics to calculate the score. One fact that makes the Halstead metrics so flexible is that their quantitative nature means they work well applied to an entire source file or a single function. In fact, running the Halstead metrics at various resolutions over the same program can give you interesting results to mull over. For the purposes of this section, though, I will be explaining these metrics as if you were going to apply them at the function level.

Program Length (N)

The program length is calculated by adding the total number of operands and operators together (N1 + N2). A large number indicates that the function may benefit from being broken into smaller components. You can express program length in this way:

```
var N = N1 + N2;
```

Vocabulary Size (n)

The vocabulary size is derived by adding the unique operators and operands together (n1 + n2). Just as with the program length metric, a higher number is an indicator that the function may be doing too much. You can represent vocabulary size with the following expression:

```
var n = n1 + n2;
```

Program Volume (V)

If your brain were a glass jar, a program's volume describes how much of the container it occupies. It describes the amount of code the reader must mentally parse in order to understand the function completely. The program volume considers the total number or operations performed against operands within a function. As a result, a function will receive the same score regardless of whether it has been minified or not. This cannot be said about other complexity metrics with factor in source lines of code (SLOC) as part of their calculations. The program volume is calculated by multiplying the program length (N) against a base 2 logarithm of the vocabulary size (n). You can write in JavaScript this way:

```
// => 11.60964047443681
var V = N * (Math.log(n) / Math.log(2));
```

Volume is an evocative name for this measure because it can take on multiple meanings. Previously, I talked about volume as a mass that displaces other mental resources, but you can also think of it as a signal to noise metric. Just as in the real world, information is optimally transmitted when the volume is set within a certain range. Imagine that you are listening to a radio; when the volume dial is set too low, you must strain to hear it. However, turning the knob to 11 will make the output too loud and comprehension will suffer.

Program Level (L)

The program level defines the relative sophistication of an approach. It uses a potential volume (V1) divided by the actual volume (V) to arrive at a perceived level of competence. The potential volume of a function is defined as if it were written in its most ideal implementation. Program level can be expressed as follows:

```
var L = (V1 * V);
```

Therefore, the closer the implementation is to one, the more desirable the approach is.

■ **Note**   Potential volume is different for each language. Higher-level languages score much better than lower-level languages because higher-level languages abstract complications away from the program source.

Difficulty Level (D)

The difficulty level measures the likelihood that a reader will misunderstand the source code. Difficulty level is calculated by multiplying half the unique operators by the total number of operands, which have been divided by the number of unique operands. In JavaScript, it would be written like this:

```
var D = (n1 / 2) * (N2 / n2);
```

This can be understood intuitively if you consider that as a program's volume increases, so too does the difficulty of understanding it. As operands and operators are reused, they ratchet up the likelihood that an error will be introduced across many control flow pathways.

Programming Effort (E)

This measure estimates the likely effort a competent programmer will have in understanding, using, and improving a function based on its volume and difficulty scores. Therefore, programming effort can be represented as follows:

```
var E = V * D;
```

Not surprisingly, as with volume and difficulty, a lower effort score is desired.

Time to Implement (T)

This measure estimates the time it takes a competent programmer to implement a given function. Halstead derived this metric by dividing effort (E) by a Stroud number.[12] The Stroud number is the quantity of rudimentary (binary) decisions that a person can make per second. Because the Stroud number is not derived from the program source, it can be calibrated over time by comparing the expected and actual results. The time to implement can be expressed like this:

```
var T = E / 18;
```

---

[12]http://www.eetimes.com/author.asp?section_id=36&doc_id=1265859

■ **Note** Valid Stroud numbers can range from 5 to 25, where 25 is the maximum number of simple decisions a person can make per unit of measurement. Halstead determined that the number 18 worked well as a surrogate for a competent programmer's performance.

Number of Bugs (B)

This metric estimates the number of software defects already in a given program. As you might expect, the number of bugs correlates strongly to its complexity (volume), but is mitigated through a programmer's own skill level (E1). Halstead found in his own research that a sufficient value for E1 can be found in the range of 3000 to 3200. Bugs can be estimated using the following expression:

```
var B = V/E1;
```

Limitations

Although Halstead metrics can be informative, some have questioned how reliable and ostensibly useful they are. Some like Lou Marco have criticized the vagueness of the scoring system and the uncertainty of how it should be applied. Marco points out that Halstead did not provide definitive direction on this matter:

> *Halstead stated that the lower the program level, the more complex the program. Unfortunately, he went no further. Is a program with level .100 complex? How about one with level .005? All you can do is compare versions of the same program and compare their program levels. Recall that the McCabe metric gives an upper limit of 10 for complexity.*

> *The computation of the Halstead metrics for the bubble sort suggest that the bubble sort, as implemented, is very complex. The problem is that the computation for the potential volume mandates the number of input and output parameters. For the bubble sort, only the array to be sorted is needed. The low number for the potential volume skews the program and language levels. Most programmers would agree that this algorithm is not complex. (Marco, 1997)*

Tooling

A primary goal of objective quality analysis is to create a series of programmatic measures, which can score complexity on-demand using a consistent and repeatable process. The procedural nature of these metrics means that they are prime candidates for inclusion in programmatic tools. Not surprisingly, there are several projects specifically designed to do just that. This section compares and contrasts two complexity analysis programs for JavaScript.

Complexity Report

Phil Booth's complexity-report[13] is a straightforward command-line tool that analyzes any JavaScript file and then generates a complexity report from it. Complexity is determined from the following metrics:

- Lines of code
- Arguments per function
- Cyclomatic complexity

---

[13]https://github.com/philbooth/complexityReport.js

- Halstead metrics
- Maintainability index

Because complexity-report is a command-line utility, deploy engineers can add it to their continuous integration workflow with little fuss. It can be configured to prevent code deploys when source files fall below an arbitrary quality threshold.

Basic Example

To see how this library works, you must first install it as an npm module:

```
npm install -g complexity-report
```

To test the output of the complexity report, you will run the tool against one of its own source files, affectionately known as *eating your own dog food*. From the command line, type the following code:

```
cr ./node_modules/complexity-report/src/cli.js
```

■ **Note**   You may need to change directories to be local to the complexity report node modules.

Once complete, the library should print the results to the terminal window. The report first scores the entire file's complexity and then evaluates each function individually. Here's an excerpt from the entire report:

```
Maintainability index: 125.84886810899188
Aggregate cyclomatic complexity: 32
Mean parameter count: 0.9615384615384616

Function: parseCommandLine
  Line No.: 27
  Physical SLOC: 103
  Logical SLOC: 19
  Parameter count: 0
  Cyclomatic complexity: 7
  Halstead difficulty: 11.428571428571427
  Halstead volume: 1289.3654689326472
  Halstead effort: 14735.605359230252

Function: expectFiles
  Line No.: 131
  Physical SLOC: 5
  Logical SLOC: 2
  Parameter count: 2
  Cyclomatic complexity: 2
  Halstead difficulty: 3
  Halstead volume: 30
  Halstead effort: 90

// report continues
```

The complexity report is useful because it not only automates the manual drudgery of scoring the source but it also analyzes the source at the file and function level. This affords the developer a mechanism to evaluate how changes at one scale affect the scores at another. Although the library's reports are information rich, they do not afford less-technical stakeholders a way to get a snapshot of the overall complexity. Fortunately, there are other tools designed expressly for this purpose.

Plato

Jarrod Overson's Plato[14] is a code quality analysis dashboard that creates a collection of visually pleasing and informative reports. Plato harnesses JSHint and complexity-report to do the actual analysis and then massages their raw reports into a collection of informative charts and graphs. Like any good visualization suite, Plato understands that data can be understood differently when viewed in alternate contexts. For this reason, Plato repurposes the raw scores into a variety of information spaces, which I will discuss next. For the purposes of this section, I will be using screenshots of a Plato report on the Grunt[15] project.

Project Quality Timeline

Plato's first reporting screen is a project quality timeline (see Figure 9-1). It offers a mile-high view of the project's changes in overall quality.

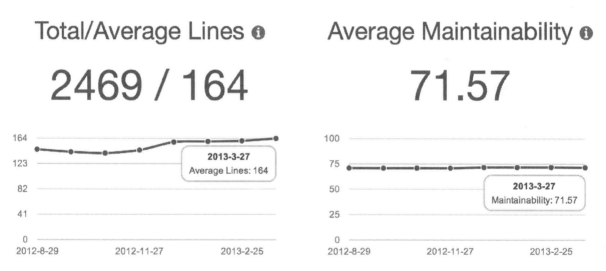

Figure 9-1. *Plato's project quality timeline charts*

Unlike other quality reports, which give you merely a snapshot at any given time, Plato's summary view, charts the project's changes in quality over time. This is extremely important because it allows the developer or manager to understand how the quality is trending.

---

[14]https://github.com/es-analysis/plato
[15]http://gruntjs.com/

Project Metric View

Below the program summary, Plato displays a collection of bar charts shown in Figure 9-2. These charts graph the various metric scores for common tests: "maintainability" (shown), "lines of code", "estimated errors", and "lint errors". Using this view, it is possible for a user to visually evaluate the files as a whole before choosing one to inspect in detail.

Maintainability ⓘ

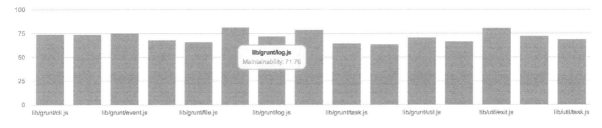

Figure 9-2. *Plato's project maintainability chart*

File Quality Overview

The last overview chart organizes the various metric scores per file as seen in Figure 9-3. The metric view allows you to mentally rank a file's performance relative to its peers; the file quality view gives you a holistic understanding of which files are the most problematic across all metrics.

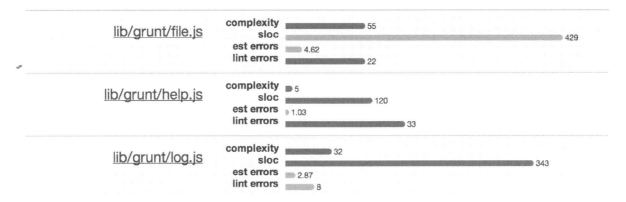

Figure 9-3. *Plato's file quality overview charts*

The point of Plato's summary view is to quickly identify global areas of concern within the codebase. Then you can drill down to inspect an arbitrary file. The file view uses the same raw data provided by the data sources, but instead scopes them to be meaningful at the file level, which I'll explain next.

File Quality Timeline

The file quality timeline charts the change of quality for a given file over time, as shown in Figure 9-4. They are very similar to the project timeline charts. Overson has made the conscious decision to chart only the maintainability and LOC metrics as timelines. He represents the difficulty and estimate errors metrics as single values. However, it would be more informative for these to be time series as well.

Figure 9-4. *Plato's file quality timeline charts*

Function Quality

Once Plato has established the global file quality, the remainder of the file level reporting is dedicated to function level analysis. Plato represents all the functions of a file as a pair of donut charts (see Figure 9-5). The slices and coloring represent the different scores per function. The choice of a donut chart is wise because a file can have a wide variation in its total number of functions. However, in terms of information density, these charts are the least successful of the bunch.

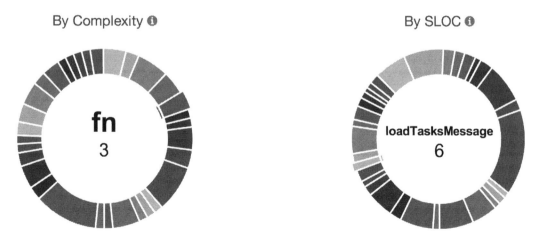

Figure 9-5. *Plato's function quality charts*

When a user selects one donut slice, it would be informative for the corresponding slice in the remaining donut to also become selected. Allowing for multiple selection would allow for the relationship between complexity and LOC to be made clear. However, two charts are not even needed. Both metrics could be easily represented in a single donut chart in which LOC controls the size of the slice and complexity controls the color. More problematic is the choice to make the chart monochromatic. Unless you knew, for instance, that a large complexity score was undesirable, you would be hard pressed to arrive at that conclusion through Plato's color choice alone. A better approach would have been to reintroduce the red, orange, blue color coding used in the overview charts. Those colors clearly delineate which score is desirable and which is not. More importantly, Plato has already trained its users to understand these color semantics, so it is wasteful not to make use of them again.

Source View

Plato's final view is not a graph at all, but rather an annotated view of the program source (see Figure 9-6). The viewer can either manually scroll to this section or click any of the donut slices in the function quality charts. Clicking a slice instantly brings them directly to the location in the source where the function appears. By clicking the name of the function, the viewer can see the various scores it received. Visually locating the scores into the source affords the viewer an opportunity to consider the scores in the context of the larger source body.

```
    21 var task = module.exports = Object.create(parent);
       Column: 12 "'module' is not defined."
    22
    23 // A temporary registry of tasks and metadata.
    24 var registry = {tasks: [], untasks: [], meta: {}};

  function task.registerTask          fied tasks message.

  Complexity : 1                      ls of recursion when loading tasks in collections.
  Length : 53                          = 0;
  Difficulty : 4.58                   the number of log.error() calls.
  Est # bugs : 0.08

    35 // Override built-in registerTask.
    36 task.registerTask = function(name) {
    37    // Add task to registry.
    38    registry.tasks.push(name);
    39    // Register task.
    40    parent.registerTask.apply(task, arguments);
    41    // This task, now that it's been registered.
    42    var thisTask = task._tasks[name];
    43    // Metadata about the current task.
    44    thisTask.meta = grunt.util._.clone(registry.meta);
    45    // Override task function.
    46    var fn = thisTask.fn;
    47    thisTask.fn = function(arg) {
    48       // Initialize the errorcount for this task.
```

Figure 9-6. *Plato's source view screen*

Plato is a fabulous tool for exploring the quality metrics of a particular codebase. It does what all good visualizations do, which is to allow the viewer to come to a deeper understanding of the data. Plato achieves this by allowing the viewer to consider the same scores at various scales and in numerous contexts. It is especially useful for nontechnical people who still have something at stake when it comes to the quality of a codebase. For this audience, it offers a way to start an informed conversation with the developers about quality, without needing to first understand the program's implementation.

Summary

This chapter considered the need and reasoning for code quality within JavaScript. A program's quality often affects a programmer's ability to maintain, enhance, or even fully understand its source. Poor quality code is often described as a form of technical debt that robs the project of time and resources that are better spent elsewhere. However, programming is a discipline that often straddles the line between art and science, making a definition of quality more complicated. Moreover, quality is simultaneously a subjective and objective measurement.

An argument can be made that quality is influenced by a person's contemporary culture, and their personal experiences. This form describes quality as having an "inner excellence" that must be identified by a person with an experience of such things. This can explain why certain movements within fields such as fine art experience an ebb and flow as the notion of quality changes. Subjective quality is often present in descriptions of artisanal programming (e.g., software craftsmen).

In contrast, objective quality analysis believes that quality can be distilled into a series of repeatable steps. These steps can be monitored by quality metrics, which afford the programmers insight into how they can improve their code. These metrics largely revolve around static analysis of the code, which is the ability to study code without running it first. This chapter examined three uses of static analysis:

- Check for syntactical correctness

- Identify areas in which the programmer deviates from established best practices

- Find code that others would find hard to understand

Much of this chapter was dedicated to the efforts by others to create algorithmic measures for scoring complex code. In programming, complexity is the measurement of the mental labor a developer must endure to completely understand a unit of code. However, many of these measures, although informative, are not without their own blind spots. Some measures, like Halstead's metrics, make use of questionable assumptions about the physiology of human cognition. Others, like NPATH, ascribe extra complexity based on certain flow structures being inherently harder to understand than others. To accommodate some of these deficiencies, it is best to use complexity measures in concert with one another and only if they mesh with your own world view of complexity.

The remainder of this chapter was dedicated to a variety of off-the-shelf tools that do the heavy lifting of quality analysis for you. Using these tools as part of a continuous integration workflow ensures that when you release code into the wild, it will have the best chance of being understood and maintained in the future.

CHAPTER 10

■ ■ ■

Improving Testability

For every complex problem there is a solution that is simple, neat, and wrong.

—H. L. Mencken

It may be impossible to completely cover JavaScript testing in a book, let alone a single chapter. When done correctly, testing should be a mentally engrossing challenge, one that offers a compelling mix of creative and technical hurdles to overcome. Many of the brightest minds in computer science have applied themselves toward the creation of tools, methodologies, and patterns that enable testers to improve the quality and reliability of the programs under their care. Therefore, leaving testing out of this book would be at the very least a disservice to the reader and might potentially minimize the importance of testing JavaScript as a whole.

Given the fact that testing is a book-sized topic, I distilled the scope of this chapter down to the subject of improving the testability of JavaScript. Through my research and personal experience as a developer, I have identified several factors that commonly prevent developers from successfully testing their code. Often failure is due to a mix of biases in how code is written and then evaluated, which are compounded when the wrong testing goals are applied. This chapter will identify the various biases and blind spots developers unwittingly fall prey to as they test their code. The remainder of the chapter will focus on tools and processes that help mitigate these issues and improve the quality of your code by refocusing your tests.

Why Testing Fails to Test

JavaScript testing fails when the test suite passes. The goal of testing is not to write tests, but to find bugs by making programs fail. I will explore this assertion in finer detail later, but for now I wanted to posit that thought into your mind. Knowing how to write tests involves more than the technical ability to do so. To test a program correctly, you must have the correct psychological mindset, and a clear definition of testing goals that are hardly ever discussed in technical material. Though, as Glenford Myers argues in his book *The Art of Software Testing*, "[A]dopting the appropriate frame of mind toward testing appears to contribute more toward successful testing than do purely technological considerations" (Myers, 1979).

Occasionally, I meet developers who postpone tests until they are done with their programs. They are not saving the best for last, as if writing tests were the dessert at the end of a meal. Instead, they are delaying what they see as an unfortunate drudgery, required merely to find the occasional obtuse error in their code. If you are a curious and creative programmer, and writing tests is not the post-meal dessert, you are most likely doing it wrong. However, in the interest of full-disclosure my feelings about JavaScript testing have *evolved* to this point of view. I spent much of the last decade trying to love testing JavaScript.

In 2005, I joined my first Agile Development team. We practiced Test-Driven Development (TDD) and pair programming. At the time, we were writing mostly Ruby web applications, which had a well-developed testing ecosystem. TDD was like any new tool; once I knew how to use it, I wanted to try it on everything. However, as I moved away from server-level Ruby code and into the JavaScript that controlled the views, my tests became nearly nonexistent. Publically, I continued to enthusiastically pump my fists in the air when talking about the importance of TDD and JavaScript testing, but privately, I was writing virtually no tests.

I remember being called out over my anemic test coverage by one of the other senior developers. In my defense, I claimed that JavaScript testing was a kind of Gordian knot, knitted together by problems unique to the language. These implicit difficulties, I argued, would intractably snag any developer's attempts to accurately test a program. These complications made testing JavaScript a time-intensive process with little opportunity to pay off. To illustrate my point, I enumerated the threads in the testability knot.

- The JavaScript community does not have the same quality of tooling needed to test code as other languages. Without quality tools, it is impractical, if not impossible, to write tests.

- JavaScript is often inextricably linked to the user interface and used to produce visual effects that must be experienced and evaluated by a human. The need for manual evaluation prevents JavaScript from being able to be programmatically tested.

- There is no way to step through a running test on the fly as you can by using command-line debuggers found in other languages. Without this capability, debugging JavaScript is a nightmare.

- The ever changing variety of host environments (browsers) make testing impractical because developers have to repeatedly retest the same program logic for each host environment.

In 2005, I was not alone in this *down-in-the-mouth* assessment of the realities of testing JavaScript.[1] Today, however, JavaScript has a robust and vibrant testing community, with an ever-growing list of tools and frameworks for hunting down program defects. Yet even seasoned developers still complain that JavaScript is hard to test. In a recent blog post, Rebecca Murphy asked for examples of why developers don't test their JavaScript. In the list of responses she posted,[2] you will find some version of every excuse I offered my coworker nearly a decade earlier. There is one exception, though: instead of there being too few tools for testing, now the complaint is that there are too many! In reality, the JavaScript language and testing tools are convenient scapegoats for the misuse and misunderstanding of testing by programmers. Much of this misapplication boils down to using the wrong definition of testing, which in turn sets the wrong goals and finally produces the wrong outcomes.

Testing Fallacies

This section enumerates and then corrects common misconceptions about testing. These misunderstandings often lead developers to adopt the wrong testing goals, which shape how and when they write tests. To fully understand how these decisions ultimately impact the quality of the final product, I will unpack these fallacies and explain the implications they have on testing practice.

Testing Proves that There Are No Bugs in a Program

> *Program testing can be used to show the presence of bugs, but never to show their absence!*

Edsger Wybe Dijkstra

Briefly consider Dijkstra's quote about testing before proceeding. It savages the common misconception that tests ensure that programs are error free. This is a fallacy because, as Dijkstra points out, it is unprovable. More importantly, when a goal is based around a metric that can't be quantified, that goal becomes unobtainable. Taking this train of thought to its rational end, testing under unobtainable goals means that the testing process is doomed because there

---

[1] http://bob.ippoli.to/archives/2005/06/02/javascript-sucks-volume-1/
[2] http://storify.com/rmurphey/what-s-making-it-hard-to-get-started-with-js-testi

is no logical conclusion to the task. Therefore, managers, programmers, and stakeholders are left with ambivalence toward the testing process because it will never end. This relegates testing to being a *de facto* tax on resources, which all parties will come to resent over time.

Successful Tests Are Those that Complete Without Errors

Glenford Myers wrote at length about the false sense of security that passing tests give development teams. He asserts that many developers and managers measure testing success in exactly the wrong way, pointing to test suites that find no bugs as a sign of their program's health. Myers uses a wonderful analogy to disparage that correlation:

> *Consider the analogy of a person visiting a doctor because of an overall feeling of malaise. If the doctor runs some laboratory tests that do not locate the problem, we do not call the laboratory tests "successful"; they were unsuccessful tests … the patient is still ill, and the patient now questions the doctor's ability as a diagnostician. (Myers, 1979)*

It is obvious why this particular testing myth is so deeply engrained in our industry. Writing software is often a highly personal and exhaustive endeavor. When bugs are found, it is easy to understand how programmers might feel that the error is a reflection on their own abilities. So programmers must fight this urge to take bugs personally. This sense of personal attachment to the code is why it often leads them to writing shallow conformational tests, which do more to protect fragile egos than they do to actually interrogate the program. As Boris Beizer wrote:

> *Programmers! Cast out your guilt! Spend half your time in joyous testing and debugging! Stalk bugs with care, methodology, and reason. Build traps for them. Be more artful than those devious bugs and taste the joys of guiltless programming! (Beizer, Software Testing Techniques, 1990)*

Testing Ensures that the Program Is High Quality

When managers use tests as a defensive blockade against poor quality software, they may be ensuring the opposite outcome. When tests are hurdles for programmers to overcome, they become obstacles, not assets. While it is true that tests that identify bugs present the opportunity to improve the quality of the program, there is a danger when making tests a formalized quality metric. Tests as a measure of quality are problematic for the following reasons:

- Tests as measures of quality demoralize programmers because of the inference that their source is intrinsically of low quality to start with.

- It constructs a useless dichotomy between the testing and development processes. It also may have the effect of stoking tensions in teams, which separate testers from developers.

- It suggests that tests by themselves can add quality to the code base.

- If tests are the arbiter of quality, they infer that there is an asymmetry in power between testers and developers, as if developers are supplicate to testers on behalf of their programs.

You cannot raise the quality of program simply by testing it. Again Beizer draws out the misuse of tests as a quality metric when he writes:

> *Programmers are responsible for software quality—quality in their own work, quality in the products that incorporate their work, and quality at the interfaces between components. Quality has never been and will never be tested in. The responsibility is both moral and professional. (Beizer, 1990)*

Testing Prevents Future Errors

Test cases are development artifacts of the program's execution context they were meant to test. As the program's goals evolve, the assumptions made in earlier tests may no longer be valid. In those cases, test breakage is welcomed because it illuminates where the test suite has become decoupled from the code base.

In other cases, new modifications to the program may break older tests that are still valid. In these cases, a new bug was immediately discovered through previous test coverage. Managers often use events like these as proof that tests prevent future errors. This view treats tests as a kind of programmatic immune system that defends the application against unknown bugs in the future.

The fallacy with this viewpoint is that it assumes that tests should have some predicative quality to them. This leads developers to write superfluous *what if* tests, which belabor the purpose of testing.

Testing Proves that the Program Works as Designed

Many development methodologies such as TDD use tests as a means of verifying that the program works as designed. Practitioners first write tests that explain the intended functionality of the method. In TDD, test suites are always running, so the new test will initially fail because the method it validates does not yet exist. One of the pillars of TDD is to write just enough code to make the test pass. Doing so ensures that extra and unwanted functionality is not added to the program as so-called *free functionality*. Additionally, tightly coupling tests as specifications to the source limits the amount of code cruft that would get introduced if the developer were just trying to infer what was needed by the feature.

The blind spot in TDD is that it can lead some developers to think narrowly about their tests and *only* as a form of *de facto* documentation that proves the function does what it should. The unintended consequence of the test-as-specification approach is that tests will be written to ensure that the approach is validated. After all, specifications should be expressive and succinct, so the tests will likely affirm an approach rather than find the limitations. Tests written with the purpose of proving functionality ignore the fact that a function can work and yet still contain bugs. Shallow affirmative tests that do not find any errors are ultimately a waste of time and effort.

For methodologies such as TDD to work correctly, they rely on a programmer who can write code while simultaneously trying to break it. That is to say, the act of designing the test is as important as writing the code that makes it pass. To quote Boris Biezer again:

> More than the act of testing, the act of designing tests is one of the best bug preventers known. The thinking that must be done to create a useful test can discover and eliminate bugs before they are coded—indeed, test-design thinking can discover and eliminate bugs at every stage in the creation of software, from conception to specification, to design, coding and the rest. (Beizer, 1990)

Adequately designing tests is not always possible for a single person to do. Confirmation biases—which I will explain in the next section—often prevent developers from thinking about tests deeply. Many methodologies mitigate this bias by making developers write code in tandem. While one programmer tries to prove an approach, the other will try to find exceptions. This pair programmer works only if the participants are relatively equal in skill and rank; otherwise, the lower of the two will tend to defer to the lead.

Confirmation Bias

A *confirmation bias* describes the likelihood that a person will favor information that supports their worldview and disregard evidence to the contrary. Politicians and religious zealots are two populations famous for their ability to live in a bubble, which is in effect the manifestation of their confirmation bias. Not surprisingly, programmers who spend much of their time inside their own heads can also suffer from confirmation bias, though its expression can be subtler.

This section explains the various factors of the software development process that contribute to the confirmation bias in programming. These causes include the inherent cognitive dissonance in developers, often unrecognized biases in testing frameworks, and the tendency for testers to look in the wrong place for bugs.

Selective Seeing

As I have completed this book, I have spent hours writing and rewriting passages, making every attempt to disarm grammatical and spelling land mines that I laid earlier. Before submitting each chapter to my editor, I first reread the chapter to myself silently and then again out loud. Yet, without fail, when the chapter is returned, it is chockablock full of corrections. I wager that many of you have had a similar experience because this tendency to selectively see is quite common in the human condition.

Like writing a book, writing software should be a personal expression of the author's craft. As such, programmers, like other craftsmen, tend to see themselves reflected in their work product. Programmers are inclined to be optimistic about their own abilities and by extension the software they write. This intimacy between programmers and their work can prevent them from evaluating it honestly. They tend to selectively see their functions from the frame of reference in which they were intended to run, not as they were actually implemented.

The Curse of Knowledge

The *curse of knowledge* is sometimes described as the inability to *unring a bell*. The metaphor offers a pleasing visual of sound waves emanating outward in space forever. It is clear how the sound wave once rippling through the air cannot be sucked back into the mouth of the bell. In programming, the curse of knowledge is the inability of programmers to think about their software from a vantage point of a less-informed user.

You might think that an intimate understanding of a program would afford the developer the ability to write a robust test around it. However, in reality these tests are less likely to find hidden edge cases within the function because programmers cannot get enough critical distance from their approach. The curse of knowledge contributes to defect density, which is the likelihood for bugs to huddle together. These bugs are shielded from the programmer's view by a misplaced assumption about how the application works.

If at First You Succeed

Imagine that you are a developer tasked to make a trivial change to an existing function in an application with plenty of test coverage. After making your change and running tests, you are comforted by the fact that they all pass. It is understandable that you feel the code is still healthy, especially when a massive test suite reaffirms this belief. However, this is called the *absence of errors fallacy*, which states that just because your tests didn't find any bugs doesn't mean there are none to be found. In order for you to be sure your change was actually safe, you must cross-reference your change with the intent of the tests. Are the tests as written meant to cover your change, or do they continue to pass for unrelated reasons? The motto I follow when fighting this bias is this: *if at first you succeed, try, try again.*

The Pesticide Paradox

Boris Beizer's first law of software testing states the following:

> *"Every method you use to prevent or find bugs leaves a residue of subtler bugs against which those methods are ineffective." (Beizer, 1990)*

The *pesticide paradox* explains the fallacy that past tests will catch future errors. In actuality, the bugs that these tests were meant to catch have already been caught. This is not to say that these tests do not have some value as regression tests, which ensure that these known errors are not reintroduced. However, you should not expect to find new bugs with tests looking in old places.

Defect Clusters

In the real world, bugs are not distributed evenly across a landscape. They instead huddle together in corners, under refrigerators, and in other hard-to-reach places. Bugs that venture out into space are easily reached by shoes and get squashed. In software, this is known as the *Pareto principle*, which states that almost 80 percent of your effects come from 20 percent of your causes.[3] Put simply, bugs are where other bugs are.

Bug clusters often occur as a result of developers falling prey to their own curse of knowledge. However, once the programmer identifies this bias, clusters can guide the programmer where to apply future efforts. For example, if the same number of tests found six bugs in one module and only one in another, you are likely to find more future bugs in the former than the later. This is because bug clusters can reveal crucial misconceptions to the programmer about their program.

Framework Bias

Test automation frameworks are software tools to programmatically run test cases in order to catch software defects. These frameworks are used to lower the cost of maintenance by making the running of tests easier to perform. Often these frameworks become a link in the development workflow chain, which allows tests to run in a context that maximizes their effectiveness. Testing frameworks are an essential component of modern development life and should be embraced where possible.

However, testing frameworks are not created in a vacuum; they are influenced by the set of assumptions and philosophies about testing that the creator holds true. Like any process that is contextualized through a metaphor, testing frameworks have the potential to make one task easier while making another more difficult. This is because metaphors allow you to port the understanding of one subject into the service of understanding something unfamiliar. Yet the affordances provided by the metaphor do not always completely overlap with the subject it is meant to explain.

For example, browser vendors initially used the metaphor of a book to explain a network of interconnected servers, which would have been hard for a nontechnical person to conceptualize. Being told the browser was a tool for reading connected books allowed new users leverage their existing knowledge of how books worked. It became natural to *read* web *pages* and place *bookmarks* in the browser. Unfortunately, the book metaphor obscured many of the more interesting potentials for accessing the web, such as thinking about data not as a series of distinct pages, but rather as a continually flowing stream of information that the user captures into pools to use and then releases.

Framework biases occur when programmers limit the scope of their tests to the framework's capabilities. For example, many applications rely on data provided by remote APIs. However, making live calls to the API during the testing process is unacceptable because it slows down the test runner and makes unwanted calls to the live API. Instead, many frameworks provide mechanisms to mock or stub out the API integration, thereby allowing the tests to accept canned answers relevant to the context that is being tested. If your test framework does not afford the test writers these capabilities, they must either short circuit the production code by overloading the function to make the tests work, or (worse yet) avoid testing these features all together.

Mitigating Confirmation Bias

The previous section covered in detail the various ways in which unintended biases can seep into a testing practice. Most of these biases cause the developer to overlook or ignore potential bugs they might otherwise catch. This section describes corrective actions, which help mitigate confirmation bias in testing.

---

[3] http://en.wikipedia.org/wiki/Pareto_principle#In_software

Test to Fail

Many biases are rooted in the fact that programmers see failing tests as a sign of their own ignorance rather than a vindication of their tenacity to track down defects. The goal of testing is to make programs fail. Test suites that run without raising exceptions should be viewed as a waste of resources, just as a trip to a mechanic who cannot diagnose the problem is seen as a waste of money.

Get Critical Distance

Confirmation bias occurs when developers lose the ability to be critical about the code they test. This can be particularly pronounced in developers who test their own code. Having an independent party write tests, or developing a series of conceptual prompts or procedural steps to follow that help frame the testing context can be helpful in maintaining critical distance.

Find the Edges

Testing is often about exploring the unknown, verifying a hypothesis and then using those findings to readjust your mental model of how the program works. To find the edge cases, developers need to fight against the tendency to selectively see what they think the code is doing. One way to find the edge cases of a function is to enumerate the assumptions you have about the method and then test them each individually. This systematic approach can force the developer to consider the functions in a fuller context. This approach helps mitigate the tendency to gloss over the details of a function that have become too familiar to be considered critically. A second option is to implement specific kinds of tests designed to use the function in ways the developer may not have intended. Fuzz tests—which you will examine in detail later—are a way to find the fringe of your program.

Finding a Baseline

Test suites are judged like bed comforters in their capability to cover all the important parts. A program is thought to be well-tested when all the paths through the application are covered by at least one test. Programs with sufficient test coverage are thought less likely to contain bugs, and therefore are often used as a measure of a program's quality. A developer's ability to maintain adequate test coverage is an important factor in the cumulative testing practice.

However, several tendencies in test writing can cause coverage to diminish. Tests can fall out of sync when they are not written in parallel with the application code. Tests can fall behind as a program under heavy development evolves. Moreover, it's hard to visualize at a glance whether the tests truly cover all the various paths through a program. Deriving an accurate measurement of the overall test coverage of a rapidly evolving application is a bit like trying to measure someone's height while they are running.

Fortunately, test coverage can be automatically calculated through the use of code coverage tools. These instrumentation libraries can be run in tandem with the test runner process. While the tests run, the coverage tool tracks which parts of the program's source is being invoked as the test executes.

After the test suite completes, the coverage tool can generate a report for the programmer to view. Many of the most robust coverage reports are interactive and highly visual. They allow the reader to gauge overall coverage across the entire application or drill down to a particular source file. At the file level, the report is typically annotated and color-coded to reflect aspects of the code coverage. Figure 10-1 shows a screenshot from the Istanbul coverage tool, which I will demonstrate later in the chapter. This view represents a coverage report for a single file. The darker lines represent areas of the file that were not tripped by tests.

```
84  29    excludes = typeof opts['default-excludes'] === 'undefined' || opts['default-excludes'] ?
85             [ '**/node_modules/**', '**/test/**', '**/tests/**' ] : [];
86  29    excludes.push.apply(excludes, opts.x);
87
88  29    if (enableHooks) {
89  28        reportingDir = opts.dir || path.resolve(process.cwd(), 'coverage');
90  28        mkdirp.sync(reportingDir); //ensure we fail early if we cannot do this
91  28        reportClassName = opts.report || DEFAULT_REPORT_FORMAT;
92  28        reports.push(Report.create(reportClassName, { dir: reportingDir }));
93  28   E    if (opts.print !== 'none') {
94  28            switch (opts.print) {
95                case 'detail':
96   1                reports.push(Report.create('text'));
97   1                break;
98                case 'both':
99                    reports.push(Report.create('text'));
100                   reports.push(Report.create('text-summary'));
101                   break;
102               default:
103  27                reports.push(Report.create('text-summary'));
104  27                break;
105           }
106       }
107
108  28    matcherFor({
109           root: opts.root || process.cwd(),
110           includes: [ '**/*.js' ],
111           excludes: excludes
112       },
113       function (err, matchFn) {
114  28    I    if (err) { return callback(err); }
115
116  28        var coverageVar = '$$cov_' + new Date().getTime() + '$$',
117               instrumenter = new Instrumenter({ coverageVariable: coverageVar }),
118               transformer = instrumenter.instrumentSync.bind(instrumenter),
119               hookOpts = { verbose: opts.verbose };
120
121  28    I    if (opts.yui) { //EXPERIMENTAL code: do not rely on this in anyway until the docs say it is a
122               hookOpts.postLoadHook = require('../../util/yui-load-hook').getPostLoadHook(matchFn, transfor
123
124  28    I    if (opts['self-test']) {
125               hook.unloadRequireCache(matchFn);
126           }
127  28        hook.hookRequire(matchFn, transformer, hookOpts);
128  28        process.once('exit', function () {
129   7            var file = path.resolve(reportingDir, 'coverage.json'),
```

Figure 10-1. *The Istanbul coverage tool in action*

This section will discuss several common coverage algorithms that these tools employ to measure test coverage. Once you have a baseline for understanding how code coverage calculation works, I will demonstrate how to use it on your own JavaScript applications. Finally, in keeping with the theme of this chapter, I will also discuss the unintended biases these tools might introduce.

Statement Coverage

Statement coverage is the most straightforward form of code coverage. It merely records when statements are executed. Consider the following example, in which a test is run in a context where user is undefined. In this example, the bolded statements represent the lines that would be counted using statement coverage.

```
var friendNames;

function findFriends(user) {
    var friends = [];
    if (user) {
```

```
        friends = user.getFriends().map(function (friend) {
            return friend.firstName + " " + friend.lastName;
        });
    } else {
        friends = ["You are unpopular!"];
    }
    return friends;
}
friendNames = findFriends();
```

Function Coverage

Another rudimentary form of code coverage is *function coverage*, which determines whether any test called a function at least once. Function coverage does not track how a test may fiddle with the function's innards; it simply cares if the function was invoked. There is a derivation of this metric called function call coverage, which calculates the total percentage of functions that the tests invoked. To reach a score of 100 percent using function call coverage, each function must be called at least once. Continuing with the previous example, you can see what parts of the code would be covered with function coverage:

```
var friendNames;

function findFriends(user) {
    var friends = [];
    if (user) {
        friends = user.getFriends().map(function (friend) {
            return friend.firstName + " " + friend.lastName;
        });
    } else {
        friends = ["You are unpopular!"];
    }
    return friends;
}
friendNames = findFriends();
```

Branch Coverage

To have sufficient *branch coverage*, every path through a function must be covered in a test. In my code example, only the else branch would be covered. This would mean that at least one other test should be added to get complete branch coverage for this function. Branch coverage is very useful for highlighting edge cases that might otherwise go untested. The following code demonstrates what the branch coverage metric would count:

```
var friendNames;

function findFriends(user) {
    var friends = [];
    if (user) {
        friends = user.getFriends().map(function (friend) {
            return friend.firstName + " " + friend.lastName;
        });
    } else {
```

```
        friends = ["You are unpopular!"];
    }
    return friends;
}
friendNames = findFriends();
```

Istanbul

Using the coverage metrics from the previous section, it is apparent how they can be combined to create an aggregate coverage score for a program. The marshalling of these metrics during the test running process is the job of the code coverage tool. In this section, I will introduce *Istanbul*,[4] which is a coverage tool created by Krishnan Anantheswaran. Istanbul is written in JavaScript for JavaScript. As such, unlike many other coverage tools, Istanbul is designed to run everywhere JavaScript can and therefore supports both browser-based execution and command-line instrumentation. According to the documentation Istanbul is designed with the following use cases in mind:

- To afford transparent coverage of nodejs unit tests

- To accommodate the use of the npm test script to allow for conditional coverage

- To allow the instrumentation of tests in batches, which is useful for browser tests

- To support integration with custom Node.js middleware that enables code coverage on the server side

Installing Istanbul

Istanbul requires Node.js to run, and can be installed as an npm package like this:

```
npm install -g istanbul
```

In the next section I will demonstrate Istanbul's cover command, which is only one of several useful tools provided by Istanbul.

cover

The cover command generates a coverage object and report for an arbitrary file. The coverage object is a JSON representation of not only the individual elements of the program (i.e., functions and statements) but also a branch map that describes the path of execution. Istanbul uses the coverage object as the input for the visual reports it creates. For example, you can run the findFriend program through the cover command like this:

```
istanbul cover find-friend.js
```

---

[4]http://gotwarlost.github.io/istanbul/

At this point, Istanbul will not only generate the coverage object but also print some helpful overview statistics to the terminal window:

```
================================================================================
Writing coverage object [/Users/heavysixer/Desktop/js/coverage/coverage.json]
Writing coverage reports at [/Users/heavysixer/Desktop/js/coverage]
================================================================================

============================= Coverage summary ===============================
Statements   : 77.78% ( 7/9 )
Branches     : 50% ( 1/2 )
Functions    : 50% ( 1/2 )
Lines        : 77.78% ( 7/9 )
================================================================================
```

Notice that this coverage summary squares with what you could confirm earlier—by manually stepping through the various coverage metrics. Because the user variable was undefined, the findFriends function was never executed. This untraversed path explains why you have only 50 percent coverage on both branches and functions, and why a little more than 20 percent of the code did not get run.

To visualize the test coverage even more clearly, open the generated coverage report that Istanbul created. It should be located in a coverage folder relative to the test file. First, open the index file in a browser; depending on your system, you may be able to open and view the file like this:

```
open coverage/lcov-report/index.html
```

Once opened, drill into the js folder and view the coverage report for the file in question. From this screen (see Figure 10-2), it should be very clear which lines were not executed.

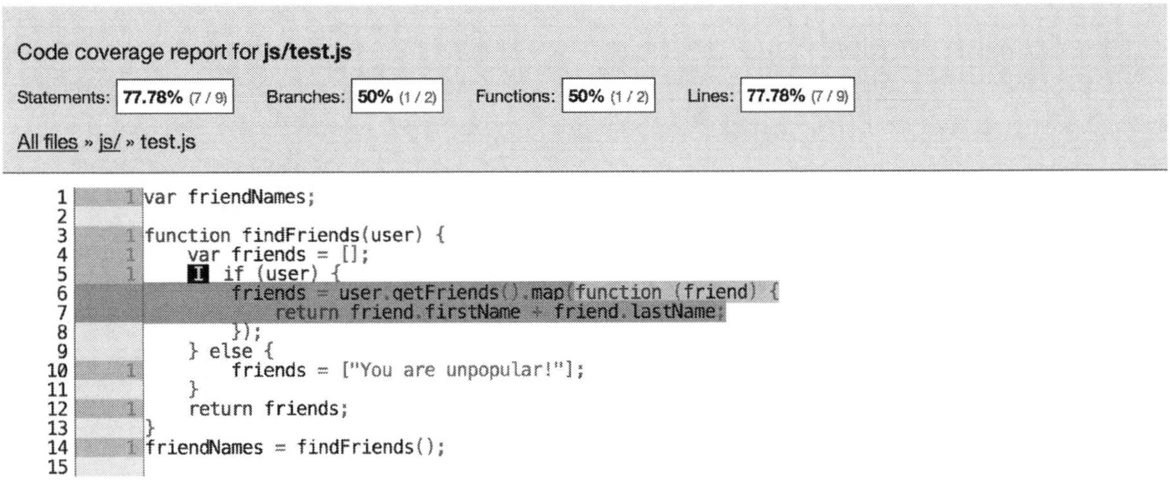

Figure 10-2. *Istanbul coverage report for a single file*

▓ **Note** The "I" surrounded by the black box in Figure 10-2 is part of the nomenclature Istanbul uses to describe the reasons for lack of coverage. In this case, *I* stands for a branch that was not taken.

Coverage Bias

Code coverage tools such as Istanbul are great for quickly and visually exploring the coverage of a program. They enable viewers to find testing deficiencies with little effort. However, coverage tools come with their own biases that you should be aware of. Executing a line of code is much different from testing a line of code. Code coverage metrics can give a false sense of security that 100 percent coverage is the same as being 100 percent tested. In order not to fall prey to this bias, the developer should use coverage tools to find the absence of test coverage, not as a way to prove it.

Bias Busting Tests

Much of a program's testability is contingent on a developer's ability to overcome the various biases that might otherwise prevent an application from being sufficiently tested. As I have discussed, these biases may include psychological barriers such as the curse of knowledge or selective seeing, which prevents the tester from thinking objectively about the tests. Alternatively, the developer might be fighting a bias implicit in another tool; for example, a testing framework that supports one kind of test while hindering another. This section offers three bias busting tests that you can use to enhance your testing approach.

Fuzz Testing

As I detailed earlier, testing bias often occurs when a developer cannot think objectively about their own code. In these cases a programmer may no longer write a test to fail the code, but instead craft the test to prove the function works as designed. In an effort to mitigate this bias, certain team structures are formed whereby a developer never tests their own code. However, this is not always possible or even desired. An alternate approach is to use a testing practice that forces the program to be used in unexpected ways.

Fuzz testing,[5] or *fuzzing*, is a software analysis technique that attempts to automatically find defects by providing the application with unanticipated, invalid, or random inputs and then evaluating its behavior. Barton Miller is credited with coining the term *fuzz*. When asked about the origin of the name, he said this[6]:

> *The original work was inspired by being logged on to a modem during a storm with lots of line noise. And the line noise was generating junk characters that seemingly were causing programs to crash. The noise suggested the term "fuzz".*

Fuzzing is especially useful for black-box testing where the goal is to discover the functional boundaries of a program. Fuzzing is also widely used by both black hat and white hat security professionals as a tool for mining a system for exploits.

The two most common forms of fuzz testing are mutation-based and generation-based. Mutation-based fuzzers understand little about the format or structure of their data. They blindly alter their data and merely record the exception as it occurs. For this reason, these fuzzers are often called (dumb fuzzers.) Generation-based fuzzers understand the semantics of their data formats and therefore create their input within those constraints. Operating within a predefined rule space generally means that their results will be more precise. However, as you would expect, it takes much more time to craft a generation-based fuzzer than one based on mutations.

The goal of a JavaScript fuzz tester is to force the host environment to execute or at least compile the fuzzed input at runtime. To achieve this goal, the fuzzer must adhere to the syntactic rules of the language. Otherwise, the interpreter will just fail to execute the code, which is not the same as finding an error. Jsfunfuzz (written by Jesse Ruderman[7]) is one of the most well-known JavaScript fuzzers. Jsfunfuzz proved to be a bit too effective in finding

---

[5]http://en.wikipedia.org/wiki/Fuzz_testing
[6]http://resources.infosecinstitute.com/fuzzing-mutation-vs-generation/
[7]http://www.squarefree.com/2007/08/02/introducing-jsfunfuzz/

exploits and is no longer publically available. In its initial fuzz testing campaign against the Firefox browser, jsfunfuzz found 280 bugs[8] in the Firefox JavaScript engine. Since then, it has located more than 1000 bugs. Think about that for a second; this testing tool found hundreds of bugs in the JavaScript interpreter whose development is managed by the creator of the language! Ruderman speculated about why jsfunfuzz could find so many bugs:

- It knows the rules of the JavaScript language, allowing it to get decent coverage of combinations of language features.

- It breaks the rules, allowing it to find errors in syntax error handling such as bug 350415 and more generally helping the fuzzer avoid having "blind spots."

- It isn't afraid to nest JavaScript constructs in fairly complicated ways, as when it found bug 353079.

- It allows state to accumulate by creating and running functions in a loop. (See bug 361346 for an example of a bug that would be hard to find otherwise.)

- It tests for correctness, not just crashes and assertions.

Since the release of jsfunfuzz, there have been other notable fuzzing tools such as LangFuzz and Crossfuzz.[9] Crossfuzz even runs directly in the browser, which makes it considerably easier to use. Many of the fuzzers not only trigger exceptions but also have the capability to transcribe the steps that produced failure into a generated test. For example, the following test[10] was generated by LangFuzz to produce an assertion failure in the Google V8 JavaScript Engine:

```
var loop_count = 5;

function innerArrayLiteral(n) {
  var a = new Array(n);
  for (var i = 0; i < n; i++) {
    a[i] = void ! delete 'object' % ~ delete 4;
  }
}

function testConstructOfSizeSize(n) {
  var str = innerArrayLiteral(n);
}
for (var i = 0; i < loop_count; i++) {
  for (var j = 1000; j < 12000; j += 1000) {
    testConstructOfSizeSize(j);
  }
}
```

---

[8]https://bugzilla.mozilla.org/show_bug.cgi?id=jsfunfuzz
[9]http://lcamtuf.blogspot.com/2011/01/announcing-crossfuzz-potential-0-day-in.html
[10]https://www.usenix.org/system/files/conference/usenixsecurity12/sec12-final73.pdf

However, although these fuzzers are incredibly powerful and effective at finding security holes and blind spots in programs, they have several drawbacks:

- Fuzzers that are mutation based can run forever. Therefore, it can be hard to choose a duration that gives you a meaningful chance at finding bugs without consuming too much time.

- Most JavaScript fuzzers are mainly directed toward the host environments such as browsers and JavaScript engines; there are limited options at directing the fuzzing toward stand-alone JavaScript programs.

- Fuzzers can find hundreds of bugs that are related through a common failure point, which can mean getting hundreds of tests with unnecessary overlap. Therefore, each defect must be considered individually and in the context of the entire collection of bugs before adding the generated test to the permanent test suite.

- Fuzzers not only find bugs in programs but also in the underlying language. Therefore, it can be difficult to distinguish between errors in your program and faults in the JavaScript interpreter.

Although fuzzing a JavaScript application can truly leave programmers gobsmacked in their ability to root out bugs, it can be hard to focus them directly on your application. However, there are "fuzzeresque" tools that can twist applications in unexpected ways and also be focused solely on the program, as you will see when I introduce JSCheck in the next section.

JSCheck

JSCheck[11] is a testing tool written by Douglas Crockford and inspired by QuickCheck.[12] In the fuzzing section, I explained that generation-based fuzzers use constraints and rule spaces to limit the type of random data they produce. JSCheck works in a similar way, but calls these constraints *specifications*. It uses specifications to verify claims about the program. For this reason, JSCheck is considered a specification-driven testing tool. JSCheck generates tests by processing claims about the program in an attempt to root out edge cases and exceptions. Just as with fuzz testing, this approach has the advantage of busting the biases a programmer holds about their program. To better understand how JSCheck works, I will take you through a basic example.

Installing JSCheck

Unfortunately, JSCheck is not available through any of your favorite package or dependency managers, so you must download the source manually from the git repo:

```
https://github.com/douglascrockford/JSCheck/archive/master.zip
```

---

[11]http://www.jscheck.org/
[12]http://en.wikipedia.org/wiki/QuickCheck

Basic Example

I will be using Node.js to run the tests, so ensure that you have it installed if you want to follow along. First, I will need a function to test. Save the following code as `flip-test.js`:

```
function flipSign(val) {
  return ~(val - 1);
}
```

The purpose of this function is take any number and flip the sign accordingly. My goal is now to test this toughly with JSCheck using Node.js. In order to include JSCheck into the test, I need to resort to some eval trickery because it is not exportable as a Node.js module. (Of course, it is not recommended for anything more than fiddling around in the example.) If you want to use JSCheck as part of an integrated testing workflow, you have to create a suitable export harness for it first. The `flip-test.js` file should now look like this:

```
eval(require('fs').readFileSync('./jscheck.js', 'utf8'));

function flipSign(val) {
  return ~(val - 1);
}
```

■ **Note**   Ensure that your path to JSCheck is correct. If you downloaded the zip file directly, `jscheck.js` may be nested inside another folder.

With JSCheck included into the test file and the `flipSign` function written, I am ready to make several claims about the functionality, which JSCheck will then validate.

Making a Claim

A *claim* is composed of three required attributes and a fourth optional one.

Name

JSCheck always expects name as the first argument. It is used by the JSCheck reporting functionality to briefly explain the context of the claim.

Predicate

All claims require a predicate argument, which specifies a function that has the capability to return a Boolean value, depending on whether the claim could be substantiated. In this case, you want to ensure that the sign was flipped, so the function could look like this:

```
function predicate(verdict, value) {
  return verdict(value === flipSign(flipSign(value)));
}
```

The predicate() method takes at least two arguments. The first parameter is always the verdict function, which is used by JSCheck to report on the result of the comparison. The verdict function is quite robust and is designed to support functions that require network transactions or asynchronous requests. The remaining arguments are values that JSCheck generates for you based on the specifiers you configure in the signature array.

Signature

The signature is an array of specifiers that describe the range of arguments, which can be supplied to the predicate function. JSCheck provides a range of specifier templates that can be used to constrain the random values. For example, JSC.integer(0,10) will generate an integer between 0 and 10. Other specifiers can be quite complex. The object specifier accepts an object as a template, which in turn leverages other specifiers:

```
JSC.object({
    left: JSC.integer(640),
    top: JSC.integer(480),
    color: JSC.one_of(['black', 'white', 'red', 'blue', 'green', 'gray'])
})
```

In the case of your program, you are expecting only a single number, so the signature array could just be this:

```
[JSC.integer(-10, 10)]
```

Classifier

The classifier is the only optional argument, and according to the JSCheck documentation, it has two main purposes:

- It can examine the arguments and return a string that classifies the case. The string is descriptive. The report can include a summary showing the number of cases belonging to each classification. It can be used to identify the classes that are trivial or problematic, or to help analyze the results.

- Because the cases are being generated randomly, some cases might not be meaningful or useful. The classifier can have a case rejected by returning false. JSCheck will attempt to generate another case to replace it. It is recommended that the classifier reject fewer than 90 percent of the cases. If you are accepting fewer than 10 percent of the potential cases, you should probably reformulate your claim.

Because your function is trivial, almost any value provided by JSCheck will be usable; therefore, you do not need a classifier for the test.

Checking a Claim

Now that I have a predicate and a suitable signature array, I am ready to wire up the JSCheck test like so:

```
eval(require('fs').readFileSync('./jscheck.js', 'utf8'));

function flipSign(val) {
  return ~ (val - 1);
}
```

```
function predicate(verdict, value) {
  return verdict(value === flipSign(flipSign(value)));
}
JSC.on_report(function(str) {
  console.log(str);
});
JSC.test("flips integers", predicate, [JSC.integer(-10, 10)]);
```

Notice that I supplied a bit of configuration to the JSC variable. Now whenever JSCheck broadcasts the on_report event, the results will be written to the console. Once configured, the script calls the test function and supplies it with the various required attributes. Save the changes to the file and then run it from the command line this way:

```
node flip-test.js
```

Once this command completes, JSCheck will output the results of the suite to the terminal window:

```
flips integers: 100 cases tested, 100 pass
```

```
Total pass 100
```

Excellent; no errors, just as I thought! However, to be sure, I will add another test that uses a number specifier in addition to the integer. This will allow me to test floating point numbers as well. The test file should now look like this:

```
eval(require('fs').readFileSync('./jscheck.js', 'utf8'));

function flipSign(val) {
  return ~ (val - 1);
}
JSC.on_report(function(str) {
  console.log(str);
});
function predicate(verdict, value) {
  return verdict(value === flipSign(flipSign(value)));
}

JSC.test("flips integers", predicate, [JSC.integer(-10, 10)]);
JSC.test("flips numbers", predicate, [JSC.number(-10,10)]);
```

Once again, I will run JSCheck against this file from the command line. However, this time I get some unexpected failures:

```
 node flip-test.js

flips integers: 100 cases tested, 100 pass

Total pass 100

flips numbers: 100 cases tested, 0 pass, 100 fail
 FAIL [1] (-4.945855345577002)
 FAIL [2] (0.6835379591211677)
 ...
 FAIL [100] (0.6536271329969168)
```

215

Looking at the `flipSign` function more closely, it becomes clear why it fails on floating point numbers. Although the bitwise NOT operator inverts the bits of the operand like I want, it also converts the result to an integer. This kind of side effect is exactly the type of bug that JSCheck is excellent at finding because it occurs outside of the mental model I had for this function. Now that I have identified the blind spot in my function, I can rewrite it this way:

```
function flipSign(val) {
  return val * -1;
}
```

Running the test again, I can see that the modification had the desired effect, and my function now works well with floats and integers:

```
node flip-test.js

flips integers: 100 cases tested, 100 pass

Total pass 100

flips numbers: 100 cases tested, 100 pass

Total pass 100
```

Automaton Testing

Many industrial manufacturers use robots as an integral part of their product testing. If you go into any IKEA store, you are likely to see one of their robots on display. Inside a giant glass case, the robot will be repeatedly and methodically sitting its simulated butt onto one of the chairs. IKEA is hoping that its consumers will draw a correlation between the robot's rigorous reseating and IKEA's own attempts to thoroughly test its products.

In the world of automated software testing, most user interactions are simulated using headless browsers such as PhantomJS or by a browser plugin such as Selenium. These tools are scripted to interact with an application much like a human would. However, they assume that the user is interacting through a computer using a mouse and a keyboard, and that interactions are composed of clicks and key presses. This is an outdated assumption in today's world, in which a program can be viewed on hundreds of different devices, which vary in their screen size, input capabilities, and responsiveness. Additionally, many devices now support complex gestures; for example swiping fingers across the screen.

I have no doubt that major hardware and software manufacturers such as Apple Computer have private armies of robot testers that can continually regression-test their products by physically *using* their devices in a scripted and automated fashion. Unfortunately, the only way for the average development team to physically regression-test its product on its target devices has been to do so in a painful and time-intensive way. With no way to reasonably test the application on the device, many teams opt for letting the end user test it for them, resigning themselves to investigating any errors as they are reported. Obviously, this is not an ideal approach. Fortunately, even small teams can now be part of the robot-testing revolution, provided they know a bit of JavaScript.

Tapster

Jason Huggins has embraced automated testing at a level many developers might find awe-inspiring. He is the CTO at Sauce Labs, which offers a variety of different products that allow its customers to farm out device testing to them. Part of Huggins's job is to find ways to weed out manual processes from their testing flows, while at the same time ensuring that the tests are as high fidelity as possible. Therefore, there is a balance that must be struck between embracing the speed of emulating a user's choices using software and re-creating the user's interactions manually by physically controlling the device. He may have found the perfect sweet spot with his Tapster project.[13] Tapster is the robot seen in Figure 10-3 that simulates a user's physical interactions in a scriptable and automated fashion.

Figure 10-3. *Tapster robot*

[13]https://github.com/hugs/tapsterbot

In a recent article for *Wired Magazine*,[14] Huggins explained why he feels projects like Tapster are essential:

> *Testing in the future will get harder to replicate in the lab or in a software simulator. My favorite example is Zipcar's iPhone app, which can open your car for you. To truly test it, you need an iPhone and a car—not something easily virtualized in the cloud. You can also use your phone to buy coffee at Starbucks or control your TV. I believe that in the future, the phone will be the remote control for everything. But with the "appification" of the world, comes a host of new problems. Digital systems are more complex and brittle than their analog predecessors. With complexity comes the higher risk of bugs. The way to hedge that risk is to do more testing—lots of testing—faster and more "real-world." And that is where the robots come in.*

The technology that drives Tapster is all open source. In fact, the bulk of the technology stack, including johnny-five, grunt, and node-serialport, have been covered in detail in earlier chapters. Even Tapster's physical parts can be printed out using your favorite 3D printer.

Tapster offers a creative attempt to bust one of the most pervasive problems in testing, which is the framework bias. As I noted earlier, developers have the tendency not to test the aspects of a program that are made difficult by the testing process. Tapster represents a solid attempt at what I see as a new field of community developed and open sourced physical testing devices. As we find new ways to embed technology into our daily life, we must also simultaneously ensure that these new forms are well-designed and well-tested.

Summary

Knowing how to write tests involves more than the technical ability to do so. To test a program correctly, you must have the correct psychological mindset and a clear definition of testing goals. These goals are often muddied by a variety of testing fallacies, which programmers can incorrectly promote. In other cases, a programmer's own confirmation bias may affect their ability to accurately write tests for their own work.

Thankfully, programmers can overcome these biases through the use of tools that help them think analytically about their code. For example, by employing code coverage tools, developers can quickly visualize the deficits in their code coverage. Additionally, developers can use fuzz testing or JSCheck to programmatically twist their code in ways that never occurred to them. Finally, the programmer can mix and match testing frameworks together to counteract any biases that one framework might have toward testing. When all these techniques are used together in a thoughtful cogent manner, you will find that the testability of your code cannot help but improve.

---

[14]http://www.wired.com/insights/2012/12/robots-at-the-intersection-of-cool-and-useful/

Index

■ W, X, Y, Z

Get the eBook for only $10!

Now you can take the weightless companion with you anywhere, anytime. Your purchase of this book entitles you to 3 electronic versions for only $10.

This Apress title will prove so indispensible that you'll want to carry it with you everywhere, which is why we are offering the eBook in 3 formats for only $10 if you have already purchased the print book.

Convenient and fully searchable, the PDF version enables you to easily find and copy code—or perform examples by quickly toggling between instructions and applications. The MOBI format is ideal for your Kindle, while the ePUB can be utilized on a variety of mobile devices.

Go to www.apress.com/promo/tendollars to purchase your companion eBook.

Made in the USA
Lexington, KY
22 May 2014